POLICY AND PRAGMATISM IN THE CONFLICT OF LAWS

To our families

Policy and Pragmatism in the Conflict of Laws

MICHAEL J. WHINCOP
Griffith University Law School, Australia
MARY KEYES
Griffith University Law School, Australia

with a Foreword by
RICHARD A. POSNER
United States Court of Appeals for the Seventh Circuit, USA
University of Chicago Law School, USA

Routledge
Taylor & Francis Group
LONDON AND NEW YORK

First published 2001 by Dartmouth Publishing Company and Ashgate Publishing

Reissued 2018 by Routledge
2 Park Square, Milton Park, Abingdon, Oxon OX14 4RN
711 Third Avenue, New York, NY 10017, USA

Routledge is an imprint of the Taylor & Francis Group, an informa business

A Library of Congress record exists under LC control number: 00053602

ISBN 13: 978-1-138-70331-5 (hbk)
ISBN 13: 978-1-315-20318-8 (ebk)

Contents

List of Figures and Tables

List of Cases

List of Statutes

Statutes of the Commonwealth of Australia

Statutes of Australian States

Statutes of the United Kingdom

United States Statutes

Other Statutes

International Conventions

Foreword by Richard A. Posner*

This is to my knowledge the first book that takes an economic approach to the important legal field of conflict of laws. The authors describe their approach as 'pragmatic' rather than economic and this is legitimate, since they do not limit themselves to economic points; their book is eclectic, properly so in dealing with any field of law and especially one to which the economic approach has been only sporadically applied. But the book is suffused with that approach, and the authors have succeeded in demonstrating the unexpected fruitfulness of an economic approach to conflict of laws.

I have said that economics has been applied to conflict of laws only sporadically heretofore, but I do not mean in saying this to denigrate the earlier contributions, which the authors fully acknowledge. For example, Roberta Romano and others have shown how the rule that the law of the state of incorporation has stimulated a competition among states to attract firms to incorporate in them and that this competition has tended to optimize (rather than as once thought degraded) corporation law. And William Baxter and others have argued that efficiency can be promoted by applying to an interstate or international dispute the law of the jurisdiction that has a comparative advantage (perhaps by reason of the site of the injury giving rise to the dispute) in regulating the parties' conduct optimally. But Whincop and Keyes's book goes far beyond previous economic analyses of issues of law, not only in comprehensiveness but also in depth of insight. And while their illustrations are taken mainly from English and Australian cases, their analysis is fully applicable to U.S. interstate conflicts of law as well as to the full range of international conflicts.

Their most distinctive analytical 'turn' is from the emphasis on government interests that has dominated the legal literature on conflict of laws to emphasizing instead the interests of the parties to disputes that pose conflict of law issues. In this respect their approach could be thought a generalization of the 'race to the top' approach of Romano and others in dealing with corporation law; there too the emphasis is on party selection of

* Chief Judge, U.S. Court of Appeals for the Seventh Circuit; Senior Lecturer, University of Chicago Law School.

the law to be applied: the choice of the corporation as to where to incorporate is a choice by the shareholders and officers to have their corporate-law disputes resolved by the law of the jurisdiction they have chosen.

The party-centered approach corresponds to the emphasis in economics on the free market, and is illuminatingly illustrated by the authors' analysis of conflict of laws in contract cases. Their essential point, simple but fresh and important — and thoroughly economic — is that the choice of law to be applied to contract disputes should be regarded as simply an extension of the parties' decision regarding what terms to include in their contract. Choice of law is just another term. If they specify a choice of law, it should be honored even if, as Whincop and Keyes argue persuasively, the choice is to circumvent the mandatory rule of a jurisdiction the law of which would otherwise apply. If they don't specify a choice of law, the court should make the choice they would have been most likely to make if they had thought about it.

The book is extremely lucid, and, as I have said, its choice of illustrative cases from the jurisdictions with which the authors happen to be most familiar in no wise detracts from the universality of their analysis. The book will be as valuable in reorienting thinking in the United States about the conflict of laws as it will be in other English-speaking countries and in the European Union. It will be the first place that judges, lawyers, and law professors interested in a fresh, pragmatic approach to conflict of laws, and in the utility of economics as a tool for reforming the doctrines of conflict of laws, will turn for guidance.

30 June, 2000
Chicago, Illinois

Preface

Conflicts scholars rarely tire of telling their students how scholars exerted more influence on private international law than on any other area of law. To such scholars, the precedent of a Beale or a Currie reminds them of Napoleon's *aperçu* that each French soldier carries a marshal's baton in his cartridge pouch. Unfortunately, private international law continues to be about as accessible as Webern's music, and its scholarship remains insular, forbidding territory. Even 'names' in the academy complain about their discipline, condemning it as 'dismal' or 'silly'. Hence, if the scholars' claim is true, it is really not something to boast about.

The primary object of this book is to break down the illusory partitions between conflicts scholarship and the rest of the academy. To do that, we extend theories proposed for substantive areas to multistate and international contexts. That means our analysis does not begin with the conflict, or the interests or powers of sovereign states. Instead, it steps back to examine the larger context, whether that be the facilitation of private ordering, the allocation of risks, the protection of property rights, or the resolution of litigation. The use of economic analysis often means that we find state interests unhelpful or distorting, just as they often are in domestic private contexts. We seek to develop a multistate legal theory that is private, pragmatic, anti-metaphysical, and liberal — not one that is statist, doctrinal, or formalistic.

This book collects, adds to, and substantially reworks our earlier published research in this area. We wish to thank the following people for their comments on this book or earlier articles: Ian Ayres, Vaughan Black, Angus Corbett, Kevin Davis, Martin Davies, Nick Georgakopoulos, Russell Korobkin, Erin O'Hara, Brian Opeskin, Patrick Parkinson, Larry Ribstein, Megan Richardson, Michael Tilbury, Stephen Ware, and participants in law and economics workshops at the University of Toronto and the George Mason University School of Law. We particularly want to express our gratitude to Tom Campbell for his enthusiasm for this project. Michael Whincop would like to thank his mother and sister for their loyalty and support. Mary Keyes wishes to thank her family.

Acknowledgements

Portions of this book are based on articles we have published on previous occasions. Chapter 2 includes material published in different form in 'Towards an Economic Theory of Private International Law' (2000) 25 *Australian Journal of Legal Philosophy* 1. Chapter 3 reworks but substantially revises material from 'Putting the "Private" Back Into Private International Law: Default Rules and the Proper Law of the Contract' (1997) 21 *Melbourne University Law Review* 515. Chapter 6 revises and expands 'Economic Analysis of Conflict of Laws in Torts Cases: Discrete and Relational Torts' (1998) 22 *Melbourne University Law Review* 370. The first half of chapter 9 is based on 'The Nexus of Forums: A Contractual Theory of Jurisdiction Over Corporations' (1998) 21 *University of New South Wales Law Journal* 681. These chapters do not, however, use copyright material from those articles.

Chapter 4 is based on, and includes passages that were first published in 'Statutes' Domains in Private International Law: An Economic Theory of the Limits of Mandatory Rules' (1998) 20 *Sydney Law Review* 435. We gratefully acknowledge the permission of the Editors of the Sydney Law Review for the use of copyright material here. Chapter 5 is based on, and reproduces passages that were first published in 'The Market Tort in Private International Law' (1999) 19 *Northwestern Journal of International Law & Business* 215. Northwestern University is the proprietor of the copyright in this article and copyright material is used here under the terms of the authors' Conveyances of Copyright Transfer.

Chapter 7 first appeared as Michael Whincop's article, 'Conflicts in the Cathedral: Towards a Theory of Property Rights in Private International Law' (2000) 50 *University of Toronto Law Journal* 41. We gratefully acknowledge the permission of the University of Toronto Press for the use of copyright material here.

Chapter 8 is based on several works by Michael Whincop. The section on the economics of forum choice and objection to jurisdiction is an informal reworking of a discussion paper called 'Choice of Forum, the Stay Application, and Jurisdictional Trade: An Economic Model of International Litigation'. The sections on anti-suit injunctions and stays of judgment in chapter 8 reproduces, in somewhat modified form, Part V(B) of Michael

Whincop, 'Three Positive Theories of International Jurisdiction' (2000) 24 *Melbourne University Law Review* (forthcoming, September). We acknowledge with gratitude the permission of the editors of the Review to reproduce copyright material from that article. The discussion of *CSR v. Cigna* is a substantially modified reworking of Michael Whincop, 'Forum Shopping Duty Free: The Law and Economics of Anti-Suit Injunctions After *CSR v. Cigna*' (1998) 5 *Canberra Law Review* 77. The discussion of judgment recognition draws its principal ideas from Michael Whincop, 'The Recognition Scene: Game Theoretical Issues in the Recognition of Foreign Judgments' (1999) 23 *Melbourne University Law Review* 416. Except where noted, chapter 8 does not duplicate copyrighted material contained in these articles.

The material on Internet conflicts in chapter 10 is based on Michael Whincop's article, 'Choice of Law, Jurisdiction and the Internet: A Policy Analysis' (1999) *National Law Review* 10. Chapters 10 does not duplicate copyrighted material contained in that article.

1 Introduction

Private International Law in the Modern Global Order

The world, we are constantly told, is getting smaller. National sovereignty is in decline, protectionism is disappearing, regionalism and globalisation are the big issues in modern policy. As global 'distances' shrink, the laws and legal systems of the world's nation states exert an increasing gravitational pull on each other. No longer are there clear definitions of, or a distinction between, what is domestic law and what is international law.

This implosion of law has two consequences, one of which is obvious, the other of which is not. The obvious consequence is that knowledge of the law of jurisdictions other than one's home base is no longer reserved to 'comparative lawyers'. Many practising lawyers and most academics have been compelled to expand their horizons beyond the domestic one. The less obvious consequence is that the role, the analysis, and the scholarship of international law are no longer tenable in their traditional forms, if ever they were. In this book, we consider this phenomenon in the domain of private international law — that part of the enterprise of international law devoted to the private law spheres of contracts, torts, and property.

The story of private international law as a scholarly discipline begins in much the same way as many areas of law.[1] Private international law rests on a tripod, the three legs of which are the jurisdiction of courts, the resolution of conflicts arising from pleas that inconsistent laws apply to transactions, and the recognition of judgments of foreign courts. The legal rules that define this corpus of law were originally viewed as logically derivable from a minimal set of essential concepts — states, courts, laws, judgments, and parties.[2] The dogma of formalism prevailed, as it did in other areas of law. Private international law's formalist pretensions were especially strong. It was, and in part continues to be, a strongly formulaic body of law, replete with a wealth of magisterial Latin and French. One need only look at the classic treatises. *Dicey and Morris*, to this day, is premised on the basis that the doctrine is capable of reduction to so many rules.[3]

The formal doctrinal approach shared by so many areas of the law generally faltered with the rise of legal realism. Yet, the jurist who contributed more to realism and anti-formalism than anyone else, Oliver

Wendell Holmes, Jr., took a metaphysical approach to rights in private international law cases that was as backward-looking as it was formalist.[4] Despite useful insights, the later realist agenda was never really fulfilled in private international law.[5] Perhaps in consequence, the broom of post-realist scholarship — critical legal studies, feminism, law and economics, theories of justice, and so on — never swept clean.[6] Policy-based conflicts scholarship did emerge in the United States. This 'government interest analysis' sought to resolve conflicts based on the respective interests of the states in the application of their laws to the case in question.[7] This theory was flawed by its statist premises, its obscure objectives, and its peculiar calculus. It had little impact across the Atlantic in England, or across the Pacific in Australia.[8] However, the academies in England and Australia failed to offer anything in place of government interest analysis, other than to explore doctrine in an atheoretical but less strongly formal manner. This is sometimes referred to as a 'pragmatic' approach.[9]

The obfuscation of policy in one academy and its neglect in others are no longer a desirable state of affairs, if ever they were. The economies of the world are much more international and interdependent than ever before. There are various ways in which one can react to such changes. One is to recognise the consequences of different private international law rules, and select the ones which maximise a norm of social choice (such as wealth, justice, or equity). Private international law would be used instrumentally to resolve the conflicts created in a global economy. The other is to achieve harmonisation at a substantive level, by minimising differences between legal rules.[10] This reduces the number and significance of conflicts. Unless, however, one has a meaningful theory to gauge the significance of changes to substantive law or conflictual doctrine, one can neither pursue the first strategy, nor choose between it and the second strategy.

One of the purposes of our book is to explore the concepts of policy and pragmatism in order to theorise and analyse private international law. We will argue in this book that contrary to the premises of English scholars, pragmatism *means* policy; a pragmatic approach must be a political one. The concept of pragmatism as it is understood in philosophy implies different things to different people; it has been a philosophy that appeals both to radicals and liberals.[11] Most strains of pragmatism have in common three features. First, they are anti-foundational. That is, they reject the need implicit in formalism to create a secure philosophical or metaphysical foundation for discourse.[12] Second, pragmatism is forward-looking. It looks backward only as a means of seeing more clearly into the future.[13]

Third, pragmatism is instrumental and consequentialist in nature. It is not (necessarily) a single-minded commitment to ends, but it does seek to clarify what ends this or that phenomenon serves, and how well those ends are served, as a way of facilitating meaningful choice and action.[14]

We argue that it is a mistake to think that government interest analysis is satisfactory in representing or furthering legitimate policy goals. However, it is also a mistake to think that a rejection of government interest analysis is a rejection of policy approaches to private international law generally.[15] Instead, one is simply recognising a need for better means of analysing policy issues. We put forward the analysis in this book as a response to this need.

A Pragmatic Theory of Private International Law

How might a policy approach to the conflict of laws be formulated? Our formulation relies on three premises. The first is that the policies that underlie what we think of as 'substantive' private law areas should, where suitable, inform the private international law rules that apply in these areas. We have mentioned that the distinction between international and domestic law is no longer easy to maintain. In this book, we intensify that view by treating private international law as a supplement to the underlying substantive law in relevant multistate cases. It follows that a pragmatic approach to policy should begin in the theories and scholarship of private law. For example, choice of law in contract cases should be considered in much the same way as other issues of the private ordering of contractual relations. Of course, policy aspirations differ between laws — conflicts would be pretty dull if that wasn't so. Thus, a choice of law rule must function as a tie-breaker in these cases. The point we emphasise is that the theory used to evaluate substantive laws may shed much light on the values that should be reflected in tie-breaking. An example is facilitating private ordering in contract cases. We maintain that this is a better approach than failing to explicate these values or assuming that none exist.

In this book, we make extensive use of law and economics scholarship. Law and economics has arguably been the dominant theoretical paradigm for the policy analysis of tort, contract, property, and civil procedure. It is equally penetrating when brought to bear upon private international law. We deny any claim to be the 'first' to develop an economic theory of private international law. There have been several fine works written by private international lawyers.[16] There have also been some powerful analyses of competitive federalism, especially in the context of the United States market for corporate charters, which have obvious implications for choice of law.[17] This book synthesises and substantially extends these literatures.

Second, as befits a theory of *private* international law, we emphasise parties and party interests.[18] This corresponds to a de-emphasis of the interests of sovereign states. Much of the conflicts literature regards a state's interests as coextensive with the application of the state's laws — and thus the policies motivating those laws — to the case. Writers have differed in the extent to which they favour the pursuit of this interest of the state, and the recognition of 'multistate' policies in addition to domestic ones.[19] Most American scholarship, adopting the methods of interest analysis, adopts a *competitive* approach, in which a state's own interests and policies are an exclusive guide to resolving conflicts. The minority American approach and the implicit assumption elsewhere are more *cooperative*, either because a state recognises the interests of other states or limits the application of its own laws.

Strategically, the choices of two or more courts to act competitively or cooperatively resemble a prisoner's dilemma game. The joint payoffs in a prisoner's dilemma are highest when both parties act cooperatively, but the difficulties of collective action combined with the strong lure of competitively seizing the surplus made possible by one party's cooperation, make self-interested competitive behaviour the dominant strategy. When parties continue to play the same game indefinitely, opportunists can be punished in the future, and cooperation may replace competition as a dominant strategy. But that is not always so, especially if the identity of a 'cooperative' strategy is not clear or is not symmetrical between the parties. Hence, self-interested states may act inconsistently in choosing to cooperate or compete.

It is clear that the concept of state interests needs to be unpacked. Laws divide broadly into two groups — those that serve the public interest, and those that serve private interests by functioning redistributively. As to the former category, most private law situations have few third party effects. Thus, welfare claims are largely subsumed by the interests of the parties. The furtherance of private sectional interests, however, raises serious dilemmas, since these interests are sometimes antagonistic to party interests. The court's choice of law method and other conflicts rules affect the scope for and cost of rent-seeking by interest groups.

The case for conflictual principle attempting to track party interests therefore has a triple motivation. First, advancing party interests is a cooperative compromise between self-interested states. As a multistate policy, it permits the furtherance of at least some of the policies of foreign states, and may encourage a more beneficial form of competition — a race for the top — that maximises social welfare. Second, furthering party interests may limit rent-seeking. This is not as simple as it sounds. In general, statutes do not come neatly labelled as 'public interest' or 'interest group' legislation — the latter is likely to be concealed in order to raise the information costs of opponents. Nonetheless, the efficiency-based approach to party interests that we will favour is likely to curtail the extent of transfers in redistributive legislation. It does this by increasing the amount of party choice and by limiting the application of the legislation. Third, the analytical inquiries are much less complex and do not depend on the investigation of the political motivations of the unrepresented state, which may be deliberately misrepresented.

Third, by extending domestic scholarship to private international law contexts, we adopt a more 'transactional' approach to private international law. Thus, the chapters of this book consider the private international law issues that arise out of transactions (consensual or otherwise) between parties. Because resolutions of conflictual issues have economic effects, they will affect how parties contract with each other, their investments in care and accident precautions, the use of property rights, and so on. For example, if legal rules affect the size of the contract surplus, *and* those effects vary between different legal systems, parties will rationally prefer that their contract be governed by the legal system whose contract law maximises the surplus. Most legal systems permit the parties to govern their contract according to an agreed law. All it takes is a simple sentence to that effect. This is equally true of jurisdiction and judgment recognition. It may maximise party wealth to litigate in the courts of a certain jurisdiction. This may be because a particular court has an established reputation in resolving disputes in a certain area, or because the parties' costs of litigation will be lowest there, or because judgments of that court are recognised in a wider number of foreign forums. Many jurisdictions recognise and enforce agreements to confer jurisdiction on a court.

It follows that if private international legal rules subject parties to substantive rules that they don't like, or direct litigation in inappropriate courts, rational parties will take this into consideration when negotiating their contracts. Unless the state has some means of preventing them, the parties will choose to contract in favour of the rules and forums that they prefer. Economists will not be surprised by this proposition. It encapsulates the insight of the Coase theorem, the foundation of modern law and economics.[20] The Coase theorem holds that the allocation of property rights is irrelevant to economic efficiency, if the negotiation and enforcement of contracts is costless. The corollary is that parties will contract around inefficient property rights and contractual terms where the benefit of doing so exceeds the costs of so transacting. This applies as much to private international law as it does to, say, corporate law. Embracing this transactional method of analysis recasts not only the function of private international law, but also the proper limits of a state's laws. In judging the limits on the application of a state's laws, it is desirable to consult the interests of the parties, especially those expressed in contracts, not just the interests of state legislatures. When viewed in these terms, the transactional approach to private international law complements an emphasis on party interests.

This is the essence of the approach we take to analysing policy issues in private international law. We have indicated that it must necessarily be complemented by a pragmatic approach to doctrinal issues. This means that policy considerations must be given some weight. It also means parting company with the conceptualism that underlies other approaches to the subject. Thus, we place little weight on 'rights' as the touchstone of policy, despite our emphasis on the interests of parties. Early Anglo-American theories argued that private international law recognised 'vested rights', that is, causes of action accruing in other jurisdictions.[21] This approach is imbued with the false scientism of formalist reasoning. Rights have been used in more recent attempts by scholars, most notably Lea Brilmayer, to construct deontic theories of a defendant's 'right to be left alone' by a jurisdiction.[22] These rights turn out to be ambiguous.

The woes of theoretical conceptualism are matched by the woes of doctrinal conceptualism. Private international law has traditionally placed a great deal of reliance on a process called *characterisation*.[23] That is, a choice of law problem is resolved categorically, according to the type of doctrinal issue it raises. For example, a tort issue may be resolved according to the *lex loci delicti* (the law of the place of the wrong). A contract issue is resolved according to the law of the jurisdiction having the closest connection to the contract. Different characterisations may give different answers. Given that doctrinal categories are, at best, matters of convenience, they do not readily bear the weight of this dispositive function. A formal conceptual approach masks the fact that the judge often has real choices. It obscures the policy reasons why those choices should be made in one way or the other. There are other examples of conceptual disorder. Prominent amongst these is the substance/procedure distinction.[24] Forum law governs procedural issues. Substantive issues are governed by the law selected by the choice of law methodology that corresponds to the problem type. Rather than relating this distinction to a policy basis, judges continue to apply it as if the terms 'procedure' and 'substance' had definite foundational content.

By contrast, pragmatism is not an unprincipled descent into uncertainty. It does not invite the judge to reconsider the merits of every legal rule or case afresh.[25] A pragmatic, economic approach often advocates a relatively conservative approach to the doctrine. The real differences are, first, a move from the generality and abstraction typical of private international law to a more specific, substantive method. Second, we seek to make doctrinal distinctions track policy issues, rather than formalist ontologies of legal rights.

An Outline of this Book

It is useful to outline the book in order to show how these objectives are pursued. Chapter 2 discusses theories of private international law. It shows that these theories can be understood according to their affirmation, first, of either party interests or state interests, and second, of either second-order rules or case-specific adjudication. This analysis brings out the theoretical and pragmatic limitations of earlier theories and lays the foundation of the theory proposed in this book.

Chapters 3 to 7 deal with choice of law issues. Chapters 8 and 9 deal with jurisdictional and other procedural issues. Choice of law and jurisdiction are not hermetically sealed from each other. The policy one hopes to effectuate with a choice of law rule can be undermined by a jurisdictional rule. Jurisdictional issues explain the content of some choice of law rules, such as the rule in *Phillips v. Eyre*,[26] that otherwise defy analysis. The chapters primarily devoted to choice of law correspond to key categories of transactions, while the jurisdiction and procedural chapters cut across these issues in a way that justifies independent treatment.

Chapter 3 begins with the simplest case — a contractual dispute. Contract law supplements the exchange process in a world where transaction costs are significant. Theories of the way in which contract laws should supplement contracts are united with the idea that private international law enables parties to select the law from which the specific supplemental rules are chosen. The traditional choice of law rules in contract further the object of maximising the parties' joint wealth, since parties are at liberty to choose their proper law. We examine how courts should proceed when the parties have not chosen the proper law. We contrast three approaches that vary in the extent to which they repose discretion in the judge to select the proper law. We return to this schema on several occasions.

Chapter 4 extends the analysis of contracts by recognising that legislatures are increasingly limiting contractual freedom by imposing 'mandatory' rules. We argue that mandatory rules are less mandatory than they appear in a world of jurisdictional diversity. Choice of law and jurisdiction agreements affect the enforceability of mandatory rules. The chapter rejects much of the current thinking about mandatory rules. We argue that a mandatory rule raises an interpretive question which has a political answer. Contrary to popular thinking, it is incorrect to say that parliament's purpose would be flouted if parties are permitted to avoid a mandatory rule by a choice of law. We examine tenable resolutions of these interpretive questions.

Chapter 5 moves from contracts to contractual ('market') torts. Tortious injuries that arise from contracts raise dilemmas for traditional doctrinal approaches. They force disjunctive answers to characterisation questions by creating a choice between contract and tort. The choice of law problems that market torts raise should be resolved in the same way as contract choice of law problems. However, there may be consequential justifications for limiting a purely contractual approach. The attributes of the market are the dispositive factors in this regard.

Chapter 6 examines non-market torts not associated with exchanges. Rules based on *lex loci delicti* are efficient when applied to torts between unrelated parties. This is not because they lead to more efficient accident precautions, but because they decrease litigation costs. We also analyse twentieth century cases involving related tortfeasors. We offer a rational basis for departing from *lex loci delicti* in these cases. This explains the results well, without resort to troublesome interest analyses.

Chapter 7 examines property conflicts. The parties' ability to choose the law applying to property rights traded — which we advocate in chapter 3 — is balanced against the fact that many property disputes involve priority competitions between parties who lack any contractual relation. We show how choice of law rules can increase coordination between independent transactions and so decrease transaction costs and strategic behaviour. We also examine the potentially inefficient referral of choice of law and jurisdiction to the law and courts of the *situs* in cases involving harmful externalities affecting land. These rules may exacerbate the inefficiencies of a jurisdiction's monopoly over immovable property.

Chapter 8 addresses jurisdictional and procedural issues. It examines a range of issues associated with the litigation of a multistate dispute, including choice of forum, objection to jurisdiction, and the allocation of legal costs. Over the twentieth century, the principles on the establishment and exercise of jurisdiction have changed substantially. We show the welfare consequences of different rules.

Chapter 9 analyses how corporations should be treated for jurisdictional purposes. Consistently with economic theory, the corporation should be viewed as a contractual arrangement, so that jurisdictional rules represent a series of supplementary provisions affecting these corporate contracts. This permits us to study the consequential properties of different jurisdictional rules without the conceptual distractions of attempting to reify the corporation. We also examine jurisdiction and choice of law rules in connection with international corporate insolvency.

Chapter 10 concludes the book by examining three pertinent issues which affect the future of private international law — the regulation of the internet, globalisation and internationalisation of laws, and the role of federalism. The purpose of this chapter is to show how the analysis in the earlier chapters can be used to shed light on these issues.

Throughout the book we argue that private international law should facilitate private ordering. Parties should be able to resolve choice of law and jurisdictional problems contractually, even where this would limit the scope of national laws. This is not because we think that private international law should subvert sovereign government. Rather, the best way to resolve the inevitable need to select one set of laws or one forum in preference to others is to permit parties to make the choice. This is not only likely to result in economically efficient outcomes, but in more liberal ones. Empowering citizens to make meaningful choices should be a policy priority of the twenty-first century.

Notes

1. See, for example, Juenger (1984).
2. The classic works in this vein are Dicey (1896) and Beale (1935).
3. Collins (1987).
4. *Western Union Tel. Co. v. Brown*, 234 U.S. 542, 547 (1914), *Slater v. Mexican National R.R. Co.*, 194 U.S. 120, 126 (1904).
5. Cavers (1965), Cook (1942), Lorenzen (1947). See chapter 2, *infra*.
6. Posner (1995) provides a crisp discussion of the changed relation between doctrinal analysis and interdisciplinary forms of legal scholarship.
7. Currie (1963). A fuller discussion and critique of government interest analysis is given in chapter 2, pp. 17-19 *infra*.
8. Fawcett (1982).
9. See chapter 2, pp. 15-16 *infra*.
10. Cf. Stephan (1999).
11. Contrast, for example, Posner (1995) and Rorty (1989).
12. Diggins (1994).
13. West (1989).
14. William James (1968) defined truth as 'the expedient in our way of thinking, just as the right is expedient in our way of behaving'.
15. Brilmayer (1989).
16. Buckley and Ribstein (2000), Choi and Guzman (1998), Hay (1992), Kobayashi and Ribstein (1999), McConnell (1988), Posner (1998a, pp. 645-646), Ribstein (1993, 1994), Ribstein and O'Hara (1997), Solimine (1989).
17. The seminal work is Tiebout (1956); the modern classic is Romano (1993). For an overview of the economics of federalism, see Posner (1998a, pp. 695-712).
18. O'Hara and Ribstein (2000) and Guzman (2000) make a similarly general claim that conflicts should be resolved by reference to party interests.
19. Brilmayer (1995).
20. Coase (1960).
21. These are described in more detail in chapter 2 *infra*.
22. Brilmayer (1989), Dane (1987).
23. Forsyth (1998), Robertson (1939).
24. Cook (1933).
25. Contrast Dworkin (1991) with Posner (1990, pp. 130-135).
26. (1870) L.R. 6 Q.B. 1.

2 Theory in Conflict of Laws

The Theoretical Context of Conflicts

Much legal scholarship begins its life as a critique, typically of some other scholar, rather than as an explanation or a prediction. This is particularly true of conflicts, and in this chapter we shall see the succession of critique-inspired theorisations of choice of law that have been offered. To begin, we first study the nature of conflicts, so that we can offer a perspective on the values underlying private international law.

Conflicts are a member of a family of legal problems in which either the legal rules applying to factual situations cease to be mutually exclusive of each other, or the scope of legal rules is not collectively exhaustive of all factual situations. These problems occur domestically as well as internationally.[1] If we ignore for a moment the issue of whether a judge should hear such a case (a jurisdiction question), there are at least three *methods* for resolving these problems.

First, the legal system may resolve the dispute by an explicit secondary rule. There are many examples. An example is to apply statute law where it is inconsistent with the common law. The traditional Anglo-American use of choice of law rules is the conflictual equivalent. These were maligned by various twentieth century scholars, especially the realists.

Second, the decision-maker may resolve the problem by reference to the primary rules in question. Since most primary rules will be silent on the resolution of the precise issue, the adjudicator may use various interpretive methods to reach a solution. These include methods which reconstruct the law-maker's relevant purposes. The many variations on interest analysis partake of these reconstructive methods. They are, however, hamstrung where there is a gap (rather than an overlap) in legal rules, or where the legal rule is evolutionary, as the common law is. Moreover, these approaches do not always avoid the need for an explicit rule of recognition, as purposive methods may not isolate a single law.

The first and second methods differ in the amount of discretion they repose in the adjudicator, and in the extent to which the content and policies of the laws in question affect determinations of their application. The first distinction is a recurring theme in conflicts, as in many other areas of law.[2]

It is often portrayed as a choice between rules and standards.[3] In this book, we refer to a related distinction between first- and second-order decisions.[4] First-order decision-making is the conventional form of choosing action on the basis of costs and benefits; second-order decisions involve constraining decisions made at later times by reference to an earlier decision. Traditional choice of law rules are second-order decisions; purposive inquiries and analysis of state interests are first-order approaches.

Third, the decision-maker may resolve the conflict by giving effect to a norm internalised by the members of the community from which the parties come. We see this in the common law's appropriation of custom, and, more pertinently, in the resolution of medieval business disputes by reference to the law merchant, a supranational body of normative principle.[5] Giving legal status to community norms has an important theoretical rationale, attributable to the limitations on information available to a law-maker.[6]

This method affects choice of law problems in two ways. As with the medieval law merchant, the norms applied in international arbitration are often used to resolve transnational business disputes. This is uncontroversial because parties agree to submit to arbitration, so these norms presumably suit their contracting purposes. Transnational solutions to other types of conflicts are proposed in the writings of such scholars as Friedrich Juenger. Juenger claims that there is a consensus opinion regarding the justice of legal rules.[7] These principles enable the judge to select the law hewing closest to that consensus. This seems to elevate intuition to the status of universality. Unlike the medieval or modern law merchant, most of the tort cases Juenger has in mind occur in situations where the parties do not draw from a single community, so there is no reason to believe the parties share normative commitments. Courts, unlike community arbitrators, may have difficulty verifying the content and scope of norms, even where they exist, and some norms may not be intended to be enforced legally.[8] In general, conflicts arise *because* there is no universal theory of the good (especially in private law areas) from which transcendent principles of fairness might be drawn. This suggests the importance of contractarian theory. Contractarian approaches to justice seek to identify means by which those with diverging values can identify cooperative solutions for their mutual benefit.[9]

An analytical method does not decide cases — it must draw its content from some objective or principle. The principal theories of choice of law can be subdivided between those which affirm party interests and those which affirm state interests. This is clear on the surface, but at another level, similar analytical methods often homogenise results, whatever the commitment. For example, Juenger is a fierce critic of interest analysis, but concedes he agrees with the outcome of most cases applying interest analysis. This may be a result of the fact that plaintiffs will try to litigate in forums whose law maximises their awards (a result Juenger favours), and these courts have strong 'homing' instincts to local law. In much the same way, there is considerable agreement amongst the various second-order proponents, who include formalists like Dicey, contractarians like Brilmayer, public choice theorists like Larry Ribstein, and pro-efficiency pragmatists like us.

The relevance of state interests depends on the sovereigns recognised as interested in particular cases, and the manner in which choices are made between interested sovereigns. The distinction is between *unilateral* theories of sovereignty, in which only the sovereign interests of the forum are recognised, and *multilateral* theories.[10] A multilateral theory will reduce the bias of the secondary rules used to resolve choice of law problems.[11] The unilateral-multilateral distinction is a continuum, not a dichotomy. Larry Kramer's version of interest analysis is more multilateral than Brainerd Currie's, but is more unilateral than conventional vested rights.

Lea Brilmayer astutely summarises the problem with the use of state interests in conflicts cases.[12] In a single state context, interests or policies may be used to ascertain the scope of the law because the capacity of the state to apply the law is rarely in doubt. That capacity is in doubt in multistate cases and should be limited according to defensible normative criteria, rather than the wishes of the state. However, advocates of party interests do not agree on what these criteria are, nor whether these should be consequentially or deontologically derived.

A Theoretical Taxonomy

We have identified methodical and normative dimensions of approaches to choice of law. Table 2.1 crosses these to form a theoretical taxonomy.

Table 2.1 A taxonomy of choice of law theories

	State Interests	Party Interests
First-order choices of law	Type B theories	Type C theories
Second-order choices of law	Type A theories	Type D theories

In practice, some theories may prove difficult to classify. The remaining sections of this chapter first explore the theories falling under each of the types in the taxonomy from a critical perspective. Second, we examine the historical momentum of choice of law theories. Third, based on the limitations of theories, we describe and justify the elements of the approach to private international law advocated in this book.

Second-order Choices of Law Affirming State Interests (Type A)

Type A theories (so coded as the starting point, chronologically, for modern theories) are characterised by analysis of the territorial limits of state sovereignty. Those limits are generally identifiable without regard to the substantive character of the laws being so limited. Vested rights is the paradigm type A theory, but it is instructive to consider other theories with similar qualities, but of more recent provenance.

Vested Rights

Ulric Huber articulated the theory of vested rights in its modern form, based on strict territorial limits on sovereignty. Huber's original articulation expresses the idea simply: 'the laws of each nation having been applied within its own boundaries should retain their effect everywhere.'[13] Hence, the law of the place that an event occurs should define and govern the right and its related obligation. Choice of law rules are directed to identifying this place. As noted above, territorial definitions of entitlements give the theory a multilateral quality.

The realists objected to the foundations of vested rights.[14] Legal causes of action were predictions of what a judge *would* do when confronted with particular facts. It was meaningless to speak of rights having vested until there had been a judicial determination that a particular jurisdiction's law applied and recognised the so-called right. Particular choice of law rules, such as choosing the law of the place of the last-occurring element to constitute a tort, were criticised as arbitrary, and their apparent derivation on logical grounds was refuted.

An alternative justification of a system of second-order rules might be certainty and predictability. However, the rules recommended by vested rights theorists had limited capacity to attain these objects. Their proposed choice of law rules corresponded to doctrinal categories — tort, contract, immovable property and so on. These rules were probably too generic, since they sought to use a single rule to embrace a heterogeneous range of cases. Their undiscriminating qualities spurred critics to offer theories based on first-order choices of law. A contrasting flaw was that the rules were sometimes not mutually exclusive — more than one rule might apply. The choice between them rests on 'characterising' the nature of the cause of action involved.[15] This ability to choose between rules permits a judge a wider amount of ex post discretion than second-order rules contemplate. This affords the plaintiff an opportunity to act strategically in formulating the suit. Chapter 5 discusses a salient example: where plaintiffs allege tort rights in contract cases. Because the justification of vested rights was pseudo-scientific in nature, its scholarship lacked a normative theory which might have enabled it to correct this problem.

Realists noted the existence of related escape devices, such as *renvoi*, the substance/procedure distinction, and the incidental question.[16] Resort to these devices effectively expands the application of the *lex fori*, and enables judges to take comparative substantive outcomes into consideration. Like characterisation, these tendencies compromised vested rights as a multilateral choice of law method based on second-order rules.

English Pragmatism

English choice of law was, compared to the continental experience, a late developer. England's unitary government and its adversarial system combined to create a unique response to choice of law.[17] The fact that England's constitutional structure is unified distinguishes it from other nations which have produced significant choice of law theorists. Dutch choice of law theory was motivated by the provincial structure of the Netherlands.[18] Similarly, most choice of law theory in the United States addresses inter-state conflicts. The adversarial nature of English civil procedure means that litigants have greater control over most aspects of litigation, compared to the practice in inquisitorial systems. In general, English courts take a passive role in the resolution of litigation. This contrasts with the position in the U.S. From early times, the Constitution confronted American courts with policy issues concerning the reconciliation of state interests and individual rights.

These influences produced a scholarship that has primarily been positivistic. That scholarship accepts the validity of a choice of law method similar to the doctrine inspired by vested rights theory in the U.S. The establishment of this method in English law was the result of A.V. Dicey's landmark *Digest of the Law of England with Reference to the Conflict of Laws*. This treatise remains hugely influential to this day. Dicey's emphasis on second-order choice of law rules as the basis for ascertaining vested rights remains substantially intact, even though few now explicitly accept the philosophy of vested rights.

Apart from the inertial momentum of doctrinal scholarship, why have second-order methods displayed greater durability in England than in the U.S.A.? There may be two reasons. First, English courts have preferred to recognise scope for (first-order) exceptions to the basic (second-order) choice of law rules, rather than rejecting the entire doctrinal edifice. This is consistent with the traditional passivity of English judging.[19] A good example is Lord Wilberforce's speech in *Boys v. Chaplin*,[20] which recognised a flexible exception to the application of the *lex loci delicti* as the law of the cause in torts cases. Similarly, some of the rules have become less precise, as they seek to identify the legal system most closely connected to the case, rather than predicating the choice on some particular fact such as the place of contracting or of performance. This enables greater flexibility after the fact. Second, it is arguable that the English bar may have preferred more predictable and less biased choice of law rules in order to increase the attractiveness of England as a forum for international commercial litigation. The willingness of English courts to enforce contractual choices of law and forum diluted the state interests the theory might be expected to serve.[21] Despite its intellectual roots in vested rights, it has claims as a Type D theory.

Lex Fori

Albert Ehrenzweig was the most authoritative advocate of the *lex fori* as a general choice of law principle.[22] He considered that *lex fori* should be, 'in the absence of a different autonomous choice by the parties', the general choice of law rule.[23] Ehrenzweig considered that accepting this proposition would concentrate attention on the development of jurisdictional principles that would ensure the forum's appropriateness to the litigation. Thus, the theory is no more unilateral than vested rights, despite its forum bias, because of its increased emphasis on the process for forum selection. Yet, there is still scope for the application of foreign law: Ehrenzweig contemplates the treatment of traditional conflicts rules as valid, but simply exceptional.

Ehrenzweig's willingness to recognise exceptions diminishes his theory's status as based on second-order principles; indeed, Robert Leflar celebrates the 'individualisation' of his approach.[24] Moreover, Ehrenzweig's belief that jurisdictional principles can constrain inefficient forms of forum shopping is offered as nothing more than a bare assertion. A choice of law approach creating variance between forums is likely to result in inefficient choices of forum. The plaintiff's private gains from selecting a judgment-maximising forum may outweigh the parties' increased joint costs of litigating in that forum. Holding all else equal, judges able to apply forum law will prefer to exercise jurisdiction rather than decline it.[25]

First-order Choices of Law Affirming State Interests (Type B)

Modern type B theories, of which interest analysis is the paradigm, grew out of the dissatisfaction with the formalism and fictions of vested rights. Their hallmark is making matches between cases and laws based either on the motivating policies, or the identity or capacity, of the law-maker.

Interest Analysis

Currie pioneered the modern form of interest analysis, having been influenced by the realist criticisms of vested rights. Currie highlighted the political function of courts in determining multistate litigation. The 'assessment of the respective values of the competing legitimate interests of two sovereign states, in order to determine which is to prevail, is a political function of a very high order'. In Currie's view, the constitutional position of courts as subordinate to the legislature required that this function 'not be committed to courts in a democracy'.[26] Accordingly, courts are bound to apply appropriately specified forum law. In general, Currie thought a choice of law problem should be resolved by an analysis of state interests in the application of particular rules. To do this, one must identify the applicable substantive rules, analyse the policies enacted in each of those rules, and determine whether the enacting states have legitimate interests in having their policy protected in the instant case by application of its law. The method therefore operates at the first-order in two ways — it examines the policies of particular legal rules and it examines the relevance of these to the case at bar. If the forum has a legitimate interest, the court must apply forum law. Another state's rule would only be applied if the forum lacked a legitimate interest in application of its law. Currie's approach had a profound effect on decision-making in U.S. litigation, and dominated American conflicts scholarship until the 1980s.

Interest analysis has provoked much criticism. Perhaps the weightiest is Brilmayer's theoretical criticism that Currie's concept of 'interest' was not gleaned from empirical analysis but was imposed by hypothesis.[27] For example, it rules out the possibility that a state might have an interest in limiting the application of its tort laws territorially.

For our purposes, three further criticisms are important. All relate to interest analysis' bias to forum law. First, these unilateralist biases create upstream pressure on jurisdictional rules, because they confer a major advantage on the litigant who chooses the forum.[28] The private gains from forum-selection may lead to excessive litigation (since both parties prefer to be the 'first-mover') and inefficient choices of forum (since the private marginal gains to the plaintiff may be less than the private marginal cost to the defendant, relative to some other forum).

Second, the active pursuit of state policies and the expansion of legislation beyond territorial limits may increase the capacity of rent-seeking interest groups to secure wealth transfers through the political process.[29] It is a hypothesis of economic analysis of law that much legislation effects transfers of wealth away from groups of citizens with limited abilities to coordinate, to groups with greater political effectiveness. Interest analysis facilitates such transfers by increasing the scope of the deal and the costs of exiting the relevant regulation.[30] This idea is related to Brilmayer's critique that state interests may lack legitimacy in multistate cases.

Third, the imprecision of interest analysis and the dependence of the *lex causae* on the eventual forum mean that legal rights and obligations may be highly uncertain. Uncertainty in ascertaining the application of a legal rule may jeopardise the achievement of the very policies the laws are supposed to be effectuating and protecting.

Fourth, states may have an interest in permitting transactions without wishing to mandate them. In those circumstances, they are unlikely to pass laws to do so unless the status quo is expressly a prohibitory one.[31] In the absence of an express law, the state's interest may well be ignored.

Larry Kramer's work addresses some of the criticisms of Currie's version of interest analysis.[32] Kramer offers a more empirical definition of a government's interest in multistate cases. A choice of law rule in a statute would be conclusive of the nature of the interest. In the absence of these provisions, or other evidence intrinsic or extrinsic to the legislation, Kramer uses canons of interpretation as constructive evidence of what these interests might be. In chapter 4, we also rely on presumptions about the application of rules applying to contracts. However, the canons are very different because we do not justify them as best guesses of state interests, but use instead the calculus of party interests. Kramer also rejects the principle that forum law must apply to true conflicts. Kramer recognises that interstate cooperation has many virtues and offers advantages of predictability and prevention of forum shopping.

Kramer's approach is more flexible than conventional interest analysis and it draws on more defensible norms of lawmaking. On the other hand, an argument so strongly based on statutory construction has the potential to rationalise virtually any result.[33]

Comparative Impairment and Regulatory Comparative Advantage

William Baxter's theory of comparative impairment is related to interest analysis.[34] Baxter relied on the heuristic of a compact that states would enter regarding the application of their laws in a hypothetical negotiation. Courts should resolve conflicts by asking what lawmakers would agree to, if they negotiated a multistate agreement. Courts can replicate such negotiations with a principle of 'comparative impairment' — law makers would agree to subordinate their own law in favour of the law of the state whose policy is most in danger of impairment by non-application. This theory is arguably more multilateral than interest analysis.

By invoking the concept of a hypothetical bargain it might be thought that Baxter's theory has a Coasean logic.[35] But it does not. If states negotiated a compact they are most likely to agree to end jurisdictional competition, in the same way that competitors find it gainful to agree to act in cartel. In cases where the application of a state's law is part of a bilateral agreement between parties (e.g., contractual choice of law clauses), jurisdictional competition should stimulate the production of efficient laws.[36] Jurisdictional competition may limit the capacity of interest groups to lobby for rent-seeking legislation. The capacity to exit the state by choosing the law of another undercuts the wealth transfer motivating the legislation.

Other faults might be mentioned, which are similar to the criticisms of interest analysis. Much depends on the ability of courts to identify policies. However, the policies of a document that reflects legislative compromises may be difficult to ascertain. In the case of rent-seeking legislation, lawmakers may want to misrepresent the policy as being in the public interest.[37] Even if rent-seeking legislation is not in point, there may be incommensurability between objectives, such as efficiency and distribution.[38]

Baxter's theory has received some imprimatur from Judge Richard Posner.[39] Posner states that the object of the law should be to ascertain the legal system which has a comparative advantage in regulating the relevant subject matter and minimising adjudicative errors. Critiquing interest analysis, Posner states that '[t]he issue ought not to be interests; it ought to be which state's law makes the best "fit" with the circumstances of the dispute'.[40] For Posner, territorial approaches will often be preferred, because they are more likely to coincide with the locus of comparative advantage. He criticises interest analysis for weakening territoriality. However, his analysis shares characteristics with interest analytic approaches since it emphasises state attributes and their relationship to the subject matter of a case.[41] The method, as illustrated by Posner, relies on identifying the purpose of legal rules, which interest analysis also does. Elsewhere, Posner has criticised such conceptualism as unpragmatic.[42] As we have seen above, apparent purposes may be misrepresented where legislation has interest group provenance. It is not clear how Posner would treat rent-seeking in analysing comparative regulatory advantage.

Posner's theory straddles the divides of the two axes of our taxonomy. It uses economics to ascertain which state has the comparative regulatory advantage. However, wealth maximisation is much more concrete when party interests are the focal units. Posner's theory also straddles the distinction between first- and second-order choice of law strategies. Posner's sympathies lie with territorial, second-order rules. Yet he proposes analysis of the purposes of individual rules, and the regulatory advantage of states in effecting those purposes.

First-order Choices of Law Affirming Party Interests (Type C)

Types A and B theories favour state interests, and so require conceptual representations of those interests such as the formal abstractions of vested rights or the reifications of interest analysis. These have been targets for criticism. Critics have turned to the interests of the parties as a basis for choice of law theory. Type C theories use the greater adjudicative discretion reposed by first-order methods to craft case-specific choices of law supposedly consistent with the parties' interests.

Better Law

Interest analysis has stimulated other American theorists to experiment with choice of law theories. Some theorists took a similar rule selecting approach to Currie, but proposed different constraints on the judicial function in resolving a choice of law issue. Robert Leflar proposed that a choice of law question be resolved to favour the 'better' of the conflicting substantive rules, having regard to their respective outcomes in the instant case.[43] This approach, of ancient heritage,[44] has also been advocated by Juenger, as we saw above.[45] Leflar, however, proposes the better law as *one* consideration which influences choice. Others, which cut in favour of second-order rules, include the predictability of results and the simplicity of the judicial task. Juenger is much more critical of second-order rules, and scorns the possibility that they may generate more predictable results.[46]

We have already argued that this approach requires a universal theory of the good, but no proponent has offered much more than an idiosyncratic notion of justice, which usually favours recovery maximisation. In addition, these approaches dubiously assume that justice is only delivered via the courtroom.[47] First-order approaches to justice decrease the predictability of legal obligations. But the stability and predictability of legal obligations should be essential to a theory of multistate justice, both to demonstrate the tractability of the theory in real world settings and as a guide to the ethics that citizens should uphold.[48]

Choice of Law Tailoring

The problems with the use of justice in multistate contexts are similar to the problems they pose in domestic contexts.[49] Efficiency yields more straightforward analytical claims. Is it possible to use it as a first-order criterion for choice of law?[50] Such an approach would have two parts — a choice-enforcing part and a choice-emulating part.

Efficiency generally requires that parties should be able to agree to the law that should apply to their relation, subject to the usual, uncontroversial limits on contractual freedom, such as incapacity and duress. The reasons why this is efficient are explored in detail in the next chapter. But there will be many cases where parties do not take — or do not have — the opportunity to make such an agreement. Some multistate contracts may not have a choice of law. Many tort cases will not present an opportunity for contracting of any kind. The question arising in these cases is whether courts should resolve the choice of law question by means of a second-order rule or a more discriminating first-order approach.

If a court took the latter approach, it would need to determine the choice of law it thinks the parties in the instant case would have agreed to, had they the chance to negotiate. This can be described as choice of law tailoring.[51] This terminology borrows from the economic scholarship of contract law, which posits that courts may, and sometimes should, supplement incomplete contracts with the legal rules the court believes the parties in the case at bar are most likely to have agreed to. In practice, such an inquiry asks which legal rule would maximise the joint wealth of the two parties.[52]

Although neither wholly undesirable nor inconsistent with some conflicts cases,[53] the appeal of choice of law tailoring is limited. First, like other first-order approaches, it makes legal obligations unclear, which complicates the decisions of the parties as to whether or not they should bother to contract ex ante. Second, its uncertainty should increase the length and complexity of litigation, and decrease the number of out-of-court settlements. Third, much important information needed to determine the efficient term may be unverifiable by a court. Choice of law tailoring is most appealing when the subject of regulation is incapable of exiting the jurisdiction selected by the second-order rule. In a limited group of cases, which we refer to in chapter 7, choice of law tailoring may respond to the problems caused by this 'jurisdictional monopoly'.

Second-order Choices of Law Affirming Party Interests (Type D)

Type D theories also affirm party interests but maintain that these are best served by second-order choices of law. Second-order rules may, however, operate either negatively or positively. Negative rules *disable* the application of certain law arrived at by other methods. Positive rules are selective in the usual manner.

Political Rights

Lea Brilmayer is the main proponent of a political rights approach to choice of law. Beginning with a critique of governmental interest analysis, she insists that the application of any particular substantive rule must be defensible in political theory. In order to justify the rule's application, an appropriate relationship must be shown between the state which enacted that rule and the individual to whom it is applied. This approach is a threshold which must be satisfied before the dispute can be resolved. Since this method only supplies a threshold fairness requirement, it does not resolve choice of law questions where more than one legal system can justify the application of its rules.

Brilmayer's paradigm signal of the legitimate application of a rule is the subject's consent to its application. Consent is also attractive to consequential theories because the enforcement of consensual decisions is likely to be wealth maximising. Brilmayer looks to three further factors in the absence of consent. The first is the domicile of the party burdened. It would be unfair to apply S's law to a domiciliary of state T. This makes an explicit link to the parties' right to voice in the polity.[54] Again, however, domicile may have consequential justifications, too. A party's information costs of ascertaining applicable laws are lowest when the laws are his 'own'. Presumably, a law's instrumental justifications are most effective when people subject to them are familiar with the laws. Second, Brilmayer calls on territoriality. Disagreeing with earlier treatments of the subject, she argues that territoriality may be a basis for political rights if the party burdened has an opportunity for a deliberate or purposeful decision to associate with the states or there is an opportunity to exit. Consequentially, this approach, like consent, gives parties an opportunity to make rational decisions based on information including legal liabilities. Third, Brilmayer relies on the concept of 'mutuality'. This is a representation of fairness which implies that the choice of law method is not biased to benefiting or burdening specific litigants. Jurisdiction-selecting rules tend to do this.

Thus, political rights constraints can also be justified on consequential grounds. The rules outlined in the remainder of the book do not infringe these constraints.

Reasonable Expectations

Party interests are also focal for writers who emphasise the importance of giving effect to the parties' reasonable expectations.[55] As Kramer has argued, many of these approaches mask underlying normative judgments regarding what courts and scholars think parties should reasonably expect; alternatively, such statements tend to be circular endorsements of current practice.[56] The best argued endorsement of reasonable expectations is Peter Nygh's. We analyse it in chapter 6. His argument about the nature of reasonable expectations in the absence of a choice of law agreement does not break free of the circularity problem.

✧ ✧ ✧

From a functional perspective, these theories differ primarily in terms of four attributes — the extent to which the rule encourages forum shopping (thus placing pressure on jurisdictional rules), the scope for extraterritorial operation, the uncertainty in ascertaining which substantive law will be selected by the choice of law principles, and the relation of the laws to private ordering and party consent. After discussing some issues in the development of theory in private international law, we will return to these four functional issues in outlining the nature of an economics-influenced, pragmatic theory of private international law.

The Momentum of Choice of Law Theory

The last sixty years of conflicts theory have been concerned with filling the vacuum the realists left after their demolition of the philosophical basis of vested rights theory. Consider again the two realist criticisms of vested rights. The first is a foundational critique of the ontology of vested rights and the formalist conception of territorial sovereignty. The second is a consequential critique about the results that second-order choice of law rules produce, given some norm of social choice.

Most American conflicts scholarship addresses the foundational critique. Currie sought to locate foundational principles from ideas about democratic government. 'Better law' theorists draw on concepts of justice. Brilmayer calls on political philosophy. Each commentator has looked to theory for a principle which imposes coherence on the subject from the top-down. This search for foundational principle will ultimately be unfruitful.

Just as Holmes considered that a constitution could not and did not embody any particular theory,[57] we doubt that there is or should be any unifying principle in private international law. In chapter 1, we noted that courts would vacillate between cooperation and competition. The relative payoffs to competition and future cooperation vary with changes in such things as technology, the amount of cross-border trade, the influence of interest groups, and the availability of alternative dispute resolution. Thus, behaviour in equilibrium will also change in ways that may be hard to predict. Private international law is a product of much larger forces, such that few consistent principles should be observed or expected.

The avoidance of foundational analysis is the identifiably 'pragmatic' quality of English scholarship. It is true that doctrinalism confers a backward-looking quality to English scholarship which is out of phase with the forward-looking quality of pragmatism. But the English experience shows that what may be indefensible in foundational terms may in practice be workable, and potentially superior to theoretically derived alternatives. The fact that English law is often selected in choice of law agreements, and English courts as a forum for litigation in international contracts may endorse its private international law as much as its substantive law and its court system.

Since the content of English conflictual doctrine is closer to the choice of law method favoured by vested rights theorists than contemporary American law, it follows that we must reconsider the force of the realists' consequential critique. The primary elements of the critique were threefold. First, escape devices such as characterisation weaken the authority and certainty of second-order rules. Second, the application of some rules, such as the last place of the tort, produces arbitrary results. Third, second-order rules are blind to the content of the selected law.

These criticisms remind one of the familiar charge that precisely described legal obligations (rules) are both underinclusive and overinclusive compared to less precise obligations implemented ex post (standards).[58] The criticisms seem to support a move towards first-order principles for choice of law. But this argument is vulnerable in two respects. First, the realists lacked the means to measure the seriousness of their criticisms, and failed to develop a theory to evaluate the consequences of moving towards first-order choice of law. Second, scholars did not consider until recently the possibility that even if more flexible choice of law principles were superior to the rules favoured by vested rights theorists, more discriminating forms of second-order rules might be even better.[59]

It is therefore important to understand that interest analysis emerged as a credible theory because the consequentialist arguments of the realists were unsophisticated. Neither Currie nor any of his followers made a serious attempt to justify interest analysis's superior consequential properties. Far more weight was placed on its foundational derivation from democratic theory — a justification that was commonly claimed by American legal scholars in the 1950s, the heyday of the legal process school.[60] This also explains why most theoretical debate since the realists has wandered further and further from the track of addressing the identified critiques and improving the choice of law rules inherited from vested rights theory. Thus, those critical of the role of government interests and policies in interest analysis either look towards overarching theories of justice without law, as in the case of the better law school, or self-consciously deny the relevance of consequentialism altogether, as Brilmayer does.

In the last fifteen years, a few scholars and private legislatures such as the American Law Institute have reconsidered the merits of territoriality and multilateralism.[61] During this period, the pro-recovery sentiments informing most first-order approaches to choice of law came unstuck in the insurance and product market crises of the 1980s. Court systems groaned under the weight of complex multistate tort actions.[62] But these moves are a cause for concern until we have the means by which to compare different doctrinal methods. The premise of this book is that progress is most likely to come from uniting a more pragmatic approach to foundational issues with a more rigorous economic approach to the consequences of legal rules. The purposes served by such an approach are described in the next section.

The Functions of Private International Law[63]

Quite apart from their content, one may criticise the focus of much conflicts theorising for its obsession with choice of law and its indifference to jurisdictional issues. In the material that follows we demonstrate how private international law's functions require simultaneous evaluations of choice of law and jurisdiction issues. These functions correspond roughly to the four issues we identified as being the principal controversies in private international law theory.

Minimising the Social Costs of Litigation

Litigation engenders major social costs, both for the parties and the state in whose courts litigation proceeds. One objective should be to minimise these costs. More specifically, where conflicts of law arise, the law should attempt to minimise the incremental costs they occasion (call these the *marginal conflicts cost*). The social costs of litigation are influenced by several factors.[64] These include the stakes and the parties' ability to settle their litigation out of court.

Consider first the stakes. The marginal conflicts cost will be minimised when the *marginal* stakes are lowest — that is, the difference between the stakes in potential forums. This is true for two reasons. First, the stakes must reach a certain level before commencing litigation is rational. Litigation may be rational in one forum (e.g., one seeking to attract plaintiffs) but not others. Second, when commencing litigation is rational, a plaintiff will maximise her net expected award. As the marginal stakes increase for both parties, the willingness to incur litigation costs also rises, and so too should the marginal conflicts cost. If the marginal stakes are low or zero, a rational plaintiff maximises her wealth by minimising costs; other things being equal, this incentive is efficient.

Out of court settlements reduce the social costs of litigation. Economic influences on the parties' willingness to settle are the degree of uncertainty concerning the likely substantive resolution of the case, the parties' costs to litigate, and inequalities (asymmetries) of information between parties.[65] The availability of settlements counters (to an extent) the effect of higher litigation stakes, since the stakes increase expected litigation costs, and thus the savings from settlement. However, uncertainty and asymmetric information may preclude settlements from occurring until substantial costs have already been incurred.

The role of private international law in reducing the marginal conflicts cost should be apparent. First, choice of law rules can decrease the marginal stakes by functioning multilaterally. Convergence on a single *lex causae* will have this effect. The more unilateral the choice of law rule, the higher the marginal stakes, and thus the expected litigation costs. Second, choice of law rules can increase the likelihood of settlement by operating in predictable fashion. Increased certainty about the likely choice of law permits parties to identify the settlement range, in which settlement terms are mutually beneficial. Related to this problem is that choice of law rules which select foreign law are likely to create errors because of the unfamiliarity of judges and lawyers with foreign law. Third, jurisdiction rules can limit the entitlement of a plaintiff to bring suit in a forum that would occasion excessive costs. The social costs of litigating in a forum with no connection to the case or either party would be high, but a plaintiff may nonetheless gain a private benefit from choosing that forum. Fourth, recognition of judgment rules can reinforce jurisdiction principles by refusing to enforce judgments entered in unsuitable forums. Fifth, private international law rules should enforce agreements regarding choice of law and jurisdiction in order to enable the parties to capture the gains from selecting, in advance, the law and forum they prefer. These considerations favour contractible, predictable, multilateral rules.

International Coordination

A central function of law in a market economy is facilitating coordination. Issues of coordination have a central place in game theory.[66] In a *coordination game*, players earn higher payoffs if they both choose the same strategy. The actual strategy chosen is less important than symmetry between the players.[67] Coordination underlies much private law, especially aspects of procedure, since it establishes a common process, even though others are equally feasible. However, if procedure differs between legal systems, there must be coordination *between legal systems* if coordination is to occur in multistate cases. Choice of law rules perform this function.

Take three examples. First, coordination is critical in property cases. The applicable law governs the existence and priority of claims to property, and so dictates the 'protocol' to be followed for transactions in property interests to be perfected. Second, although coordination is easier in contract cases where parties communicate, it arises centrally where procedure and matters of formal validity affect the existence and terms of contracts. In these cases, the parties must be able to coordinate in order to adopt the procedure necessary for the contracts they want to enter. Third, tort choice of law rules have coordinating properties. By enabling the parties to know what liability rules will apply to their actions and omissions, they allow the parties to take rational actions to further their own ends. Social costs, including those associated with risk bearing, may rise if the parties do not act on the basis of the same assumptions about liability.

Parties often achieve coordination where a focal point is available — an equilibrium solution that parties psychologically favour.[68] Choice of law rules can assist coordination by selecting a law of the cause that is focal in this sense. This requires multilateralism, and perhaps also differentiation between categories of cases. For example, the place of the accident may be focal in a motor vehicle accident, but not in a products liability case.

Optimal Contracting

We have already mentioned the desirability of enforcing choice of law and jurisdiction agreements to minimise litigation costs, and the need for choice of law rules to coordinate matters affecting formal validity. Facilitating contracting is a long standing private international law norm.[69] In a general sense, there are two basic issues in contracts conflicts — to what extent should parties be able to choose the law applicable to their contracts, and what should courts do when parties might have, but have not, chosen a law?

The absence of a choice of law in a contract with international elements is an instance of incomplete contracting. Economists ascribe incompleteness to transaction costs, and posit that the law can often increase efficiency by filling the contract gaps with legal rules. In the absence of a contractual choice of law, the law can do this by determining the proper law of the contract. What means of selecting the proper law would maximise the contract surplus? Economists have often reformulated this inquiry by asking what term (choice of law) the parties would have agreed to. Here, there is a basic tension — more exact replication of the parties' wishes may create uncertainty inimical to the law's capacity to provide coordination. We study these issues in chapter 3.

Contractual choices of law and forum not only allow for certainty, but also allow parties to opt into legal rules that maximise the exchange surplus. Even if contract law is completely enabling, a contractual choice of particular legal rules should occasion lower transaction costs than attempting to replicate those rules by formal contract. However, contractual choices of law and forum can be controversial when the law the parties would otherwise be subject to is not enabling, but mandatory. Permitting contractual choices enables parties to avoid mandatory rules in a way foreclosed in that domestic system. Our principal arguments for contractual choice are threefold. First, enforcing choices limits the inefficiencies of attenuated foresight by parliaments, who may not have thought about international contracts. Second, the parties most likely to opt out are often the least likely to be protected by paternalistic laws. Third, contractual choices of law counter inefficient rent-seeking interest groups whose political deal requires mandatory rules. These arguments are addressed in chapter 4.

Limiting Regulatory Monopolies and Spillovers

Where the amount of cross-border activity is high, as is the case in products markets within federations, states are increasingly able to enforce their laws against the residents of other jurisdictions.[70] This is to some extent inevitable because behaviour occurring outside the territory of a state has local effects.[71] In these cases, the laws are really attempting to force the person engaging in that behaviour to internalise its costs. However, there are several problems.[72] First, these spillovers increase coordination problems because of the risk that inconsistent laws apply to particular behaviour. Second, states may pass inefficient laws at the expense of out-of-state interests. The ambit of these laws is extended if pro-forum choice of law methods are used. Interest groups within the state can be expected to lobby for such laws. The inefficiency of these laws depends on how parties might avoid these laws and the costs of doing so.

Avoidance may occur either by a party attempting to physically exit the jurisdiction, or by ousting particular laws by express contractual choice of other laws. Physical exit costs depend on four things — the jurisdiction specificity of the subject of the regulation,[73] the scope of operation expressed in the relevant law;[74] if the scope is not stated, the choice of law method used by in-state courts;[75] and the capacity of the in-state law to be enforced.[76] Contractual exit costs are very low. Multilateral choice of law rules and limits on the circumstances in which a forum may accept jurisdiction over a forum defendant can increase coordination, decrease physical exit costs, and thus the extent of regulatory spillovers.

Conclusion

Private international law theory has struggled to fill the vacuum left by the realists' attack on formalism. The American literature has claimed policy and ignored pragmatism; the English literature has done the opposite. In this chapter, we first rejected transcendental approaches to conflicts based on the absence of universal norms or theories of the good. Second, we have shown that private international law can serve important functions that further party interests in a non-partisan way. Third, the unilateral, pro-forum biases of first-order approaches are likely to thwart these functions and increase the social costs of international activity. The following chapters of this book evaluate the extent to which theoretically informed second-order approaches can do a better job.

Notes

1. Kramer (1990).
2. The distinction is basically the same as Cavers' (1933) historic distinction between jurisdiction-selecting and rule-selecting choice of law methods, which was central to the realist critique of vested rights theory.
3. See, e.g., Kaplow (1992).
4. Sunstein and Ullmann-Margalit (1998).
5. Trakman (1980).
6. Cooter (1996).
7. Juenger (1993).
8. Bernstein (1996).
9. Sugden (1993). Brilmayer (1989) adopts a contractarian approach to choice of law.
10. On multilateralism, see Fruehwald (1996).
11. Whether the theory can eliminate bias in the manipulation of second-order rules (e.g., by characterisation) is another matter.
12. Brilmayer (1989).
13. Translated by Llewellyn Davies (1937, p. 65).
14. See, e.g., Cook (1942).
15. Forsyth (1998).
16. *Renvoi* arises in the application of a jurisdiction selecting choice of law rule: does the reference to foreign law include choice of law rules (which may refer the issue back to forum law or some other system) or only the domestic rules of the foreign system. The substance/procedure distinction distinguishes matters of procedure (governed by the *lex fori*) and matters of substance (governed by the *lex causae*). Expanding the scope of 'procedure' enables a greater application of the *lex fori* (Cook 1933). The incidental question refers to the determination of an issue incidental to the main issue in dispute by reference to the *lex causae* applicable to the main issue. By alleging that an issue is incidental to another, application of an unfavourable rule can be avoided.
17. Llewellyn Davies (1937), Anton (1956), Nygh (1964).
18. Yntema (1953, p. 306).
19. Posner (1996, pp. 31-37).
20. [1971] A.C. 356, 391.
21. Graveson (1962, pp. 355-356) has argued that the 'great lines of principle' in English private international law include policies in favour of individual

freedom, multilateralism and the upholding of agreements, and the confining of public policy within the narrowest possible limits.

22. Ehrenzweig (1960).
23. Ibid., 669.
24. Leflar (1966, p. 269).
25. Kobayashi and Ribstein (1999), Posner (1993).
26. Currie (1963, p. 182).
27. Brilmayer (1995, pp. 116-117).
28 Kobayashi and Ribstein (1999).
29. Becker (1983), Peltzman (1976).
30. O'Hara and Ribstein (1997).
31. Guzman (2000).
32. Kramer (1985, 1990).
33. Brilmayer (1980a). See generally Sunstein (1989).
34. Baxter (1963).
35. Coase (1960).
36. Kobayashi and Ribstein (1999).
37. Macey (1986).
38. Kramer (1990, p. 317).
39. Posner (1985, p. 305).
40. Posner (1998a, p. 646).
41. Solimine (1989).
42. Posner (1990, p. 430).
43. Leflar (1966).
44. Yntema notes this approach was proposed by Aldricus, just before the thirteenth century (1953, pp. 301-302). See also Juenger (1993, p. 12).
45. Juenger (1993). See also Borchers (1997).
46. See, e.g., Juenger (1994). Cf. Juenger (1998), where the rule-based law on jurisdiction in the European Brussels and Lugano Conventions on jurisdiction is described as a 'resounding success' (p. 116), and the vague constitutional constraints of American case law on jurisdiction are described as 'chaotic and incoherent' (p. 118). Juenger observes that the aim of a jurisdiction convention should be the statement of the bases of jurisdiction in 'clear and concise terms' (p. 122).
47. Rabin (1996).
48. See chapter 6, pp. 99-102 *infra*.
49. A. Schwartz (1997).
50. See Gergen (1988).
51. For advocacy of choice of law tailoring, see Whincop and Keyes (1997). As to the literature on tailoring, see Ayres and Gertner (1989) and Ayres (1993).
52. Cf. Coleman et al. (1989).
53. Courts often resolve choice of law questions in a manner calculated to uphold the terms of contracts: e.g., *Coast Lines Ltd v. Hudig & Veder Chartering N.V.*

[1972] 2 Q.B. 34, *Seeman v. Philadelphia Warehouse Co.*, 274 U.S. 403, 407-408 (1927), Nygh (1995, pp. 340-346), Ehrenzweig (1962, p. 465). More significantly, international arbitrators often select whichever rules are thought appropriate to the litigation (Juenger 1997).

54. See chapter 10, p. 195 *infra*.
55. See, e.g., Kincaid (1996), Nygh (1995), Shreve (1996), Twerski (1971). Some courts have endorsed this approach: *Phillips Petroleum Co. v. Shutts*, 472 U.S. 797, 822 (1985), *Breavington v. Godleman* (1988) 169 C.L.R. 41, 77.
56. Kramer (1990, pp. 336-337).
57. See, e.g., *Lochner v. New York*, 198 U.S. 45 (1905).
58. Diver (1983), Dworkin (1967), Ehrlich and Posner (1974), Kaplow (1992), Kennedy (1976), Posner (1990, pp. 42-53), Rose (1988), Schauer (1991).
59. Kaplow (1992).
60. Amar (1989), Posner (1996, p. 96).
61. American Law Institute (1994), Brilmayer (1989), Kozyris (1987), Symeonides (1997). Cf. Juenger (1994).
62. Huber (1988), Priest (1987).
63. This section is based on Whincop and Keyes (2000).
64. Cooter and Rubinfeld (1989).
65. Shavell (1982).
66. See, eg, Baird et al. (1994, pp. 35-44).
67. However, in some coordination games, players may have different preferences for one particular set of coordinated strategies. An example is the battle of the sexes game, in which a husband and wife must choose whether to turn up at a boxing bout or the opera, not knowing for sure which the other will choose. The husband prefers boxing to opera, and the wife prefers opera to boxing, but each prefers to be with the other at the less preferred event than being alone at the more preferred event. A number of conflicts problems fit the battle of the sexes paradigm.
68. Schelling (1980).
69. Graveson (1962).
70. McConnell (1988).
71. *Laker Airways Ltd v. Sabena, Belgian World Airlines*, 731 F 2d 909, 923 (D.C. Cir. 1984). See generally *The Case of the SS Lotus (France v. Turkey)* [1927] P.C.I.J. (Ser. A) No. 10.
72. Trachtman (1997).
73. Compare land (which is jurisdiction-specific) and a contract for the supply of goods.
74. Compare 'the consumer purchased the product within the state' to 'the injury occurred within, or the products were brought into, the state'.
75. O'Hara and Ribstein (1997).
76. Goldsmith (1998b).

3 Contracts

The Functions of Contract Law

The phenomenon of exchange has been a vital part of the evolution of human civilisation.[1] Consensual exchange is the most reliable way to improve the welfare and the utility of all involved. The institution of contract permits parties to project exchanges into the future by promissory and other means.

Contract's welfare properties and the liberal values associated with the common law underwrite the principle of freedom of contract — that parties are substantially free to bind themselves to whatever obligations they like. If, however, contract law's only purpose was to ascertain what parties had agreed, and what that obliged them to do, it would collapse into the law of evidence and processes of interpretation. Instead, contract law does many other things. It specifies formalities, such as obligations to commit certain types of contracts to writing. It imposes disclosure obligations on the parties. Perhaps most importantly, it specifies a range of supplementary obligations that the parties have not expressly provided for in their agreement. For example, it provides that certain conduct by one of the parties entitles the other to terminate the contract and sue for damages, the measure of which it specifies should the parties not have done so.

The significance of these doctrines and the importance of contract law generally are attributable to an economic insight — contracting is costly.[2] Therefore, the parties will often be unable to write a contract so complete as to leave nothing for a court to do save enforce it. The costs of doing so are greater than the benefits. Real world contracts are therefore *incomplete*. This term has two different meanings.[3] A contract can be incomplete in an 'obligational' sense — it fails to specify the parties' obligations in possible future states of the world. A contract failing to specify the consequence of breach is obligationally incomplete. A contract can also be incomplete in a 'contingent' sense, because it is insensitive to possible future states of the world, and so does not realise all possible gains from trade between the parties. This problem may motivate one of the parties to renegotiate this contract in certain future situations, or to breach it.[4]

'Transaction costs' are not limited to the costs occasioned by the search for counterparties, negotiation and drafting. The existence of asymmetric information is a powerful source of transacting problems. Imperfectly informed parties may enter contracts which do not maximise their joint wealth because one of the parties suppresses important information.[5] To take a much-used example, parties may differ in the damages they sustain from the same breach of contract.[6] In those circumstances, it may be efficient to offer two or more types of contracts, involving different types of precautions. High precaution contracts would be offered to high damage buyers, who would pay a higher price (corresponding to the marginal cost of greater precautions) than a low damage buyer. However, where the cost of ascertaining what sort of party one is dealing with is high enough, separation of high and low risks may not occur. A party may suppress private information because she is better off staying silent, notwithstanding the greater joint welfare gains from revelation.

Much of the enterprise of law and economics has been directed to determining the form that legal rules should take where contracts are incomplete and contracting is costly. This scholarship recognises that contract law functions to reduce contracting costs. One way it can do this is to fill gaps in the incomplete contract. By filling gaps, the law spares the parties the need to reach agreement themselves. This also implies a suitability criterion for the content of a legal rule. Given some assumptions, the best legal rule is the one that a majority of contracting parties would prefer. What this majoritarian approach does not tell us is how to define the contractual population. Is one looking for a rule to apply across all contracts, or to all sale of goods contracts, or to sale of goods contracts involving consumer purchasers? The more heterogeneous one's field, the less confident one can be in claiming a majority preference.

Law and economics scholars generally advocate that contract law rules be themselves subject to contract. It is customary to describe such rules as 'defaults'. As is implicit in the above discussion, legal rules are only ever likely to command majoritarian acceptance. Unanimity is rarely achievable. The ability of the minority to contract around the legal rule is something that efficiency requires to be preserved. This is consistent with the implications of the Coase theorem — parties will contract around inefficient property rights allocations, including those created by contract law rules, subject to transaction costs.

From a systemic perspective, the economic objective is to minimise not only the sum of the parties' transaction costs and welfare losses resulting from lost opportunities to exploit gains from trade, but in addition the costs of rule promulgation and application. It is unlikely that this cost function can be minimised without default rules. There is a tradeoff between the costs of rule-making and transaction cost reduction. The joint cost function is likely to be minimised by shifting some of the costs of differentiating rules to the parties. Nor should one expect rule-makers, such as parliaments and courts, to be particularly good at ascertaining contractual preferences. Parties will usually know their own preferences better than rule-makers.

This analysis implies a simple prescription — choose rules that have majoritarian appeal, and permit parties to contract around them. However, this proposition has been contested. First, the literature sometimes advocates defaults that parties *do not* want.[7] This proposition follows from the earlier suggestion that contracts may be left incomplete by parties with private information. If parties were fully informed, contract terms would frequently be differentiated to reflect relevant risk and cost attributes. In the absence of full information, high risks may attempt to 'pool' with low risks by imitating their behaviour. This is the economic problem of *adverse selection* — differentiation of risks may be efficient, but it may suit high risks to stay mum where they are able to obtain a larger share of a smaller pie.[8] An undesired default rule — a 'penalty default' — may compel such parties to disclose their private information when they contract around the default for the legal term they do want. Because risks and term preferences should be correlated, the default rule achieves the separation of risks.

Second, in some circumstances, a default that expands contractual choices may be preferred, whether or not it has majority appeal. For example, it may be difficult to write contracts that emulate the complex balancing of merits implicit in some legal standards.[9] It may expand contractual choices if the standard is made the default, and parties are permitted to contract out of it in favour of a simple obligation.[10]

Third, default-setting may be shifted from before the fact, to after it. An adjudicator may ask what rule the actual parties would have contracted for, had transaction costs not prevented them from doing so.[11] We discussed tailoring in chapter 2. The concept of a tailored default presupposes, not uncontroversially, that courts are competent and can verify necessary information to ascertain what parties would contract for.[12] Tailored defaults may be appealing where transaction costs are substantial and preferences heterogeneous.[13] The merits of a tailored rule resemble the merits of a standard administered ex post, compared to a rule formulated ex ante.[14] It may also be that the content of a default rule itself influences party preferences.[15] Parties may prefer to retain the default, rather than contract out of it, because they have a cognitive bias in favour of the status quo. Tailoring may reduce the significance of such a bias.

Finally, the optimal form of default rules may depend on learning and network externalities associated with contract terms.[16] Parties may prefer to adopt terms that have been commonly used in the past because of the institutional learning available in respect of them. They are, for example, easier to draft, more certain in their operation, simpler to explain to others, and so on. For similar reasons, parties may prefer to adopt terms that are contemporaneously used, or expected to be used in the future, in other contracts. The pioneering work in this area demonstrates that the presence of such effects may lead to suboptimal contracting, either because there is too much standardisation, or too little. The optimal response may not be single default rules, but the construction of menu-like options.[17]

There is an active debate in the law and economics community concerning the optimal form of defaults, but there is a fiercer debate between its members and non-members over the advocacy of default rules. Contested here is the claim that contractual freedom will make both parties better off. This might not follow if parties lack sufficient information about the costs associated with the options they must choose between.[18] This is particularly intense in cases involving tort-like injuries. Paternalism may justify conversion of majoritarian defaults into mandatory rules, although law-maker competency must be a maintained hypothesis here.

This discussion of mandatory rules and default rules can be used to analyse conflictual issues associated with contracts. Here, too, we confront issues associated with the scope of contractual freedom, the interpretation of mandatory rules, and the judicial method that courts should use in default of agreement. These issues will occupy this and the following two chapters. The remainder of this chapter discusses the nature of contractual choice of law and jurisdiction. Chapter 4 extends the analysis by examining the relation between the proper law of the contract and mandatory rules established by domestic law. Chapter 5 considers a special case of this relation — where the mandatory rules are tort laws that apply to contractual exchanges, such as products liability statutes.

Choice of Law and Jurisdiction in a World of Costly Transacting

In a world of complete and costless contracting, choice of law issues would, like contract law itself, collapse into procedural, evidentiary, and interpretive doctrine. Outside of that world, choice of law matters for at least three reasons. First, the proper law of the contract settles the procedural and formal obligations necessary either to enter contracts, or to agree certain terms. Included here are formal obligations, disclosure requirements, and requirements to give notice of terms such as exclusion clauses. We refer to this as a *procedure-settling* function. Second, the proper law determines whether or not the provisions the parties have agreed are valid. We call this a *contract-validation* function. Some contracts will be inconsistent with the public policy or the mandatory rules of a jurisdiction. Third, it selects the body of law from which default rules will be drawn to supplement the gaps in the contract. This is a *default-selection* function, although the rule selected may not always be a default.

Each function is important economically. The procedure-settling function may help to resolve, or it may exacerbate, the coordination problems we studied in chapter 2. It may affect formal disclosure obligations and penalty defaults designed to increase informed contracting. Contract-validation either limits or expands the parties' contractual freedom to exploit gains from trade. Default-selection is as important as default rules themselves. Multistate contracting therefore creates both problems and opportunities. A range of potentially applicable legal regimes increases information costs. Parties must understand how the rules of these regimes can affect rights under the contract. A wider range of rules may increase opportunistic litigation. A party wanting to renegotiate a contract may assert rights unilaterally that neither party would have expected to exist when the contract was formed. But there are advantages as well. The multistate world adds a dimension to the contracting process. Parties need not be limited to domestic laws or courts. This increases choice and may blunt rent-seeking. Comprehending these advantages depends on how the law resolves conflicts. We now turn to this inquiry.

The most salient feature of the law's method for determining the proper law of the contract is that, except for the procedure-settling function, parties may choose it themselves.[19] This is usually done by a choice of law clause, which stipulates that the contract is governed by, for example, English law. Thus, the law delegates the contract-validation and default-selection functions to the parties. Historically, the absence of any connection between the law chosen and the contract is irrelevant.

By permitting parties to control contract-validation, the law effectively expands the permissible number of contracts the parties can write. These rules help to control problems associated with learning and network externalities. One of the implications of the research in this area is that the default rule itself can be a barrier to parties contracting out of it.[20] This is because defaults, being the subject of so much case law, generate powerful learning effects. However, the ability to opt for a different law, rather than a different contract term, sanctions a wide range of effective choice. Parties may prefer to opt for a legal system offering different rules than attempt to contract out of defaults in the domestic system. Contractual choice of law resembles a potentially vast menu of legal systems.

The economic advantages of contractual choices of law have been extensively explored in federal contexts. The best known instance is competition between the American States for corporate charters. Corporations can opt into the corporate law of any state they choose by incorporating or reincorporating there. Although this 'internal affairs' rule is sometimes thought to reflect the artificial status of corporations, it is economically a contractual choice of law.[21] The appropriateness of permitting parties to choose their corporate law has been questioned, but empirical evidence indicates that shareholders have gained from wider choice and state competition.[22]

A notable feature of the U.S. charter 'market' is the existence of supply side competition. States actively compete to enact corporation statutes that attract incorporations. Permitting parties to choose the proper law may not always have this effect. The American charter market is special because a state can levy a franchise tax on incorporations within the state. This makes competition worthwhile. In other types of contracts, it is harder for states to exclude non-residents from the benefit of their rules.[23] However, some interest groups in the state may attract benefits from choices of law (e.g., litigation instructions for lawyers).

The procedure-settling function is a qualification to the general rule. Issues associated with whether a binding contract exists are not easy to resolve by a contractual choice. That would beg the question regarding the existence or terms of the contract. There is some confusion about how these issues should be resolved. The law selected needs to be adapted to the economic problem that parties may not be aware of the terms (including choices of law) that they are agreeing to. In the case of sophisticated buyers or repeat transactors, the procedure-settling function may not matter much. In the case of one-off transactors dealing on standard form terms, it may matter significantly. The law chosen needs to exhibit two virtues. First, it must be tolerably certain at the time of transacting, to enable parties to coordinate. Second, it needs to economise on the parties' (especially one-off transactors') information costs.

Perhaps the stronger view in English law is that procedure-settling and formation issues are determined by the contract's 'putative' proper law — the law that applies in the absence of an express choice.[24] That is normally the legal system with which the transaction has its 'closest and most real connection'.[25] We analyse the merits of this rule below. However, it seems to be as good as any other rule in this context. The rule will be reasonably certain in simple cases, although not in some complex transactions. It is less easy to know for sure whether this is the rule that economises on information costs. This depends on the procedural content of domestic law. Although it is ultimately an empirical question, it seems intuitive that the parties most in need of protection by formation procedures (one-off transactors contracting on standard forms) will not go very far afield in searching for contractual counterparties. This will substantially limit them to domestic markets.[26] In these circumstances, the putative choice of law rule is very likely to select the law of that place. The consumer will be more familiar with the contracting procedures there, so reducing the need for extra search and investigation. A rule selecting the place of contracting would have similar virtues and may be more certain.

The putative proper law is superior to the most commonly used alternative — the law of the forum.[27] The obvious problem with forum law is that it is not known ex ante. This contradicts the very concept of procedure-settling and precludes coordination. The plaintiff's incentive to select a forum with procedural law that favours the plaintiff is strong — perhaps by enforcing a concealed term, perhaps by avoiding the contract.

Although an expressly chosen law will apply to substantive issues, it generally does not apply to issues of procedure.[28] The law of the forum governs procedure. This is the substance/procedure distinction in private international law — venerable to some, disreputable to others.[29] Trying to ascertain the features of a procedural law is a vexed enterprise. 'Procedure' is unlikely to have any coherent meaning that could be prescribed ex ante or applied deterministically. But there is a pragmatic justification for it, once it is understood that forum, like substantive law, is within the parties' contractual competence. Under English law, parties may agree to submit to the jurisdiction of a court, to the exclusion of all other jurisdictions if they please.[30] So, in consequence, parties can select procedural law, by way of a choice of jurisdiction.

Jurisdiction clauses are motivated by minimising litigation costs and facilitating optimal contracting — two of the basic functions of private international law. First, particular courts may resolve certain types of cases expeditiously. Such expedition is a consequence of the court's procedural rules. Because a court applies its procedural rules, whatever the *lex causae*, a substance-procedure distinction enables the parties to make these comparisons and choices. This implies a pragmatic criterion for separating substance and procedure — which rules should be kept constant to permit parties to choose between jurisdictions? Case management, discovery, pleading and evidence rules are clear examples, but caps on damages and statutes of limitation are almost certainly not procedural in this sense.

Having said that a substance/procedure distinction permits a choice of forum independently of substantive law, other factors encourage law and forum to be 'bundled'. The procedure for raising issues of foreign law is messy. In the absence of full faith and credit provisions, it has to be proved as a 'fact' by expert testimony. Given a judge's unfamiliarity with foreign law, this method is likely to result in a higher incidence of errors in the application of foreign law. As a result, a choice of the same substantive law and jurisdiction is a means to control the costs of judicial errors.[31]

Second, apart from issues of substantive law, a choice of forum may economise on the parties' joint costs. Litigation in a forum handy to the parties' residences or places of business or to the place the contract was performed is likely to involve lower costs than in a far-flung forum.

Finally, some courts may have a reputation for neutrality that wins favour. A state *may* have incentives to attract choices of its law. Lawyers, as a potent interest group, will stand to gain if parties contract to submit to the jurisdiction in which the lawyers practice. They may get advisory work. If the contract becomes litigious, they are likely to act for the parties.[32] Hence, lawyers may lobby states to invest in facilitative law and unbiased judges to attract contracting parties.[33]

So far, we have discussed the effect of express choices of law, and of jurisdiction. In a majority of cases, the parties will opt for a single choice of each. However, it may be that parties would prefer a more complex arrangement, particularly in the context of choices of law. First, parties may choose to refer different parts of their contract to different laws. For example, despite a general choice of the law of New York State, matters relating to damages payable for breach of contract might be governed by English law. This is called *depeçage*. It has long been permitted. Why would parties agree to such a thing? Recall the risks for parties making a disjunctive choice of law and forum — courts are more likely to err when applying foreign law. Depeçage has the advantage that parties might carve out a smaller domain of foreign law, the substantive content of which is relatively clear. This means that parties are not restricted to taking 'bundled' or 'tied' goods, a dilemma well-known to anti-trust lawyers.[34]

The tolerance of depeçage contrasts with the reception of the second complex arrangement, which is sometimes called 'floating' law. Floating law makes contingent choices of law. For example, the law of J applies while *x* holds, otherwise the law of K applies.[35] Floating law serves the needs of contracting parties. Given uncertainty as to the future, the comparative costs and benefits of different laws will be unclear. Contingent and flexible choice of law arrangements may thus address the problem of contingent incompleteness, outlined above. Also, if the parties have not made an exclusive choice of jurisdiction, they may prefer to link the choice of law with the eventual forum.

English courts have had difficulty with floating law arrangements where the proper law is not determinate ex ante. We find formalism running rampant here. Courts have articulated a contractual archetype which requires at all times a strict, one-for-one correspondence between a contract and the law governing it. A pragmatic approach rejects the need for such a severe, unrealistic ontology of contracts. The role of courts is to ascertain what the parties have agreed, and to supplement it with suitable default rules. Floating law arrangements are compatible with this function, provided they have an ascertainable meaning at the time of the litigation. If they do not, one can revert to the default methodologies for ascertaining the proper law in the absence of choice.

This section has vindicated a 'transactional' approach to private international law. It has shown how choice of law and forum issues are contractible, and the considerations that might influence party choices. The next section analyses the proper law of the contract in the absence of choice.

Default Choices of Default Rules

What does the law do when the parties have not made a choice of law? In answering this question, we are describing default choices of law, since the last section shows that the law yields to party choice. Hence, these rules are a species of 'metadefault'[36] — a default rule that chooses rules which, in contract law at least, will usually be defaults. The multistate context of private international law opens out the dichotomous mandatory/default distinction. To explain this, we establish a taxonomy of defaults.[37]

A legal rule that permits parties to contract out of, or around, it, is a *substantive default*. What is not a substantive default in a domestic system is not necessarily a mandatory rule in an international context. The parties may be able to choose a different proper law. Whether they should be able to do that is examined in the next chapter. Unless the domestic jurisdiction prevents them from doing so, we say that a *choice of law default* has been preserved. Even if the choice of law default is not preserved, a court may nonetheless enforce a choice of foreign forum. The foreign forum must then decide what effect to give to the chosen law. Where the parties are at liberty to make a choice of forum, we say that a *forum default* has been preserved.[38] The difference between these two forms of default is that a choice of law default should require the *domestic* forum to enforce the selected proper law, notwithstanding its mandatory rule. An *international mandatory rule* eliminates all defaults, and compels a domestic forum to accept jurisdiction and apply local law. This section examines the content of choice of law defaults, with a glance at forum defaults. The next chapter analyses the relationship between domestic mandatory rules and choice of law and forum defaults.

The current approach to choice of law defaults in English and U.S. law is to locate the legal system with which the transaction has the closest connection.[39] Various factors are considered in this inquiry, including the places the contract was made and performed, the residences or places of business of the parties, and the subject matter of the contract. In many cases, this will be straightforward, but genuinely international cases are difficult.[40] This approach is sometimes called a *jurisdiction-selecting* one;[41] it locates the most closely related jurisdiction, without explicitly considering the suitability of its legal rules to the contractual exchange.

'Closest connection' choice of law defaults can be compared to two alternatives, one of which confers less, and the other more, discretion on the trial judge.[42] The first is to use rules, such as adopting the law of the place of contracting (the *lex loci contractus*). English and U.S. law used these some time ago but they have fallen out of favour. The second alternative draws on the concept of choice of law tailoring described in chapter 2. It would select on a case-by-case basis the legal system that provides the gap-filling rules the parties are most likely to have contracted for, had they been able to do so. Where rules are a second-order approach to choice of law, choice of law tailoring requires a first-order adjudication. The number of factors that closest connection tests rely on determines which side of the line they fall.

According to the Coase theorem, the legal rule is irrelevant if transaction costs are low. Parties will contract around inefficient choice of law defaults. We suspect, although we cannot prove, that the rule does not matter that much in many contract cases. Casual empiricism suggests that choice of law clauses are common in international agreements. For example, this book is written pursuant to a contract selecting English law. An interesting question to ponder, however, is how often the express choice of law deviates from the default law selection? There may be a status quo bias that deters parties from contracting for other law.[43] If such a bias exists, choice of law tailoring may be the optimal response.

If choice of law rules don't matter much, or matter in only a small fraction of cases, rules make good sense. A rule such as *lex loci contractus* is simple to understand and administered at low cost, so economising on state judicial resources.[44] Private international law cases are rarities, and create an availability bias for a law-maker when it comes to rule formulation.[45] That is, one thinks that ex post discretion is needed to deal with these cases because we are only familiar with the complex cases raising these questions. The representativeness of these cases may be vastly overrated. A simple rule may suit a substantial majority of cases. Complex contracts may be best dealt with passively, by enforcing the parties' agreement, or a simple default if no agreement exists.[46] This analysis explains why, in the European Union, the Rome Convention adopts presumptions, since these tests are closer to pre-emptive rules.[47]

The optimal complexity of untailored choice of law rules is unclear. One or two generic rules are less likely to capture majority preferences.[48] A place of contracting rule may be a good rule for a sale of goods, but less good for a contract involving services. A place of performance rule may be the opposite. We concur with the argument of some authors that formulating rules specific to transaction types (e.g., charterparties, franchises, sale of goods, insurance) is a better option.[49]

There are arguments for tailoring choices of law ex post. These are strongest in the context of long term contracts. The relation may change substantially over its term, and so too may the parties' choice of law preferences. Tailoring may be necessary if courts refuse to countenance floating or contingent choices of law.[50] But this is not a sufficient argument. Litigation is rarely a preferred means of achieving cooperation and adaptation in long-term relations.[51] The court is often unable to verify information needed for a more active function. The other problem with tailored rules and even closest connection methods is that courts may use the greater discretion conferred on them in a partisan way. The local party may be favoured over the alien. There are instances of this in tort cases, but not very many in contract law to make it a serious consideration.

Our discussion of choice of law defaults so far has juxtaposed untailored and tailored defaults. We have said nothing about penalty defaults — those designed to induce parties to communicate private information regarding contractual preferences. In a limited sense, an untailored default, such as *lex loci contractus*, may operate as a penalty default if preferences for choices of law are heterogeneous. Such a rule will force more parties to contract explicitly.[52] However, the use of information-forcing penalty defaults is not simple in a multistate context. Contracting around a choice of law default has an inherently lower information content than contracting around a substantive default. Opting out of rule *r* indicates something about a contracting party's preferences for a term governing that aspect of the exchange. However, contracting for the legal rules of system *s*, compared to the default alternative, *t*, is a less clear signal. There are inevitably a large number of rules in each system, many of which may differ. Only where very few rules are saliently different, or where there is a consistent correlation between the differences (e.g., they all favour 'high-risk' consumers) can the expression of a preference have a signalling effect.[53]

The information-forcing effect of penalty defaults can therefore be blunted in a multistate context. If the penalty default exists in all relevant jurisdictions, its effect will be preserved. But if it only exists in, say, one out of two jurisdictions, it may not induce information-forcing. Whether it does depends on (a) the beliefs of the privately informed party about the likely proper law; and (b) the pay-offs to disclosing and not disclosing under the different choice of law possibilities.[54] There will be more 'pooling' and less disclosure where choice of law rules operate uncertainly. This is a further argument for clearer choice of law rules.

Finally, what of forum defaults? This is a complex question which we consider in more detail in chapters 8 and 9. The assertion of jurisdiction depends on a two-stage process. The first stage, which we may call the *establishment* stage, invokes a set of jurisdictional limitations. In English, and also Australian law, the basic rule is that the court will only assert jurisdiction against a person present, in the physical sense, in the law area of its jurisdiction.[55] This rule is extended by procedural rules of court, which permit service out of the jurisdiction. Some rules require the plaintiff to obtain the court's leave to serve out. Others require leave where the defendant does not enter an appearance.[56] The second *exercise* stage requires the court to consider whether the established jurisdiction should be exercised by hearing the matter. A court may stay its own process. The law on stays in England and Australia has changed substantially over the last twenty-five years. Both jurisdictions, although more particularly England, have liberalised the previously onerous criteria for a stay.[57] English courts will grant a stay where there is another forum, having jurisdiction over the parties, which is a more appropriate, or 'natural' forum in which to resolve the matter. An Australian court will grant a stay where it is a clearly inappropriate forum.[58]

We expect that forum defaults matter more than choice of law defaults, at least in contract cases. Moves towards harmonised law decrease the significance of substantive conflicts. By the time of litigation, choices of law certainly affect the distribution of exchange surplus. However, choice of law decisions may have no more than indirect influences on efficiency, because they lengthen the litigation process, change the applicable defaults, or create more uncertainty. Jurisdiction issues, however, have first-order impacts because they affect the decision and cost to litigate. A crucial empirical question is whether it is possible to establish majoritarian forum defaults if the forum in which litigation costs are minimised is heavily fact-contingent. We return to this issue in chapters 8 and 9.

Of course, if transaction costs are low, the unrepresentativeness of the establishment rule is irrelevant, as parties will simply contract around it by way of jurisdiction clauses. But making a choice may be difficult. The appeal of a particular forum may depend on the nature of the dispute. Thus, choice of forum may be particularly affected by contingent incompleteness. If so, much weight rests on the exercise stage and the resolution of stay applications. Chapter 8 examines how these applications should be resolved, and how they are in fact resolved. There is a case for a 'tailored' approach to the discretion to grant a stay. The court on a stay application would consider which forum minimised the costs to the parties of resolving the rights they have contracted for. Advocacy of tailoring depends on the heterogeneity of the jurisdictional preferences of parties to similar contract types, and the ability of courts to verify information relevant to costs.[59] This depends on the hypothesis we have posited — the relation between the parties' costs and case type is heavily fact contingent in multistate cases. If it holds, we would have a striking contrast in our approach to choice of law and forum defaults — untailored defaults suit the former, but ex post tailoring suits the latter.

Conclusion

This chapter is a reference point for the remainder of the book. We have shown how private international law can be treated as simply another aspect of exchanges. Parties can and often will contract for their preferences. The law largely permits this. The economic logic of this is clear. The multistate world is both a problem and a boon. Domestic objectives underlying rules (such as penalty defaults) can be thwarted. The availability of different rules may induce opportunistic litigation. On the other hand, private international legal rules expand contractual choices and limit the lock-in effects of learning and network externalities. Many recent changes in choice of law and jurisdictional doctrine can be explained on efficiency grounds.

So far, we have described a world in which the only legitimate concern of states is formulating contract-facilitating default rules and maintaining competent, unbiased courts. Contracting parties are assumed to act consistently with a rational maximising model. The following two chapters examine the strain on the liberal, transactional model of private international law in contexts where these assumptions may not hold.

Notes

1. Macneil (1974).
2. Coase (1937, 1960).
3. Ayres and Gertner (1992).
4. Ayres and Gertner (1992), Shavell (1980).
5. Ayres and Gertner (1989, 1992), Johnston (1990), A. Schwartz (1992).

6. *Hadley v. Baxendale* (1854) 156 E.R. 145. Apart from the references in note 5, see also Bebchuk and Shavell (1991).
7. Ayres and Gertner (1989). After criticism by Johnston (1990), Ayres and Gertner (1992) revised their treatment of strategic contractual inefficiency. The concept has nonetheless stuck, perhaps because it is able to explain a range of phenomena: see, e.g., Whincop (1997a, 1998a), and chapter 9.
8. The 'pie' metaphor comes from Ayres and Gertner (1989, p. 99). See note 54 *infra*.
9. Rose (1988).
10. Ayres (1992, 1993). Cf. Kaplow (1992).
11. Ayres (1993), Ayres and Gertner (1989).
12. A. Schwartz (1992, 1993). Cf. Hadfield (1994) and Johnston (1995).
13. Ayres (1993). In these cases, higher transaction costs decrease the amount of contracting. Heterogeneity means that any single rule will leave a larger number of parties with a suboptimal rule.
14. On the rules and standards literature, see Diver (1983), Ehrlich and Posner (1974), Hadfield (1994), Kaplow (1992), Kennedy (1976), Posner (1990, pp. 42-53), Johnston (1995), Rose (1988), Schwartz and Scott (1995).
15. Korobkin (1998).
16. Kahan and Klausner (1997), Klausner (1995).
17. Klausner (1995).
18. Cf. Schwartz and Wilde (1979).
19. *Vita Food Products, Inc. v. Unus Shipping Co. Ltd* [1939] A.C. 277, 290, *Suisse Atlantique Société D'Armement Maritime S.A. v. NV Rotterdamsche Kolen Centrale* [1967] 1 A.C. 361. European law endorses party autonomy (Juenger 1997). U.S. law at first refused to enforce choices of law, but now substantially accommodates them: *Restatement (Second) of Conflict of Laws* § 187 (1971).
20. Klausner (1995). This idea is anticipated in Goetz and Scott (1985).
21. Ribstein (1993).
22. Romano (1985, 1993, 1998) and Winter (1977) are the classic references in the area. Macey and Miller (1987) extends the debate by analysing interest group effects. Bebchuk (1992) provides the most important critique. For wider perspectives than the American one, see Charny (1991), Daniels (1991), Drury (1998), Ramsay (1990), and Whincop (1998b).
23. It is the ability to tax which is the key issue, not the excludability problem. A state cannot stop another state replicating its rules — this happens all the time in U.S. corporate law. Thus, some leading theorists have argued that Delaware's seemingly invincible lead has more to do with its court and political systems than the rules per se (Romano 1985, cf. Black 1990). Klausner (1995) attributes it to network externalities.

24. *White Cliffs Opal Mines Ltd v. Miller* (1904) 4 S.R. (N.S.W.) 150, *The Parouth* [1982] 2 Lloyd's Rep. 351, Nygh (1995a, p. 304), Sykes and Pryles (1991, pp. 611-613).
25. *Bonython v. Commonwealth of Australia* [1951] A.C. 201, 219.
26. Internet transactions are an exception: see chapter 10, p. 191 ff. *infra*.
27. *Oceanic Sun Line Special Shipping Co. Inc. v. Fay* (1987) 165 C.L.R. 197, 222 (Brennan J), 261 (Gaudron J), *Mackender v. Feldia A.G.* [1967] Q.B. 590, 602-603. See generally *Green v. Australian Industrial Investment Ltd* (1989) 90 A.L.R. 500, Australian Law Reform Commission (1992, paras 8.12, 8.59), Bell (1996), Briggs (1990), Garner (1989).
28. Here, procedure does not refer to the law's procedural requirements for a contract's formal validity, but to non-substantive matters of civil procedure.
29. Contrast the majority and minority judgments in *Stevens v. Head* (1993) 176 C.L.R. 433. See chapter 6, p. 97 *infra*.
30. *The Eleftheria* [1970] P. 94, *Huddart Parker Ltd v. The Ship Mill Hill* (1960) 81 C.L.R. 502. The U.S. courts now take a similar view, after historical antipathy: *The Bremen v. Zapata Off-Shore Co.*, 407 U.S. 1 (1972), *Carnival Cruise Lines, Inc. v. Shute*, 499 U.S. 585 (1991), cf. *Davenport Mach. & Foundry Co. v. Adolph Coors Co.*, 314 N.W.2d 432 (Iowa, 1982), *Montana Uniform Arbitration Act*, Mont. Code. Ann. § 28-2-708 (1999). See generally Carrington and Haagen (1996), Mullenix (1988).
31. Fentiman (1992).
32. Macey and Miller (1987).
33. Ribstein (1994). The reverse is also possible: lawyers lobby for plaintiff-friendly legal rules in non-contractual cases (Epstein 1988). For example, England and Delaware may be the forums most friendly to contracting parties; Texas may be the tort plaintiff's best friend.
34. Daniels (1991, pp. 146-147). Bundling also increases the lock-in effect caused by learning and network externalities.
35. Examples include *Armar Shipping Co. v. Caisse Algerienne d'Assurance et de Reassurance* [1981] 1 W.L.R. 207, *Black Clawson International Ltd v. Papierwerke Waldhof-Aschaffenburg A.G.* [1981] 2 Lloyd's Rep. 446, *The Mariannina* [1983] 1 Lloyd's Rep. 12.
36. Whincop and Keyes (1997).
37. This taxonomy was first developed in Whincop and Keyes (1998a).
38. It has also been suggested that the parties' rights to refer their case to arbitration also excludes the default because arbitrators infrequently apply the law directly (Ware 1999).
39. *Bonython v. Commonwealth of Australia* [1951] A.C. 201, 219, *Akai Pty Ltd v. The People's Insurance Company Ltd* (1996) 188 C.L.R. 418. U.S. law is similar: *Restatement (Second) of Conflict of Laws* § 188(1) (1971).

40. *Coast Lines Ltd v. Hudig & Veder Chartering N.V.* [1972] 2 QB 34, 44, *Stanley Kerr Holdings Pty Ltd v. Gibor Textile Enterprises Ltd* [1978] 2 N.S.W.L.R. 372.
41. Cavers (1933). Jurisdiction-selecting rules are typically second-order rules.
42. See the references in note 14 *supra*.
43. Korobkin (1998).
44. Epstein (1995), A. Schwartz (1993).
45. Tversky and Kahneman (1982).
46. A. Schwartz (1992).
47. *Convention on the Law Applicable to Contractual Obligations* 1980, art. 4.
48. O'Hara and Ribstein (2000) advocate majoritarian preferences as the principal guide to choice of law.
49. Delaume (1981), Horlacher (1991).
50. Ayres (1992).
51. Bernstein (1996), Hadfield (1990), Johnston (1996), Macneil (1978), A. Schwartz (1992), Williamson (1985, 1996), Whincop (1997b).
52. Ayres (1993).
53. See generally Baird et al. (1995, pp. 122-156).
54. Take an example involving negotiation between B and C for a contract. B is a high risk, and can choose either to disclose or not to disclose. Disclosure is efficient because C will take an efficient precaution, but will charge B for it. Assume that if B discloses, there is an exchange surplus of 100 shared equally (50/50). If B does not disclose, there is an exchange surplus of 80. If the law of r applies, B gains 30, and C, 50. If the law of s applies, B gains 70, and C, 10. B's payoff from disclosing is 50; his payoff from not doing so is $30p_r + 70(1 - p_r)$, where p_r is the probability of r's law applying. It can be seen that unless B believes that p_r is greater than 50%, B will not disclose.
55. *Laurie v. Carroll* (1958) 98 C.L.R. 310.
56. Examples of the former type are O. 10 r. 1 of the *High Court Rules (High Court of Australia)* and O.11 r. 1(1) of the *Rules of the Supreme Court of Judicature*. An example of the latter type is r. 7.04 of the *Supreme Court Rules 1996* (Vic.).
57. The old law is exemplified by *Maritime Insurance Co. Ltd v. Geelong Harbour Trust Commissioners* (1908) 6 C.L.R. 194 and *St. Pierre v. South American Stores (Gath & Chaves) Ltd* [1936] 1 K.B. 382. The modern Australian position is described in *Oceanic Sun Line Special Shipping Co. Inc. v. Fay* (1987) 165 C.L.R. 197, *Voth v. Manildra Flour Mills Pty Ltd* (1990) 171 C.L.R. 538, *Henry v. Henry* (1996) 185 C.L.R. 571. English law has now adopted a doctrine of *forum non conveniens*: *Spiliada Maritime Corp. v. Cansulex Ltd* [1987] 1 A.C. 460.
58. See also *Piper Aircraft Co. v. Reyno*, 454 U.S. 235 (1981).

59. Ayres (1993) hypothesises, consistently with our analysis, that the case for tailored defaults or the use of standards is strongest in cases where preferences are heterogeneous. Untailored defaults correspond to more homogeneous preferences.

4 Mandatory Rules and Statutory Interpretation

Domestic and International Mandatory Rules

In chapter 3, we described the default rule concept and its conceptual opposite, a mandatory rule. Parties are entitled to vary or exclude a default rule, but not a mandatory rule. We also stated that matters are not quite so simple in a multistate world. The existence of multiple courts and legal systems implies that parties may be able to dissociate with an undesirable mandatory rule. This opens out the mandatory/default dichotomy into a fourfold classification.

Legal rules that are not contractible *substantive defaults* need not govern the contracts of parties if the law permits the parties to make choices of law. Common law systems determine the proper law of the contract either by party choice, or in default of choice, by presumptions or by closest connection tests. Therefore, a mandatory rule in jurisdiction J can be avoided in two ways. The first is an express choice of the law of K, K not having the relevant rule. If the parties can do that, we describe the mandatory rule as being subject to a *choice of law default*. Second, the parameters of the contract can be changed so that the law of J does not apply, under J's choice of law rules. The feasibility and cost of this depend on J's choice of law rules.

If the parties contract out of J's choice of law default in favour of the law of K, the rights under their contract should be enforceable in any jurisdiction, even J's. In practice, things may not be so easy. J's courts may not permit the enforcement of those rights. If they do not, the rule ceases to be subject to a choice of law default. However, it may be subject to a *forum default*. That is, a court of J would be prepared to enforce an exclusive jurisdiction clause in favour of K, even if it will not enforce the contracted rights. The J court would enforce the exclusive jurisdiction clause by ordering a stay of its own proceedings, so permitting the plaintiff to proceed in K. This will enable the parties to avoid the application of J's domestic mandatory rule. The rights the parties are able to enforce in K will depend on K's private international and substantive law.

If a court will neither recognise a choice of law rule inconsistent with the domestic rule, nor stay its own process, the legal rule is an *international mandatory rule*. Such rules commit domestic courts to *both* the exercise of jurisdiction and the application of the rule.

The use of domestic mandatory rules increased with the advent of consumer protection legislation. Some of these Acts explicitly provide for the status of intermediate defaults; some don't.[1] This chapter introduces a method for reconciling state interests with party rights, which we call *interest positivism*. To do this, we revisit our understanding of mandatory rules and their efficiency effects. Given their apparent inefficiencies, why are mandatory rules used at all — and why are they being used more often? This poses a further question — would a parliament choose to use a domestic mandatory rule, but preserve intermediate defaults? We show that preserving intermediate defaults is desirable in a multistate world.

Endowed with this analysis, we examine how courts should, and how courts do interpret contracts statutes. We see this as an issue of pragmatic statutory interpretation. We take issue with recent judicial approaches to interpretation of apparently mandatory rules. These have used purposive approaches inimical to the existence of intermediate defaults, which are unsupportable in their own interpretive terms. We consider the possibility that canonical approaches to interpretation may balance the facilitation of private ordering, the effectuation of legislative purposes, and the minimisation of judicial error.[2] We suggest what canons in this area might look like, as starting points of an increasingly important debate.

The Relation Between Mandatory Rules and Intermediate Defaults

Economic analysis has admitted little or no scope for mandatory rules in contract cases. A few economic writers have justified them in some special cases such as corporate law.[3] These justifications, however, tend to be based on collective action problems which do not apply to most other contracts. Most lawyer-economists would accept that there is scope for a mandatory rule only where (a) contracting parties agree with sufficient frequency to terms that are contrary to their interests; and (b) law-makers are better judges of the preferences of contracting parties than the parties themselves. It is hard to be sanguine about these conditions being met. Mandatory rules are most problematic if preferences are heterogeneous.

There is a clear welfare loss if contracting parties would prefer but are not permitted to contract for terms other than the mandatory provision.

The inability to choose may fortify information asymmetries between the parties. We noted in chapter 3 that one way to address these problems is by using penalty defaults. By offering defaults that are not what some or all parties would contract for, the rule encourages contracting and, thus, the disclosure of preferences. Parties may be able to replicate this effect for themselves, if transaction costs permit, by offering multiple kinds of contracts, which counterparties self-select. If the ability to do this is taken away, there will inevitably be more pooling and less information.

Despite the inefficiencies of mandatory rules, their bite and their bark are not coextensive.[4] This is especially true in a multistate world. First, the parties may re-order their contract to take it out of the reach of the jurisdiction applying the mandatory rule. The jurisdiction with the closest connection to the re-ordered exchange would be one supplying a preferred rule. Second, the parties might make credible commitments not to invoke a mandatory rule by agreeing to remove assets from the jurisdiction, so that a judgment based on the mandatory rule would be nugatory.[5] Third, the parties might alter the character of their contract where they have agreed to exclude a mandatory rule. M might assure N that he will not invoke those rights. That assurance is not credible in a one-shot contract, as M always has an incentive to defect. However, in longer-term contracts, the parties may renegotiate the contract periodically. N has an opportunity, when renegotiating, to punish M for earlier defections. In these contracts, an assurance by M that isn't binding can nevertheless be credible.[6]

The implication is that many mandatory rules are avoidable, provided the gain from doing so exceeds the transaction costs. However, the parties' ability to avoid mandatory rules is reduced if nations adopt uniform mandatory rules (e.g., by convention).[7] The likelihood that preferences are homogeneous internationally is even lower than on a domestic basis, so this is a radical solution in terms of both welfare loss and the costs of international agreement. That legislatures must go so far makes the case for default rules a persuasive one.

The primary justification for mandatory rules may come from interest group effects or violations of standard economic assumptions. Contract law is not an ideal tool for the redistribution of wealth from one contracting party to another.[8] The terms of exchanges may adjust to reflect any change in marginal cost resulting from the new mandatory rule. However, interest groups would favour a mandatory rule fixing prices or providing barriers to entry.[9] Choice of law is an important limit on the rents that interest groups gain from mandatory rules. It provides low-cost exit compared to physical relocation and limits regulatory spillovers.[10]

Interest groups representing lawyers may prefer mandatory terms because the expected litigation or advisory work associated with them is higher than under other terms that parties might contract for. Richard Epstein has attributed mandatory products liability provisions to the advocacy of lawyer interest groups.[11] Lawyers benefit from litigation under these laws compared to more contractible tort rules.[12]

What of possible violations of economic assumptions? Mandatory rules might protect third parties against external effects of the exchange. But as economists point out, externality is not a password for legal intervention. There is no case for regulation unless marginal costs cease to equal prices; mere changes in prices or wealth effects ('pecuniary' externalities) are not enough.[13] Using mandatory rules to rectify genuine externalities is, in most cases, unappealing. It would often be better to give the injured third party a right to enjoin injurious conduct that occurs without his or her consent, or a right to damages.[14]

That leaves the argument that contracting parties do not act rationally in choosing between contract terms. They may systematically err in estimating the costs and benefits associated with different rules.[15] They may be inadequately informed, especially in cases where terms are contained in standard form documents.[16] In such circumstances, they may make choices contrary to their best interests. There may be a paternalistic justification for limiting choices. The problems of the law-maker's competence in limiting choices are not diminished, but the comparison is between imperfections.

If we admit that behavioural problems are substantial concerns in making policy decisions about contractual freedom, we merely raise a question. We do not thereby supply an answer. Behavioural analyses of law have properly stressed the empirical nature of many research issues. Moreover, cognitive capacity varies between individuals. The essence of the policy problem is preserving contractual freedom for those able to look after themselves, limiting it for those unable, while supplying information to all parties that will assist in making those choices properly left to them.

Our concern is to show how private international law can reinforce contractual freedom without subverting policy, while also dealing with information problems. In the last chapter, we introduced the procedure-settling function of contract choice of law rules. Unlike the contract-validation or default-selection functions, this function is not directly amenable to contractual choice. Since procedure governs the existence of a contract and agreement to terms, direct choice would be circular. Instead, procedure-selection is governed by the 'default' proper law methodology.[17] This can be used to respond to the problem of uninformed selection. Legislatures can mandate procedures to be used in contract cases. The use of disclosure requirements to deal with information deficiencies of consumers may have lower social costs than mandatory substantive rules.[18]

A legislature wanting to go further and adopt a mandatory rule might nonetheless retain intermediate defaults. One common feature of both choice of law and forum defaults is that they require contracting parties to take the legal rules of any particular jurisdiction as a bundle. That bundle includes the jurisdiction's mandatory rules. We have noted that many jurisdictions have adopted mandatory rules in their consumer legislation. A legislature may take the view that there is a lower risk of systematic unfairness for the least informed contractors if parties must take a country's law as they find it, as opposed to having an unrestricted right to customise. The retention of intermediate defaults is not therefore inconsistent with substantive paternalism.

Why would a legislature restrict choices of law but permit choices of forum? The answer lies in why a law-maker might permit rights to be enforced abroad but not domestically. Courts probably make more errors in applying foreign law, given their lack of familiarity with it. Those errors may exacerbate the plight of uninformed contractors. Hence, the legislature precludes only the local court from applying that law.

Another, more interesting answer is that forum defaults provide a self-regulatory mechanism for limiting the international operation of a statute. Legislatures may strongly desire to further the policy behind a mandatory rule but may also desire that the rule not be overextended. States may have 'multistate' policies that limit the prosecution of substantive policies to an extent less than the sovereign's fullest competence.[19] The problem lies in formulating a rule for a statute's operation that balances substantive and multistate policies. One solution is to let the parties decide by retaining a forum default. If, as we posit, the litigation costs to contracting parties differ substantially between forums, parties are unlikely to opt for a foreign forum simply because they want to evade a mandatory rule.

Consider a world with two jurisdictions, J and K, each of which has a different mandatory rule. Parties who are only connected with J would find the marginal cost of litigating in K very high. Even if there are benefits in avoiding J's mandatory rule, they would often be dominated by the marginal cost of an inappropriate forum. Other parties, however, may have connections with J *and* K. If these parties agree to submit exclusively to K's jurisdiction, this should be enforced. A decision to 'exit', manifested in excluding a forum default, can have very real costs.[20] It is therefore a credible signal. The people most likely to give that signal are the ones who are less likely to be the beneficiaries of choice-restricting domestic policies. They are likely to have broader international affiliations. Therefore, leaving the exit decision to contracting parties by preserving forum defaults is a sensible strategy for a legislature in a multistate world.

Recall that an international mandatory rule only applies to a transaction which satisfies the criterion of operation of the said rule. For example, a statute may apply to all contracts the proper law of which would be English, but for a contrary express choice. The parties who are most likely to be able to submit to a foreign forum are also those who are most able to reorder their transaction in order to avoid the criterion of the statute's operation. They could use foreign subsidiaries, foreign agents, negotiate and enter the contract offshore, denominate it in foreign currency, and so on. Very little is truly immutable. Destroying a forum default simply increases the deadweight costs of avoiding a jurisdiction with unsuitable rules. Thus, legislatures should retain forum defaults, even where the domestic context requires the use of mandatory rules.

This idea can be presented in another way.[21] The coexistence of mandatory rules and intermediate defaults may be part of the deal cut by the interest group. Consider an example in which the members of an interest group, A, transact with the members of two other groups, B and C. B's members are repeat transactors, who can negotiate their contract terms. C's members are either not repeat transactors or are term takers. The lobbyists for A seek legislation enacting a mandatory rule which would transfer wealth to its members, from the members of B and C. For B's members, the transfer is once-off (e.g., because it applies to current contracts), since they can alter other terms of later contracts, albeit without transaction costs, without members of A being worse off. For C, the transfer is continuing if they are term takers. A may not lobby to preclude choices of contrary law as a means of limiting political opposition by B. Since B's members can avoid future transfers in any event, preserving low-transaction-cost means of doing so (such as intermediate defaults) limits the deadweight transaction costs they incur, and thus the extent of their opposition. As Gary Becker famously argued, political competition can limit the inefficiencies of rent-seeking.[22] This is another reason why treating domestic mandatory rules as international mandatory rules is untenable.

We have treated choice of law and forum defaults as separable concepts. This treatment may be problematic. It assumes that even if a court in J enforces a submission to the jurisdiction of K, the K court will apply either the law of K or the proper law the parties have agreed. A forum default is meaningless if the K court applies J's law. Generally, courts have not done this. However, the Rome Convention on the Law Applicable to Contractual Obligations[23] *permits* a court to apply mandatory rules of a country with a 'close connection'. The court must have regard to the nature and purpose of those rules, and to the consequences of their application or non-application.[24] However, that rule does not qualify a forum's right to apply its own mandatory rules. Our analysis suggests that parties who have submitted to the jurisdiction and chosen the law of K should not be subject to the mandatory rules of J. Consistently with our focus on party interests, that sort of party agreement should take precedence over a generic domestic policy in a foreign jurisdiction.

An important theme of our analysis is adapting the law to information cost problems. We have noted that the procedure-settling process of contract adjudication permits a domestic forum to prescribe pre-contractual information obligations. These could be extended to apply to choice of law or forum agreements. The information costs associated with a choice of law, for example, may be significant. To make a rational decision, parties must know the differences between the rules of the chosen jurisdiction and the laws of the default jurisdiction. For many parties, such information may be costly. It may be desirable for a legislature to require a party proffering a contract adopting a choice of law other than that of the default jurisdiction to give reasonable notice of the differences between these two jurisdictions' laws. A repeat contractor offering a standard form is likely to have lower marginal information costs than the other party.[25]

There may also be cases where a party uses unconscionable conduct to procure the agreement of the counterparty to choice of law and jurisdiction clauses. The party might provide false information regarding the clause or use unfair forms of pressure to enter the agreement. Most jurisdictions provide statutory or equitable relief in these cases. Given this convergence, conflicts may not be very severe. To the extent that unconscionability relates to entry into the contract, it seems sensible, if unorthodox, to treat this as a procedure-settling issue, and so apply the putative proper law.[26]

Consumers, for example, would typically get the benefit of their local law when contracting in domestic contexts.

To conclude this section, the ability to opt out of intermediate defaults not only increases contractual options, but provides a valuable circuit breaker for the overinclusiveness of domestic legislation. The retention of intermediate defaults is not inconsistent with the use of domestic mandatory rules. The next section shows how this theory can be incorporated into a normative theory of interpreting statutes in a multistate world.

Interpreting Contracts Statutes in a Multistate World

A premise of our analysis is that legal rules are capable of hierarchical classification according to the presence of substantive and intermediate defaults. A court's classification of a law within this hierarchy matters. Take a case where a rule is mandatory in a domestic context, but is coupled with a forum default in an international context. It would be undesirable for a court to apply that legal rule as an international mandatory rule. It would decrease the number of contracts the parties could write. It may increase the costs of transacting if the parties try to avoid the rule's operation by changing the contract's parameters. If parties have contracted on the basis of a specific forum applying a law inconsistent with a domestic mandatory rule, the lure of being able to change the rule to international mandatory status encourages opportunistic litigation. Dispute resolution becomes a rush to enliven the jurisdiction of preferred forums, followed by a complex gavotte of interlocutory manoeuvres.

If classification matters, then statutory interpretation matters. This is an area of law which is undergoing reconception. At one stage, it was chic to dismiss the area as indeterminacy masquerading as scientific method. But whatever one thinks of the conventional tools, interpretive problems have not gone away. Indeed, they have been intensified by increased statutory intervention. Because modern statutes are often complex, interpreters continue to turn to extra-textual means to resolve ambiguities and gaps. Prominent here are interpretive techniques that rely on legislative purpose.

Purposive interpretation resolves ambiguities by resort to what can be discerned of the legislative intention from textual and extrinsic material. Judge Richard Posner describes the method thus: 'The judge should try to think his way as best he can into the minds of the enacting legislators and imagine how they would have wanted the statute applied to the case at bar.'[27] There is an affinity between this approach and the tailoring of a default rule. Both methods permit drafting economy since the court will supplement the formal instrument in a sympathetic way. Drafting, like contracting, is not presumed to involve full specification.

It has been a short step from purposive interpretation to the advocacy of international mandatory rules. Because many domestic mandatory rules are enacted to reform some area of law, the reform purpose is often thought to require that the rule be placed outside the party's contractual competence. James Fawcett considers that a party's right to opt out should be limited when the law expresses a 'strong social or economic policy'.[28] Ironically, Fawcett's use of substantive purpose is conceptually similar to deciding choice of law issues in interest analysis.[29] Yet Fawcett considers interest analysis to be inappropriate to English law.[30]

Our analysis highlights the problems of this approach. We have shown that a domestic mandatory rule can coexist with intermediate defaults. There is a flaw of different kind. Purposive interpretation allows a legislature to economise on drafting costs, while permitting courts to fill gaps and resolve ambiguities in the legislation when the facts of actual cases have crystallised. This approach may improve the quality of interpretation. The mandatory rule approach shares none of these virtues. It does not seek to reconstruct legislative intent based on the circumstances of a particular case. Instead, it generalises about the application of certain rules *independently* of the factual matrix of individual cases. The judge is enjoined to ignore the specific merits of the written contract. The mandatory rule approach is better considered not as a purposive method, but as an approach which generates a *presumption* about certain rule types.

Legislatures may want rules to apply in every possible case.[31] If this intention is clearly stated, a court should give effect to it. The issue is how far a court should go in turning a domestic mandatory rule into an international mandatory rule when such an intention is *not* stated. In deciding whether to expand the literal scope of a legal rule, the court may be influenced by the ease with which the legislature could have expanded the rule's application. Liberality in interpreting substantive provisions is appropriate because it will be difficult for the legislature to provide for every situation that might arise. But when the issue is a provision's susceptibility to private ordering, the possibilities are not endless. There are only four ways avoidance can occur — by avoiding the statute's criterion of operation, by agreement to an inconsistent provision, by choice of law, or by selection of a foreign forum. These methods do not depend on the context but apply whenever the subject is contract regulation. Substantially the same provisions could be used in *any* statute to control avoidance.

Some statutes make it clear which provisions are substantive defaults and which are not. Likewise, statutes are increasingly uniting criteria of operation with the effect of choice of law. It is common enough now to provide that a statute applies to all contracts, the proper law of which is, say, Australian. Where the statute applies, an express choice of other law will be disregarded. It would be easy to stipulate that, where the statute applies to a contract, a forum court must not grant a stay in aid of a submission to the exclusive jurisdiction of a foreign court.

If these provisions are easily drafted, and they resolve the existence of substantive and intermediate defaults, their presence or absence can be used to attribute meaning to the text. Those provisions present will exclude the defaults they refer to. Absence can be equated with a legislative intent of maintaining contractual freedom. O'Hara and Ribstein argue that forcing legislatures to expressly exclude choice of law defaults encourages opposition and thus interest group competition from those adversely affected by the choice of law rule.[32]

An interpretive model can only be justified pragmatically — it can never claim to offer a privileged account of textual truth. What, then, justifies our approach? There will often be no useful material from which one might make informed guesses about the legislative intent with respect to, say, forum defaults. There will either be a provision or silence. One can resolve the silence by presuming it to be enabling, or disabling, or by interpreting it statute by statute, case by case. Any of these interpretations will involve value judgments. The case by case analysis makes for the greatest uncertainty, but still requires the judge to decide whether or not contractual freedom should be respected. The mandatory rule approach is illogical because it attaches the same meaning to silence as to cases where the actual provisions appear. Our approach to interpretation is based on the idea that contracts legislation is based on a model of party autonomy to the extent that it does not specify to the contrary. Interpretive deadlocks should be resolved by elevating party interests over state interests. We call our approach *interest positivism.* It recognises government interests only in so far as they comply with rules for the recognition of positive law. Given that the number of legislative strategies needed to control substantive and intermediate defaults is small, and the strategies are both simple and general, this approach provides legislators and contracting parties with greater ability to predict the effect of legislation on contracts.

An interpretive method needs to be adapted to dealing with the four dimensions that define the scope of legal rules — the statute's criterion of operation, domestic contractibility (whether the rule is a substantive default), choice of law, and choice of jurisdiction.

Criteria of Operation

A statute applying to contracts can define its operation in two ways.[33] First, it may adopt a fact-based criterion called a *localising* rule.[34] An example is that the contract is entered into in New York State. Second, the statute may use private international law concepts, such as the proper law of the contract. Where the proper law is used, the statute might direct that it be determined without regard to express choices of law.

When the statute uses a localising rule, it must be construed. The greatest risk is that courts will construe the provision reactively by reference to transactions seeking to avoid the statute. For example, courts may fall into the mandatory rule 'mindset' by thinking that the legislature would not have intended parties to be able to avoid the legislation by manipulating the transaction's parameters. A court that thinks this way will be tempted to change the localising rule. We see this as undesirable, unless there is an inconsistency between the substantive provisions and the localising rule. Otherwise, parties should be able to rely on the legislation's self-declared scope. To repeat, much 'avoidance' is costly to the parties — it will not occur unless there are genuine gains. Localising rules are not difficult to extend if a parliament is prepared to define them cumulatively.[35] For example, the statute applies to a contract where *a* or *b* or *c* holds. The fact that a legislature has chosen a less expansive localising rule (*a* or *b*) more likely implies that a wider one (*a* or *b* or *c*) would be over-inclusive, not that a narrow one is underinclusive.

Where a statute's operation is defined by, say, the proper law of the contract, a question arises about the relevance of party autonomy. Should an express choice of law determine the proper law? Again, the answer is yes, if the parliament has not otherwise made provision. Statutes commonly make contrary provision, so the answer seems reasonable.

Even if a statute has made contrary provision, how far should that be construed? When a court is instructed not to have regard to an express choice of law, would it flout the statute to consider evidence about the rules the parties favoured or did not favour? In determining the proper law of the contract, it is impossible to draw a fixed line between objective facts and subjective intentions. The court can only work with the contract as formed by the parties; objective facts take their form from the parties' shared intentions. A court ought to ignore only what statute tells it to ignore. The more it considers, the more likely a proper law test is to ascertain an answer suitable to the actual contract. This chapter has shown, for example, that a choice of forum is a particularly important and credible signal about the parties' preferences. If evidence indicates that the parties do not favour local law or courts, that should be weighty evidence in determining the proper law. If legislatures do not want this evidence considered, they can use fact-based localising rules.

Finally, how should a court treat a silent statute? Our argument is that contract laws should be treated as supplements to contract. This is best achieved by treating the statute as being subject to the usual rules of private international law. Authority supports this approach.[36] Courts should not imply localising rules unless there is a clear textual basis in the substantive provisions. It is more certain and more efficient to permit parties to use choices of law and forum to define the scope of the legislation, than for them to be at the mercy of judicial invention.

Substantive and Intermediate Defaults

In our default taxonomy, we placed substantive defaults at the top, because they preserve the greatest amount of contractual freedom. Choice of law defaults trump forum defaults because the former should permit a wider choice of forums in which contracted rights can be enforced. Interpretive principles should be based on a similar presumption — if a higher level default has been retained, the lower level defaults should be presumed to be retained also. On the other hand, the elimination of a higher level default does not carry a similar presumption about lower level defaults, because a domestic mandatory rule can coexist with intermediate defaults.

The first interpretive principle presumes that unless there is an express indication or necessary implication to the contrary, rules affecting contracts (other than procedure-settling rules) are substantive defaults. This would entitle parties to contract around or out of legal rules, provided they comply with any specified procedural obligations.

The second principle presumes that unless there is an express indication or necessary implication to the contrary, parties are entitled to enforce a choice of foreign law clause in their contract. This result is not changed by the fact that the choice of law would avoid a domestic mandatory rule. In principle, the chosen law could be enforced in any forum, *including a domestic one*.

The final principle presumes that unless there is an express indication or necessary implication to the contrary, parties are entitled to enforce a choice of foreign jurisdiction in their contract. This result is not changed by a direction in the statute that choices of foreign law are to be disregarded. Where substantive and choice of law defaults are eliminated, the parties' rights can only be enforced negatively by a stay of proceedings in favour of the agreed forum. The court hearing a stay application should not consider the rights a party foregoes under domestic law.

Australia's *Trade Practices Act* 1974 eliminates the effect of choices of foreign law on the legislation's operation. In doing so, it refers to choice of law clauses and 'terms to like effect'.[37] Should that provision be interpreted to eliminate the forum default? Choices of jurisdiction may arise in a similar context to choices of law but are not otherwise 'alike'. If there is no necessary implication, forum defaults should be taken to survive. This does not render the statutory language meaningless, as it can apply to clauses which courts have held to choose law without expressly saying so.[38] Statutes that arguably extinguish the forum default include legislation implementing the Hague and Hague-Visby Rules on the carriage of goods by sea. An example of such a provision is 'an agreement has no effect so far as it purports to preclude or limit the jurisdiction of a court of the Commonwealth or of a State or Territory in respect of a bill of lading or a document' to which the legislation applies.[39]

Having established a framework for interest positivism, we now compare our principles with how courts have resolved the application of contracts legislation in a multistate world.

Judicial Approaches to Interpreting Contracts Statutes

The most commonly cited contract case in English private international law is the Privy Council decision in *Vita Food Products, Inc. v. Unus Shipping Co. Ltd.*[40] That case involved the carriage of goods from a port in Newfoundland to a destination in New York. The bills of lading were inconsistent with a Newfoundland statute, which applied to the contract by virtue of a localising rule. The bills of lading stated that they were subject to English law. The case endorses the principle that courts should enforce party agreement on the proper law, provided the choice is '*bona fide* and legal, and provided there is no reason for avoiding the choice on the ground of public policy'.[41]

The opinion is significant because it accepts that while a Newfoundland court might refuse to enforce the contract, foreign courts might well enforce it. The action was commenced in Nova Scotia. Foreign courts will enforce contracts, which are valid by their proper law, whether or not they are contrary to the law of the place the contract was entered. The opinion is consistent with our theory, because it preserves intermediate defaults. However, the court was adjudicating a foreign statute, which limits the generalisability of the case's defence of the choice of law default.

Likewise, most Anglo-Australian cases emphasise the importance of enforcing jurisdiction clauses. These cases accept that a court has a discretion *not* to enforce the clause, although strong reasons must exist to justify this course.[42] The prima facie preference to enforce jurisdiction clauses conforms to our theory. But the ability of a court to review ex post which forum agreements it will enforce weakens the significance of forum defaults and erodes the certainty of the contract. The most problematic trends in the case law have stemmed from this questionable discretion, and the vague qualifications in *Vita Food* quoted above.

Consider, for example, *Golden Acres Ltd v. Queensland Estates Pty Ltd*.[43] *Queensland Estates* involved a contract appointing the plaintiff as sole agent for the sale of the defendant's land, which was situated in Queensland. The plaintiff's entitlement to commission was inconsistent with Queensland legislation, which regulated commissions and required that agents be licensed. The contract featured a choice of law clause opting for Hong Kong law. The plaintiff was incorporated there, and the land was expected to be sold to Hong Kong residents. The selection of law was held not to be 'bona fide' as it avoided the local law. Hoare J. considered that it would be contrary to public policy for the legislative intention to be stultified by choice of law clauses.

Realistically, one expects courts to enforce local legislation. But the blatancy of the interest group derivation of this legislation — barriers to entry, cartel protection, and price fixing — makes a strict construction desirable. A court cannot refuse to enforce such legislation, but it should not widen its scope by eliminating choices of law that the parliament has not eliminated.[44] The case invites examination of what the Privy Council meant when it referred to choices of law that are not bona fide. It cannot be right, as Hoare J. implies, that a choice of law is not bona fide because the parties intend to avoid the effect of certain laws. If that were so, the scope for choices of law would be very small. Apart from the case where one of the parties uses bargaining tactics lacking in good faith to conceal the term from the other party, we would limit the exception to sham agreements. That is, to cases where the parties never intended their contract be governed as they appear to have agreed. Where the parties intend that their rights be governed by the chosen law, the choice is bona fide — the only issue is whether the legislation proscribes it.

We come now to the House of Lords decision in *The Hollandia*,[45] and the Australian High Court decision in *Akai Pty Ltd v. The People's Insurance Company Ltd.*[46] Both involved statutes that eliminated the choice of law default, but said nothing in respect of forum defaults. Both involved applications to stay local proceedings on the basis of foreign jurisdiction clauses, which the respondent resisted successfully by arguing that a stay would deprive them of the protection of local legislation. Both judgments rested in part on the argument, exposed as deficient above, that the legislative purpose would be thwarted if the applicant was granted a stay. *The Hollandia* can be justified more easily than *Akai* because the legislative text (which enacts the Hague-Visby rules) states a much stronger case for extinguishing the forum default.[47] The minority judgment in *Akai* is preferable. It held that the application of substantive Australian legislation should only be considered once it is determined that Australia is the proper forum for resolution of the dispute. Non-enforcement of a jurisdiction clause was an unwarranted interference with the parties' contractual rights — especially because the applicant had refused to contract on the terms of an Australian choice of law. This approach recognises the difference between choice of law and forum defaults, and that elimination of the former need not eliminate the latter.

The majority in *Akai* concentrated on the 'objective' aspects of the contract. However, as we said above, when choice of law is used as the criterion of operation, a simple distinction between objective facts and subjective intentions does not exist. If the parties were compelled to contract on the basis of Australian law, there may have been no contract at all, or one in very different terms.

Neither case identifies an actual legislative purpose which is furthered by these specific results. All the court can rely on is the fact that *some* defaults are eliminated. We have shown why this argument is insufficient. Given that choice of law defaults were eliminated in these cases, the cost of opting out of a forum default would be substantial for many contracting parties. That the remedial purposes of substantive provisions will be thwarted by the costly use of foreign forums is not a tenable argument.

The Australian litigation in *Akai* had an interesting sequel.[48] Parallel litigation was on foot in England. PIC, the insurance company relying on the choice of English law and forum, sought an anti-suit injunction against further Australian proceedings. Akai sought a stay of proceedings in England. It argued that the English court should, as a matter of 'comity' give effect to the Australian High Court decision, not least because its reasoning was similar to *The Hollandia*. Thomas J. rejected the submission. Relying on *Vita Food* and the earlier House of Lords decision in *Re Missouri Steamship Co.*,[49] he said that the court should give effect to the parties' contract. The matter fell outside the exceptions Lord Wright enumerated. Thomas J. refused to stay proceedings in England, as it was the contractual forum and English law was the proper law of the contract. The judge granted an anti-suit injunction in support of that finding.

This case reinforces our analytical method. If a foreign court will enforce contractual rights to the extent of granting an anti-suit injunction, there is no justification for a domestic court expanding the scope of local mandatory rules beyond the meaning the text reasonably bears. By doing so, it simply encourages parallel litigation and international stand-offs. Those stand-offs should be resolved by emphasising party interests, while addressing state interests in the positivist manner we describe. Our approach brings greater certainty to contracts and to the effect of legislation. It encourages less litigation and less opportunism between contracting parties. It requires less reconstruction of legislative intentions. And it resolves ambiguities with a liberal, pro-autonomy value.

Conclusion

We have explored why contractual freedom has been substantially wound back by mandatory rules. Interest groups and paternalism are alternative explanations. However, the multistate world of the late twentieth century makes mandatory rules hard to effectuate. Committing courts to the exercise of jurisdiction and application of local rules is inconsistent with liberal, economic, and legal values. Permitting parties to make choices of law and jurisdiction is a better strategy, especially when it is combined with intelligent procedure-settling legislation. Interest positivism can be embedded in principles designed for the interpretation of contracts statutes with potential multistate application. These principles are superior to the flawed inconsistencies implicit in recent authorities.

The next chapter remains in the domain of mandatory rules, but departs from a purely contractual orientation. We examine the private international law issues that arise in torts actions arising from contracts. This is a crucial area since much recent statutory intervention has used mandatory tort norms. Nonetheless, the issues remain very similar, once the obfuscating effect of the law is clarified pragmatically.

Notes

1. Amongst Australian legislation, see, e.g., *Carriage of Goods By Sea Act 1991* (C'th Aust.) ss. 11, 16, *Civil Aviation (Carriers' Liability) Act 1959* (C'th Aust.) s. 41H, *Health Insurance Act 1973* (C'th Aust.) s. 126(3), *Insurance Contracts Act 1984* (C'th Aust.) s. 8(2), *Trade Practices Act 1974* (C'th Aust.) s. 67.
2. Easterbrook (1983), Eskridge (1990), Kramer (1990), Macey (1986), Macey and Miller (1992), Mashaw (1997), Sunstein (1989).
3. Bebchuk (1989), Gordon (1989). See also Ayres and Gertner (1992).
4. Black (1990).
5. Williamson (1985). This argument assumes the judgment will not be recognised in other jurisdictions.
6. Telser (1980), Klein and Leffler (1981).
7. Stephan (1997, 1999).
8. Demsetz (1972), Polinsky (1989, pp. 122-123).
9. As to regulation of quality, see Spence (1975).
10. Kobayashi and Ribstein (1999).
11. Epstein (1988, 1995).
12. Cf. Geistfeld (1994).
13. Haddock et al. (1987).
14. Calabresi and Melamed (1972), Radin (1987).
15. There is an extensive literature using behavioural evidence to criticise economic assumptions and predictions: Edwards and Von Winterfeldt (1986), Eisenberg (1995), Ellickson (1989), Jolls et al. (1998), Sunstein (1997). Cf. Posner (1998b).
16. Katz (1990a, 1990b).
17. An exception is where the procedure is specified by a statute which has a specified mode of operation that does not include the use of private international law concepts such as proper law.
18. A. Schwartz (1988).

19. Brilmayer (1995, ch. 4).
20. Hirschman (1970). Brilmayer (1989) makes use of the concepts of exit and voice in defining moral rights in private international law.
21. This argument is substantially influenced by O'Hara (2000).
22. Becker (1983).
23. 1980 O.J. (L. 266). Adopted as English law under the *Contracts (Applicable Law) Act* 1990 (U.K.), and referred to *infra* as the 'Rome Convention'. See similarly *Restatement (Second) Conflict of Laws* § 187(2) (1971).
24. Article 7(1). This article does not have effect in English law: *Contracts (Applicable Law) Act* 1990 s. 2(2).
25. Ribstein (1993). Similar comments might apply regarding the principal rules of the agreed jurisdiction's procedural law (e.g., costs orders, trial by jury).
26. Cf. *Dimskal Shipping Co. S.A. v. International Transport Workers Federation* [1992] 2 A.C. 152, *Mackender v. Feldia A.G.* [1967] Q.B. 590, 596, *The Chaparral*, 407 U.S. 1 (1972).
27. Posner (1983, p. 817).
28. Fawcett (1990, p. 53).
29. See also chapter 2, p. 11 *supra*.
30. Fawcett (1982).
31. In practice, their choice of law rules suggest they do not (Brilmayer, 1980a).
32. O'Hara and Ribstein (2000).
33. Dutson (1996a). It is also common for the statute not to make an express provision at all.
34. Kelly (1974).
35. Cf. Opeskin (1996).
36. *Barcelo v. Electrolytic Zinc Co. (A/sia) Ltd* (1932) 48 C.L.R. 391, *Wanganui-Rangitekei Electric Power Board v. Australian Mutual Provident Society* (1934) 50 C.L.R. 581.
37. *Trade Practices Act 1974* (Cth) s. 67.
38. *B.H.P. Petroleum Pty Ltd v. Oil Basins Ltd* [1985] V.R. 725, *British Controlled Oilfields Ltd v. Staff* [1921] W.N. 319. Cf Opeskin (1996).
39. *Carriage of Goods By Sea Act 1991* (C'th Aust.) s. 11(2)(b).
40. [1939] A.C. 277.
41. Ibid., 290.
42. See, e.g., *The Eleftheria* [1970] P. 94, *W.C. Thomas & Sons Pty Ltd v. Bunge (Aust.) Pty Ltd* [1975] V.R. 801, *Huddart Parker Ltd v. The Ship Mill Hill* (1960) 81 C.L.R. 502, *Oceanic Sun Line Special Shipping Co. Inc. v. Fay* (1987) 165 C.L.R. 197, 224, 230-232, 259-261, *Leigh-Mardon Pty Ltd v. P.R.C. Inc.* (1993) 44 F.C.R. 88. As to U.S. law, see chapter 3, note 30 *supra*.
43. [1969] Qd. R. 378. Affirmed on other grounds, *sub. nom. Freehold Land Investments Ltd v. Queensland Estates Pty Ltd* (1970) 123 C.L.R. 418.
44. Easterbrook (1983), cf. Macey (1986).
45. [1983] 1 A.C. 565.

46. (1996) 188 C.L.R. 418.
47 See also the Canadian Federal Court decision in *Agro Co. of Canada Ltd v. The 'Regal Scout'* (1983) 148 D.L.R. (3d) 412.
48. *Akai Pty Ltd v. People's Insurance Co. Ltd* [1998] 1 Lloyd's Rep. 90.
49. (1889) 42 Ch. D. 321.

5 Market Torts and Concurrent Liability

Contract, Market Torts, and Non-market Torts

Chapters 3 and 4 discuss how courts should respond to private international law problems in contract cases. We endorsed the law's deference to the parties' agreement on choice of law and jurisdiction. We also showed why a legislature wanting to limit contractual freedom in a domestic context might retain choice of law and forum defaults. This chapter studies a subset of these issues: how does private international law deal with rights that arise *in tort* when a person is injured in a situation arising out of a contract? These include rights under such important bodies of law as products liability and industrial law.

A distinction between rights in tort and rights in contract in this context is an unsatisfying one for a pragmatist. It implies an ontology of rights based on metaphysically sound classifications — an ontology that few people today believe exists. The only meaningful basis for a tort-contract distinction is that some rights have different consequences. When a plaintiff asserts rights arising out of a contract, designating them as tortious or contractual is often an index of the extent to which the legal system permits private ordering of the right. A right arising in contract is easier to modify contractually than a right arising in tort. Tort is a synonym for 'mandatory'. But the distinction is not fixed. What was contractible in 1900 may be immutable in 2000.

Contract rights and tort rights form part of the law's allocation of property rights. The Coase theorem indicates that the parties will trade these rights when there are gains from doing so. If transaction costs are significant, trade will occur only where the gains from trade exceed the associated transaction costs. Tort rights create duties which should resemble the obligations that parties might contract for in a zero transaction cost world.[1]

So far, the explanation of tort rights is practically identical to the account we gave in chapter 3 of contract default rules. The similarity implies that if contracts are formed in a well-functioning market, a regime of contractual freedom should produce an equilibrium level of care which is socially optimal. Even where tort rules underestimate the optimal care level, the high value that consumers place on care and safety will induce providers to supply it. Contracts would credibly signal the provider's investment in care. If tort rules overestimated consumers' valuations of care, parties would scale back contractually the scope and consequences of liability. If mandatory law prevented these contracts, the cost burden would be reflected in higher prices.[2] Well-functioning markets would be fatal to a tort-contract distinction.

Tort law is also important in contract-based tort cases because it allocates accident costs between providers and consumers.[3] If care is costly, accidents will always occur, as some cannot be efficiently prevented. Tort laws determine who bears the costs of these accidents. The revolution in tort law over the last four decades has been the gradual allocation of most losses to providers through strict liability principles. This is sometimes described as *enterprise liability*. Its effect is to require the provider to supply a product with an implicit insurance policy covering accidents that reasonable care would not avoid.[4] The supposed merits of enterprise liability include its insurance of persons unable to afford to insure themselves, the cost of which is passed on to all consumers in prices.

The insurance function of enterprise liability has been criticised. Any form of insurance — whether first-party or third-party insurance — relies on the ability of the insurer (the provider in the case of enterprise liability) to segregate insureds into narrowly defined risk classes. It is difficult for many providers to segregate risks, since they typically must sell to anyone prepared to pay the price. This makes the risk pool a heterogeneous one. An overall increase in the incidence and extent of liability destroys the independence of the risks in the insured pool. Both effects are fatal to the insurance function. Equally problematic is the tendency of courts to award damages for non-pecuniary loss for accidents incapable of prevention by reasonable care. First-party markets have never developed for these forms of loss as consumers are unlikely to value such coverage. The total effect is the unravelling of insurance markets, increased prices and product withdrawals. In these circumstances, contracts may have a crucial role. Contracting around liability rules can reduce risk pool variance and, hence, prices, while reallocating to consumers the risks they are better positioned to bear (e.g., by first party insurance).[5]

There are two reasons why tort law has not, and will not, collapse into contract law, even in the case of exchange-related injuries. First, care is a difficult subject for contracting. Problems of verifying precautions limit the number of contracts parties can write.[6] Second, there may be impediments to the formation of an efficient market for care and safety. Consumers face high costs of acquiring and processing information about product risks, injury costs, and contract terms.[7] This may explain why the law in these areas has moved to resolve these problems by mandatory rules.

However, experience shows that the move from contract to tort is not a solution free of problems. Consistently with the theory just expounded, the 1980s witnessed crises in insurance and product markets. Just as an earlier generation of scholars thought they were witnessing contract's last rites,[8] the current generation sees answers to these crises in market contracting.[9] In the United States, many states have scaled back the possible recovery under tort rules, leaving liability beyond that point to markets.[10]

Private international law scholarship must confront these issues. Historically, it has been built on doctrinal tort-contract distinctions without recognising their instability or addressing their consequences. In this book, we develop a different distinction — torts that arise out of exchanges, and torts that do not. The former, studied in this chapter, we call *market torts*. We study and endorse with qualifications the case for permitting the parties the freedom to make choices of the tort law applying to their transactions.[11] This chapter shows how the conflictual treatment of market torts can be integrated with contracts. Chapter 6 examines *non-market torts*. In these torts, transaction costs preclude any form of contracting. We first describe and critique the conventional apparatus used to resolve tort problems. Using our transactional approach, we examine the reasons for permitting choice of law problems to be resolved by express choice in the first instance, and otherwise by contract-like choice of law defaults.

Tort Choice of Law

In English law, a tort conflict was historically subject to the rule in *Phillips v. Eyre*,[12] which referred the tort not to one law, but two. The wrong alleged must be 'actionable' had it been committed in the forum, and must not have been 'justifiable' by the law of the place of the wrong (*lex loci delicti*). This rule has been extensively studied but it remains, in jurisdictions where it survives, miserably unclear.

There are three areas of uncertainty. First, the meaning of justifiability under the *lex loci delicti* is unclear. Various interpretations have been offered.[13] The most demanding definition is that if suit was brought in the *locus delicti*, the plaintiff would recover the liability claimed in the forum. The weakest definition is that the defendant's conduct is not legally 'innocent', irrespective of whether or not the *locus delicti* recognises a civil cause of action. The weaker the definition of justifiability, the more liability turns on the *lex fori*. Hence, forum shopping is encouraged. Second, *Phillips v. Eyre* is not necessarily a choice of law rule. It could be simply a threshold requirement for a claim to be justiciable in the forum. A further choice of law rule would then be needed, the most likely (and problematic) candidate being the *lex fori*.[14] Third, as earlier chapters mention, *Phillips v. Eyre* only applies to 'substantive' conflicts.[15] Procedural law is governed by the *lex fori*. We suggested in chapter 3 that the substance/procedure distinction assists the plaintiff to compare the likely costs of proceeding in alternative forums. However, courts have used the distinction to preserve the application of a forum's law on recoverable heads of damage. This is unjustifiable and encourages forum shopping.

Phillips v. Eyre has met with different reactions internationally. Although strictly a minority position, Lord Wilberforce and Lord Hodson in *Boys v. Chaplin*[16] held that the *lex loci delicti* should be the primary *lex causae* in torts cases. However, they indicated, with a nod to government interest analysis, that the facts of some cases would justify application of the *lex fori*. This is often described as a *flexible exception*. This approach has been influential. English legislation now substantially adopts it.[17] The Canadian Supreme Court has rejected *Phillips v. Eyre* in favour of a *lex loci delicti* rule.[18] Australia, however, retained the old rule up until June 2000. The High Court had adopted a more demanding definition of justifiability while maintaining a substance/procedure distinction that classified many important laws as procedural.[19] Shortly before this book went to press, the High Court fell in line with Canada and England by holding that *lex loci delicti* applied to Australian conflicts. It rejected a flexibility exception for these torts. The rules applicable to international conflicts are left open.[20] The Court also confined the ambit of 'procedural' laws in a narrow but readily defensible manner.

The use of the *lex fori* creates ex post forum shopping incentives. These are inefficient if they cannot be controlled by contract. However, the *lex loci delicti* itself can be a suboptimal rule if the exchange relations from which market torts arise have significant multistate elements. As costs of transacting fall, markets become increasingly international. The *lex loci delicti* becomes highly uncertain where manufacturers have multinational operations, global distribution arrangements are in place, and consumers enjoy substantial freedom of movement. Products liability cases struggle with these problems.[21] Does the tort occur where the product was designed? Where it was manufactured? Where the sale took place? Where the accident occurred?

Consider the use in *Distillers Co. (Bio-chemicals) Ltd v. Thompson*[22] of the concept of a 'duty to warn'. It was held there that the tort occurs where the product is sold if the product was dangerous to certain types of people entitled to be warned of the product's risks. Where there is a manufacture defect, the tort occurs in the place of the manufacture. It is unclear why the victim of a generally unsafe product would be subject to (typically) foreign law, but the other victim will typically be able to rely on local law. The distinction has real consequences, because the plaintiff will not know which law his rights will fall under — to know the rights would imply, absurdly, a knowledge of the form of the negligence. Subjecting the plaintiff's right to foreign law also imposes costs of information, as regards the content of that law. Given the matter can only be resolved in court, uncertainties will complicate product market pricing and insurance arrangements. These problems reflect the inadequacy of doctrinal solutions to policy problems.

Characterisation

A similarly unedifying problem arises when one must determine the cases in which tort choice of law rules are applied. The applicable choice of law rule is established by *characterisation* of the juridical nature of the legal problem. This involves selecting amongst doctrinal categories. Forum law recognises a choice of law rule for each identified category. Thus, in the context of market torts, the characterisation problem requires the judge to decide whether to resolve the matter according to contract or tort choice of law rules. The difference is important. If a contract choice of law rule is applied, the parties might refer the legal issues to an agreed law. A tort choice of law rule would not permit this, except where the selected law coincided adventitiously with the law the parties would choose.[23]

Many market torts will be characterised as tortious, simply because there may not be a privity relation between plaintiff and defendant (e.g., a products liability suit by a consumer against a manufacturer). The absence of privity is not fatal to private ordering, because manufacturers could specify the terms on which consumers buy their product as they do with warranties. However, characterisation tends to follow doctrine, and therefore leans towards tort where the law does not recognise a contract.

Employment contracts are a subset of market torts where there often is a privity relation. These have been the setting for some instructive analyses of characterisation of market torts. In *Coupland v. Arabian Gulf Petroleum Co.*,[24] an industrial accident occurred in Libya, in which a Scottish plaintiff was injured. The plaintiff sought damages in tort in England. The court was prepared to accept for the purposes of a strike-out action that the proper law of the contract was Libyan law. It held, however, that the plaintiff was entitled to advance a claim in tort. As the alleged tort would have been actionable in Libya, that part of the rule in *Phillips v. Eyre* was satisfied, and the matter could be resolved according to English law. The Court of Appeal held that the proper law of the contract had no relevance to the tort claim. The plaintiff was entitled to sue in tort, if he thought it advantageous to do so. The plaintiff therefore has a substantial ability to answer the characterisation question by how she pleads her case.

Denying the relevance of the proper law of the contract to the adjudication of the tort is undesirable. As we have argued, parties to a contract need to know the liability rules that apply to them. An employee needs to know the risks that the law allocates to him in order to make a rational decision regarding the compensation he should demand to bear them. The employee may want to effect first-party insurance coverage, and the employer may want third-party insurance against liability. This is much harder if the applicable tort rules cannot be known ex ante. Markets will also be affected adversely. Plaintiff-selected tort rules make the risks to which the employer is exposed much harder to segregate into risk pools. The employer's insurance against third party claims will become more expensive.[25] The extreme case for hazardous occupations is that insurance may become unavailable, which may in turn decrease employment. These consequences imply that the parties should be able to know, and, ideally, be able to choose the tort law that applies to claims between them.

In *Coupland*, the court stated that the contract could be relevant to a tort claim if it excluded or restricted the tort claim. How have courts responded to exclusion clauses? Peter North has argued that these clauses can be analysed in four different ways.[26] First, one could refer the validity of the exclusion to the law selected by the tort choice of law rule. Second, one could vary this method slightly by inquiring as to the validity of the exclusion under the proper law of the contract, once one has ascertained that the *lex causae* applicable to the tort permits exclusions. In *Brodin v.*

A/R Seljan,[27] a court refused to enforce a contract excluding an employee's rights to compensation apart from what was available under Norwegian law. The employer was a Norwegian company, and had employed the Scottish plaintiff to work on one of its ships. The accident occurred when the ship lay in a Scottish port. The limitation of liability was invalid under Scottish law. The case is an example of the first approach, but the second would produce the same result.

Our criticism of *Coupland* substantially applies here. Referring the *lex causae* to a tort choice of law rule is inefficient. By increasing the uncertainty associated with applicable liability rules and risk-bearing arrangements, it adversely affects insurance and labour markets, and complicates the underlying contracting process.

North describes two other methods which may, in part, overcome these problems. One uses the proper law of the contract to adjudicate the validity of the exclusion. The other uses a unique choice of law rule, which would have regard both to the circumstances of the contract and the tort. Both approaches are used in the Court of Appeal decision in *Sayers v. International Drilling Co. N.V.*[28] That case also involved an industrial accident, this time involving injury to an English plaintiff, employed by the Dutch defendant to work outside of the U.K. The injury was sustained on board a Nigerian oil rig. The plaintiff's contract provided for a compensation scheme should the plaintiff be injured, but excluded his rights under English tort or workplace insurance law. The plaintiff sued for tort damages in England. The limitation was held valid under Dutch law, but not under English law. Stamp and Salmon L.JJ. held that the proper law of the contract was Dutch, and that the limitation should apply. This is consistent with North's contractual approach. Lord Denning M.R. sought to locate a unique choice of law rule (essentially on a first-order basis) which would resolve the conflict between the proper law of the contract (which he thought was English) and of the tort (which he thought was Dutch). The contract resolved the deadlock, since it could only be valid under Dutch law. A choice of law approach designed to uphold the express provisions of a contract is likely to be transaction cost-reducing.[29]

Our analysis of tort choice of law rules and characterisation raises two issues. First, should parties be able to choose the tort law that applies to injuries arising out of a contract? This question raises the matters we explored in chapter 4, in particular the extent to which parties have sufficient information and ability to make a choice that is in their best interests. Second, what are the optimal choice of law rules for market torts?

Were we to admit scope for direct choice, this would be an inquiry about the optimal choice of law default for market torts. The optimal choice of law rule may take different forms, depending on whether or not it is subject to displacement by express choice. The answers to these questions must be derived consequentially. An analysis of consequence must have regard to aspects of the market in which the tort occurs. The efficiency of markets and the nature of transactions affect one's confidence in contractual solutions and the suitability of the underlying choice of law rule. We will not analyse every possible market tort, but we will specifically address products liability issues and professional negligence alleged by investors in corporate securities. These show how choice of law depends on market context.

Contractual Choices of Tort Law

Contractual choices of tort law should be significant in a case like *Coupland*, where there is no express contractual limitation on liability, as well as in *Brodin* or *Sayers*, where limitations do exist. There are three reasons why resolving tort choice of law problems by contract is efficient.

First, contractual choices increase the number of contracts the parties can write. Even in the unlikely event that tort law rules are completely contractible, learning and network externalities may preclude the parties from varying defaults. If tort rules are mandatory on a domestic basis, choices of foreign law are the only way to contract on other, preferred terms. This is especially important when consumers have heterogeneous preferences for tort rules. Second, contractual choices of law, if enforced, reduce the plaintiff's incentive to select a forum that has tort rules that will maximise his damages. Since tort choice of law rules have forum biases, this is a real concern. Third, because tort choice of law rules continue to rely on the *lex loci delicti*, contractual choices of law provide a crucial circuit breaker for the current of indeterminacy that runs through multistate market torts. Contractual choices provide certainty at the time of contracting, which will facilitate both product and insurance markets.

Thus, we can take much the same position as in the last two chapters — courts should enforce parties' choices of law (and forum), unless the parliament has legislated in a way which is inconsistent with choice of law and forum defaults.[30] There may be substantial market failures but legislatures are in a better position to ascertain these than courts are. This justifies passivity in both contract enforcement and statutory interpretation.

The law's procedure-settling function is as important to market torts as to other contracts. There are real information costs associated with choices of law, especially information about the effect of the selected law. Statutes might usefully require notice of (a) a foreign law agreement included in the terms, and (b) the differences between the foreign legal rules and those applicable by default, as a precondition to making an effective choice of law agreement. Alternatively, judges could shape extant common law principles (such as duties to warn) to have this effect in cases involving contractual choices of law. Statutes might also require that the manufacturer provide information about risks associated with the product, in order to facilitate informed decision-making.[31] Below, we analyse contractual choice of law in the context of specific torts.

Choice of Law Defaults for Market Torts

If current tort choice of law rules do not suit market torts, what rules would be more appropriate? To answer this, we apply the theory of contract choice of law defaults described in chapter 3. We outlined three conceptual alternatives to selecting the proper law. In ascending order of the degree of ex post discretion conferred on the judge, they are (a) pre-emptive rules; (b) closest connection tests; and (c) tailored choices of law. While the ultimate choice inevitably depends on many factors, we favoured pre-emptive rules. Do these conclusions apply to market torts? We divide our analysis to correspond with the case where contractual choices of law are enforced, and the case where they are not.

Tort Choice of Law Defaults

The key trade-off between these choice of law methods depends on the extent to which pre-emptive rules capture the preferences of a substantial majority of contracting parties. The less representative the rule, the stronger the claims of tailoring, at least where transaction costs are not trivial.[32] But 'representativeness' is not exogenous to the rule. While it depends on the distribution of preferences, it also depends on the form of pre-emptive rules. We believe that generic formulations are likely to be unrepresentative. Formulations based on single transaction types stand a greater chance of reflecting majority preferences.

While closest connection tests involve a degree of tailoring, they assume a strong correlation between jurisdiction and preference — that where parties' contracts are most closely connected with jurisdiction J, they prefer J's law. If preferences vary, or jurisdictions supply substantially inefficient rules, this assumption is hard to maintain. If, however, that assumption is correct, well drafted rules would achieve most of the advantages of the closest connection test, while adding greater clarity to harder cases.

We said earlier that apart from its ability to select more often a preferred law, tailoring rectifies the problem of contingent incompleteness. That is, because circumstances change over time, rule preferences change, too. Ex ante choices of law may induce costly renegotiation or breaches. We doubted in chapter 3 the significance of this point. For it to be a significant point, it would imply that the parties' demand for reasonable precautions or for insurance will change over time. With the exception of industrial accidents, most market torts do not arise from long term relations between the parties. Therefore, the need for tailoring to track longer term agreements will frequently be low. The characteristic problems of tailoring, such as verifying information concerning the optimal rule, judicial competence, and possible forum biases, also apply to market torts.

Pre-emptive rules respond directly to the problems of tort choice of law rules. First, in conjunction with procedure-settling rules, they can economise on information costs. A rule, based on one or two factors, reduces the information the parties need to acquire to ascertain the applicable law, compared to the much broader inquiry tailoring implies. If the rule operates in a conventionally territorial manner it will economise on information costs, since conflicts issues can be substantially ignored in a majority of apparently domestic transactions. Parties are not precluded from adopting foreign law where they prefer it, but if they do, the party proffering a choice of foreign law should be obliged to bear the counterparty's information costs. A territorial rule may also limit the extent to which states can externalise the costs of their laws on out-of-state defendants. Second, clearer rules facilitate pricing in product markets, and (depending on which tort rules they select) insurance markets. Third, they set clear benchmarks at the time of contracting, which would permit parties to decide whether they want to remain with the default, or contract out of it. Fourth, they mitigate forum shopping incentives. Fifth, they should be simpler and take less time to litigate. Sixth, rules facilitate class actions. The court can reduce the extent to which it must make individual findings on the *lex causae* applying to a class member's transaction. Our ability to say more about market tort choice of law defaults than contract defaults stems from the higher information and transaction costs likely to characterise markets in which these torts occur.

Thus, pre-emptive rules are optimal for market torts, where they are differentiated by tort transaction types, and the rule for each type is based on criteria which are common knowledge, and corresponds to the locus of the market in which transactions occur.

Mandatory Tort Choice of Law Rules

Most of the advantages of pre-emptive rules are intensified when the choice of law rule becomes mandatory. Under a choice of law default, parties could contract around the rule by a choice of law clause. They cannot do so here, irrespective of transaction costs. In theory, the parties could attempt to take the transaction outside the criterion of operation of the tort statute. This will be costly, however. The optimal approach may be to retain pre-emptive rules but to dilute them to presumptions, rebuttable where another jurisdiction is more closely connected with the transaction, and there are sound reasons to believe the parties would have contracted in favour of that system. Presumptions are not an ideal solution because they share some of the flaws of tailoring. However, some flexibility in choice of law is needed where preferences are heterogeneous and contracting is not permitted. Ex post tailoring takes the place of ex ante contracting.

Choice of Law in Products Liability Cases

We explored above the considerations relevant to choice of law rules for market torts. The advocacy of contractarian solutions to choice of law problems in market torts depends on the market and the nature of the transaction in which torts occur. We show how important these contextual factors are. First, we analyse whether markets may fail in a way that militates against contractual choices of law. Second, we analyse the choice of law rule that should apply in the absence of a choice or where choices are not permitted.

Contractual Choice and Market Failure

Should we permit a manufacturer and a buyer to subject their tort rights to an agreed choice of law? This question is similar to another vexing dilemma: whether liability rules applicable to products cases should be subject to contract? William Landes and Richard Posner argue that contract may often not be an efficient solution to liability because the information costs associated with generally low accident risks may swamp benefits from contracting.[33] They recognise that markets can function well, even if some consumers are poorly informed, if they clear at prices that reflect the presence of other, well informed consumers. However, there may only be a trivial fraction of consumers with any feel for product risks.[34]

Alan Schwartz takes a different view.[35] He points out that the case for enforcing contracts depends on three things. First, consumers must know the content of their contracts. Not enforcing contracts is not the best means to achieve this. Procedural means such as disclosure and plain English requirements may be a better solution. This is consistent with our analysis of the law's procedure-settling functions. Second, consumers must know the alternative terms offered in the market, and opt for the terms they prefer. While Schwartz recognises that comparison shopping is probably limited, firms will profit if they offer substantially preferred contract terms.

Some scholars are sceptical of such a claim.[36] This intuition has been formalised by Avery Katz.[37] Katz analyses contracts in which the buyer places value on aspects of the exchange which she cannot costlessly evaluate. These include the quality or the risk of the goods, as well as warranty and contractual provisions. The problem for the buyer is that once she sinks the costs of investigation, they will cease to be relevant to a decision to enter that contract. Reading the contract terms will not change the reservation price that bounds the contracts she will accept had she *not* investigated them. Thus, the seller will want to offer terms that put buyers in the position of wanting to accept the contract, but only just. The buyer who reads will be in the same position as a buyer who does not read, but the former will wish she had not incurred the cost to do so. So, in equilibrium, buyers will not read, and sellers will offer low quality terms. Katz acknowledges that sellers may profit by offering higher quality terms where consumers are willing to pay more for higher quality, but this will depend on sellers being able to make information regarding this attribute of the contract costlessly assimilable by buyers.

Third, consumers must perceive risks correctly and appreciate the effect on risk of product alterations. Schwartz argues that there is no theoretical or empirical reason to believe that consumer estimates err systematically in one direction or the other.[38] Much behavioural research over the last two decades shows that human decision-making is often substantially flawed, because of the tendency to use informal heuristics to analyse risks.[39] These heuristics may lead to overestimation (or underestimation), for example, because of the vivid (or bland) nature of the risk. Failures of rationality need not be uniform across all transactors. Repeat transactors may be more accurate than one-time transactors.

So the case for contractual choices of law is not compelling, but neither is the case against it. This dilemma is compounded by the fact that the problem arises in a conflictual context where accepted doctrinal approaches admit either *all*, or *no*, contractual choices of law. Intermediate positions are possible, but these would require that courts use standards to adjudicate the validity of choices of law. If forums apply different standards, plaintiffs will simply be drawn to those applying the most favourable standards.

This is why courts should adopt a passive approach to the enforcement of contracts not prohibited by legislation. Courts are in a poor position to assess aggregate welfare effects. If procedure-settling rules do their job, it will be relatively exceptional that parties with some connection to jurisdiction J will choose to exit it completely in favour of jurisdiction K. As we said in chapter 4, the cases where this does occur are often the ones with the most credible claims to enforcement.

Choice of Law Defaults

Our analysis of choice of law for products liability cases substantially follows our general analysis. The optimal products liability default is a pre-emptive rule, and the optimal mandatory rule is a presumption, both selecting the law of the place of sale. This rule economises on information costs, as it minimises the amount of information about legal rules that buyers need to have. The rule's greatest advantage is that it enables the seller to decide whether or not to distribute its product within a jurisdiction, based on its markets and potential legal exposure. Although some manufacturers may not have direct control over their product distribution, it seems most practical to make the manufacturer bear the risk, given that they have lower transaction costs than buyers in making arrangements with the distributor regarding final markets.

Although mostly a certain rule, the place of sale may not always be apparent. For example, what happens where a buyer litigates in respect of a product, such as a drug, from which she suffered adverse effects as a result of long-term administration? The answer is difficult if buyers have moved between jurisdictions over the period in question. But it is no easier to resolve using the *locus delicti*, which engrafts an added layer of complexity regarding duties to warn. Few rules giving certainty at the time of the contract will be completely certain ex post.

Choice of Law in Investor Suits

In recent years, there have been many negligence suits by investors against professionals, such as auditors, retained by a corporation.[40] An investor typically alleges loss sustained as a result of the defendant's negligence. With increasing internationalisation of securities markets, there is a greater likelihood that choice of law issues will be raised in future suits of this kind. Admittedly, much of this territory is covered by the mandatory disclosure and fundraising provisions of securities statutes,[41] but tort actions remain alive and well.

Some may find it hard to regard these cases as contractual. There is not even a direct line between the parties as there is between consumer and manufacturer. However, economic analysis explains the provision of (for example) an audit by a company offering its securities.[42] Investors value the certification of company information, and would be prepared to pay for it because it is relevant to security returns. There are barriers to them doing so, because a producer of information can rarely capture all of its benefits. The company will benefit if it can provide certification most cheaply, since investors will pay more for these securities. Thus, the audit commissioned by the company economises on third party information and transaction costs. The rights investors have against professionals are a subset of the rights that accrue to them by virtue of their membership of the corporation.

We have said above that the optimal choice of law rule for a transaction type must flow from a study of the market context. An important aspect of securities markets is that the transaction cost of trading is very low. For most transactions, exchange-traded securities can be reduced to their risk-return properties, giving them a uniquely high degree of substitutability. These features give securities markets a high degree of efficiency in the response of securities prices to new information. One of the consequences of efficient markets is that territoriality concepts wither. It matters not at all that X bought securities in Black, Inc. in Tokyo, Sydney, or New York. Low transaction costs mean that price differentials persist only very briefly, before they are 'arbitraged' away.[43]

These features affect the optimal choice of law rule. Rights ought to be constant across all investors in a corporation's securities. Place of sale of securities is a meaningless datum. The place where audit services are performed may also be an undesirable criterion because ascertaining it may be costly, especially when the corporation has multinational operations. *Locus delicti* rules create similar problems.

The best choice of law rule is to select the law of the place of incorporation. The place of incorporation is used in common law countries to resolve conflicts regarding the corporation's 'internal affairs', such as shareholders' rights and governance issues.[44] It has formed the basis of jurisdictional competition for incorporations in the United States. We noted in chapter 3 that empirical evidence indicates that such competition has value to shareholders.[45] However, the rule does not apply to all corporate affairs. The characterisation process would refer rights asserted in tort to tort choice of law rules. Rights arising from securities regulation are most commonly referred to the law of the place of the transaction.[46] We have seen that these rules are inappropriate.

The advantages of applying the internal affairs rule to shareholders' rights in tort are that, first, it provides a simple rule which minimises information costs. Shareholders only need to know the place of incorporation. Second, it provides a single body law for all of the rights a shareholder asserts. This makes for consistency between the rights forming the corporate contract between shareholders and managers, and the tort rights shareholders assert against other defendants. Third, the rule controls the future provision of information by professionals retained by the corporation. Shareholders know that they will be able to enforce the laws of the place of incorporation. Fourth, this predictability facilitates the pricing of shares. Incorporation in a jurisdiction is a credible way to lock in the application of laws (subject to reincorporation), the quality of which should be reflected in the price of securities offered by the corporation. The value of the corporation will be maximised by choosing the jurisdiction with the best corporate and securities laws.

Roberta Romano has used this argument to advocate the devolution of securities regulation authority by the federal government to the American States.[47] However, Romano takes the argument further, by advocating a right to select a securities 'domicile', which could be separate from the place of incorporation. This feasible approach uncouples securities law from other corporate law, potentially permitting greater choice. This has not gone without criticism.[48]

It will be noted that so far we have only advocated a *single* solution: apply the law of the place of incorporation. Since every corporation must be incorporated somewhere, this contractual solution cannot be obligationally incomplete. Hence, a distinction between contractual and default choices of law has no real content. It is conceivable that at some time after a corporation goes public, an auditor might negotiate with the managers for some other less demanding choice of law. There is a case against permitting that to be enforced against the shareholders, even where the choice is disclosed. Managers do not bear the costs of this choice — the existing shareholders will, as their shares may drop in value if the choice of law is perceived by the market as an adverse signal. Short of a decision by a majority of shareholders to reincorporate elsewhere, only the laws of the place of incorporation should apply.

Conclusion

This chapter has shown that market torts raise the same analytical issues as other contract cases. They raise a prima facie case for being dealt with under a contract choice of law methodology, rather than being characterised as tort cases and analysed under tort choice of law rules. That is not to say that contractual choices of law are always the appropriate solution. The information that potential victims have about risks and contract terms, and their ability to process it may be highly attenuated. However, this chapter shows that rejecting private ordering as a solution does not compel us to reject contract choice of law rules. Choice of law rules must recognise the characteristics of the basic transaction and of the efficiency of the market. The private international law rules that apply to market torts need to achieve the same goals as those that apply to contracts — predictability, satisfaction of majority preferences, reduction of information costs, and so on. We have argued for the use of untailored, transaction-based, pre-emptive principles that apply as rules where contracting is permitted, and as presumptions otherwise. Our analysis demonstrates the importance of a pragmatic, policy-based approach to private international law, and the deficiencies of foundational doctrinal approaches.

Notes

1. See generally A. Schwartz (1988). Cf. Coleman (1992).

2. Craswell (1991).
3. Priest (1987).
4. See generally Ehrenzweig (1951). For more recent analyses, compare Priest (1985) with Croley and Hanson (1993).
5. Priest (1987), A. Schwartz (1988).
6. A. Schwartz (1988, pp. 367-368).
7. See Landes and Posner (1987, pp. 280-284).
8. Atiyah (1979), Friedman (1965), Gilmore (1974).
9. Buckley (1999), Epstein (1995), Huber (1988), Rubin (1993).
10. Cf. Bell (1990), Geistfeld (1994).
11. And choices of forum, too. This chapter will mostly focus on the choice of law issue, however, because it provides a better context in which to contrast our theory with conventional approaches.
12. (1870) L.R. 6 Q.B. 1, 28-29.
13. Contrast *Stevens v. Head* (1993) 176 C.L.R. 433, 441 with *Machado v. Fontes* [1897] 2 Q.B. 231.
14. *Anderson v. Eric Anderson (Radio & T.V.) Pty Ltd* (1965) 114 C.L.R. 20.
15. See chapter 3, p. 40 *supra*.
16. [1971] A.C. 356.
17. *Private International Law (Miscellaneous Provisions) Act* 1995 (U.K.) s. 11.
18. *Tolofson v. Jensen* [1994] 3 S.C.R. 1022.
19. *Breavington v. Godleman* (1988) 169 C.L.R. 41, *McKain v. R.W. Miller & Co. (S.A.) Pty Ltd* (1991) 174 C.L.R. 1, *Stevens v. Head* (1993) 176 C.L.R. 433.
20. *John Pfeiffer Pty Ltd v. Rogerson* [1998] H.C.A. 36.
21. See, e.g., *Distillers Co. (Bio-chemicals) Ltd v. Thompson* [1971] A.C. 458, *Castree v. E.R. Squibb Ltd* [1980] 1 W.L.R. 1248, *Metall und Rohstoff A.G. v. Donaldson Lufkin & Jenrette Inc.* [1990] 1 Q.B. 391. These cases have often arisen in the context of jurisdiction disputes, rather than specifically in the context of choice of law problems. See also Morse (1989) and Harris (1998).
22. [1971] A.C. 458.
23. In theory, the *lex loci delicti* could be displaced in favour of the agreed proper law under the flexible exception: *Red Sea Insurance Company Ltd v. Bouygues S.A.* [1995] 1 A.C. 190.
24. [1983] 3 All E.R. 226.
25. Priest (1987).
26. North (1993). See also Morris (1951).
27. 1973 S.C. 213.
28. [1971] 1 W.L.R. 1176.
29. See also *Coast Lines Ltd v. Hudig & Veder Chartering N.V.* [1972] 2 Q.B. 34.
30. Tort legislation has often been imprecise in formulating its criteria of operation, which in turn affects intermediate defaults (Dutson 1996b).

31. Simply providing the requisite information is no guarantee that it will be properly used. See generally Beales, Craswell and Salop (1981), Croley and Hanson (1993), Geistfeld (1994).
32. Ayres (1993).
33. Landes and Posner (1987, pp. 280-282).
34. See also Shavell (1987, pp. 61-62).
35. A. Schwartz (1988). To similar effect, see Rubin (1999).
36. See, e.g., Rakoff (1983).
37. Katz (1990a, 1990b).
38. See also Shavell (1987, p. 54).
39. The classic is Tversky and Kahnemann (1974). See chapter 4, note 15 *supra*.
40. See, e.g., *Caparo Industries plc. v. Dickman* [1990] 2 A.C. 605, *Columbia Coffee & Tea Pty Ltd v. Churchill* (1992) 29 N.S.W.L.R. 141, *Esanda Finance Corporation Pty Ltd v. Peat Marwick Hungerfords* (1997) 188 C.L.R. 241.
41. *Corporations Law* (Cth) s. 1022, *Financial Services Act* 1986 (U.K.) ss. 144, 146, 150, 154A, 156A, 156B.
42. Easterbrook and Fischel (1984), Watts and Zimmerman (1983).
43. See generally Gilson and Kraakman (1984), Gordon and Kornhauser (1985), Stout (1988), Kahan (1992).
44. Collins (1993, pp. 1109-1113), Sykes and Pryles (1991, pp. 398-399), *Restatement (Second) of Conflict of Laws* § 302(2) (1971).
45. See the references cited in chapter 2, note 22 *supra*.
46. *Uniform Securities Act* § 414, 7B U.L.A. 672 (1985). Alternatively, the processes used to define the operation of statutory rules, described in chapter 4, might be used: see generally Dutson (1996a).
47. Romano (1998).
48. Fox (1999).

6 Non-market Torts

Non-market Torts and Efficiency

Dividing torts into market and non-market torts seeks to reduce the weight placed on characterisation processes. Market torts raise issues of contract *and* tort; the characterisation process requires the judge to choose one *or* the other. Since non-market torts by definition do not involve contracts, a contractual approach to choice of law ceases to be relevant. What, then, should a 'tort' approach involve?

This question requires that we revisit the tort choice of law rules that the last chapter rejected as unsuitable to market torts. Does that conclusion hold when the tort no longer arises from an exchange? That question depends on whether the move away from contracts should change the law's underlying objective. Efficiency is a defensible objective when the subject is contract, as contract provides a means by which all relevant parties can be better off than they initially were. But non-market torts do not involve exchanges because transaction costs are prohibitive. Maybe justice is a better objective for these wrongs.[1]

This is not the place in which to resolve the philosophical objectives of tort law. Our argument is that there is little friction between these objectives in the situations we analyse, whatever dissonance there may be elsewhere. In resolving non-market torts conflicts, we show that the legal principles that satisfy an efficiency objective also happen to be *just* rules, having regard to both John Rawls' contractarian definition of justice,[2] and corrective justice approaches. The analysis below deals first with torts where there is no relation at all between the parties, and then with those torts where is a relation, albeit not a contractual one. We shall refer to the two tort types as discrete torts and relational torts.[3]

The Costs of Non-market Torts

The costs of non-market torts divide into three types — the expected cost of the injuries suffered by the victim, the cost of precautions that might be taken to prevent the accident (both by the injurer and the victim), and the cost associated with the litigation of the claim. Efficient rules will minimise the total of these costs, rather than any one component. Economic analysis shows how different liability regimes affect total accident costs.[4] For example, Steven Shavell has demonstrated that in a case where both parties should take care, the use of a negligence rule should induce efficient investments in care by both parties.[5] So, too, would a strict liability rule coupled with a defence of contributory negligence. The costs of accidents may depend not only on the actual precautions an injurer takes against an accident, but the extent to which the injurer engages in the accident-causing behaviour. Unless the definition of negligence takes activity-level issues into consideration, strict liability may be superior. So far as settlement is concerned, negligence is more difficult to prove than strict liability, but more cases may be litigated under strict liability.

If the victim and injurer could contract costlessly, they would agree to apply the wealth-maximising rule, and plan their conduct accordingly. Does that imply that the law should emulate that bargain by its legal rules? Naturally, the normative thesis of economic analysis of tort law favours that course. But the situation *we* are studying is not the formulation of tort rules, but the selection between them in order to resolve a conflict of laws. This context affects our normative analysis. It is a premise of economic analysis that tort rules induce injurers and victims to take due care because of the liability deterrent.[6] The deterrent effect relies on the fact that the parties are, or act as if they are, aware of the liability rule. But choice of law problems are rare occurrences. Resolving a choice of law problem by applying the efficient law will only have the desired effects on accident precaution if parties expect the law to apply.

The efficiency effects of particular substantive law turn on the circumstances of the tort and the choice of law rule. In market torts, the application of foreign law can be predicted, depending on the choice of law rule. Discrete non-market torts, however, imply that the parties are unrelated to each other; neither will know much or anything about the other. Choice of law rules impact on the problem by the criteria used to select the *lex causae*. For example, if they rely on personal attributes of victims or injurers (such as their respective domiciles), it will be practically impossible for the party whose criteria are *not* the basis for selection to learn the standards the law will apply. If choice of law rules rely on the *lex fori*, as *Phillips v. Eyre* does, it will be *completely* impossible to learn those standards until litigation commences. Victims and injurers will choose their precautions based on their best guess of what the applicable law will be. This is likely to be based on the *lex loci delicti* since most torts are purely domestic.

The Effect of Tort Conflicts on Accident Precautions

Assume that Victim is struck when crossing a road by the car that Injurer is driving. The accident occurs in jurisdiction J, where Victim is resident. Injurer resides in jurisdiction K, but is temporarily present in J on a holiday. Assume that the only possible forums are J and K, the domestic tort laws of which are different. A conflict can be resolved either by applying the *lex loci delicti* or the *lex fori*. K's law will be applied only if suit is brought there and the court applies the *lex fori*; otherwise J's law will apply. We also assume that Victim chooses the forum. To analyse the effect of the choice of law rules, let us investigate the effect of three different conflicts.

Strict liability versus negligence Economic analysis shows that, compared to negligence, strict liability is more likely to cause the injurer to moderate the level of accident-causing *activity* to the efficient level. Assume first that J applies strict liability. It would not matter what choice of law rule would be applied as Victim will only bring suit in J, which is both forum and *locus delicti*. The choice of law rule matters if K applies strict liability but J applies negligence. Victim may decide to sue in K in the hope that it applies the *lex fori*. However, Victim will only do so if Injurer exercised reasonable care, as Victim could otherwise establish liability in J. If Injurer knew for certain that Victim could invoke strict liability, it would affect activity-levels.[7] But there can be no certainty. First, litigation in K will presumably cost Victim, a J resident, more, as there may have to be two sets of lawyers, transit costs for witnesses, and so on. Second, a court in K may refuse to invoke more onerous liability rules if a K resident bears the burden. Third, unless the choice of law rule in K is a strict *lex fori* rule, many judges may regard *Injurer v. Victim* as most closely connected with J, and apply J's laws under a flexible exception. Fourth, a K court may grant Injurer a stay of proceedings.

Undercompensation versus full compensation J may limit recoverable heads of damage, but K may not. Again, there is an incentive for Victim to sue in K. If Injurer knows that she will bear a higher proportion of Victim's losses, Injurer's investment in care may be closer to the optimum. But for the same reasons that we explored when discussing the last conflict, the likelihood of the rule applying drops substantially. The rate of change in probability would appear to depend on the difference between recoverable heads of damage. The greater the difference, the greater the incentive to bring suit in K.[8]

Contributory negligence The two previous conflicts examine Injurer's incentive to take care. What happens if the conflict arises because J offers a contributory negligence defence but K does not? There is likely to be no effect on Victim's self-care. Litigation should only occur in K *if* reasonable self-care is *not* taken.[9] But this outcome should not often occur in equilibrium. Victim must choose a level of care based on the expectation that he will be injured by another resident of J. The effect of this expectation is that a rational Victim will expect the contributory negligence defence to apply, so leading him to invest in reasonable self-care.

Itinerant Victim Our analysis suggests that choice of law rules have no effect or a very minor positive effect on efficiency. Any positive effect may reflect our assumption that there are only two possible jurisdictions, each of which had some chance of supplying the *lex causae*. Once the number of jurisdictions from which parties may come, the number of forums, and the number of potential conflicts escalate, any benefit from deterrence is likely to be overwhelmed. This is apparent when one reverses the origins of Victim and Injurer. The Injurer is now the local based in J (which remains the *locus delicti*), and the Victim based in K. The Victim will litigate in K when a conflict favours suit there. The Injurer will invest in care based on the reasonable belief that the Victim will be a resident of J. The conflict should have little effect on the Injurer's incentives. What of Victim? If J and K both apply contributory negligence, Victim has no incentive to be careless. If K offers strict liability, does not apply a contributory negligence rule, *and* does not undercompensate plaintiffs, the Victim may underinvest in care. Unlike the itinerant injurer cases, a court in K is more likely to favour the Victim, who is now a local.

This inefficiency may be constrained by jurisdictional rules. If Victim sues in K, Injurer will have to be served *ex iuris*. K's law would have to recognise a right to serve out of the jurisdiction in a case to which it is only connected via Victim's residence.[10] A K court may grant a stay of proceedings, given its weak connection to the suit. Likewise, if Injurer has no assets in K, other courts may refuse to recognise the judgment.

The Effect of Tort Conflicts on Litigation and Settlement Costs

Choice of law rules do not have substantial efficiency effects on accident precautions in cases of discrete non-market torts. However, they may affect settlement cost, which we define as all costs associated with the resolution of the parties' rights. The following analysis foreshadows aspects of our consideration of jurisdiction in chapter 8.

Choice of law rules affect settlement costs in two ways. First, they influence the costs associated with the application of the choice of law rule and of the *lex causae*. More complex or discretionary rules make for longer litigation.[11] Rules more likely to select foreign law increase litigation costs because of the awkward procedures for its proof. Second, choice of law rules influence the forum in which the plaintiff sues, other jurisdictional manoeuvres by the parties, and the causes of action asserted. If the choice of law rule has these effects, it may also influence the willingness of the parties to settle given that the stakes are likely to be affected. We shall describe the two as *law costs* and *litigation costs*. Law costs and litigation costs may be inversely related, since the *lex fori* is a simple rule to apply and never selects foreign law (*renvoi* aside) but increases litigation costs.

Litigation costs may rise if choice of law rules increase the variance of a plaintiff's outcomes across forums. Rational plaintiffs will maximise their expected recovery. If expected awards are stable across forums, plaintiffs would select jurisdictions that minimise their settlement costs. The more variable the expected awards, the greater the willingness to incur high litigation costs. For example, if Victim could recover $100,000 in forum J, and $1,000,000 in forum K, with 75% probability in each case, Victim will spend as much as $675,000 more on litigation costs to prosecute in J.[12] The Injurer has a corresponding incentive to avoid the greater expected loss. Each party is pursuing a private gain which has no social value, because a damages award is zero-sum as between Victim and Injurer.

However, a willingness to pay is not enough by itself. The inefficiency with respect to litigation costs depends on two things. First, the parties' costs to prosecute, and to defend, the litigation must differ across forums. Attorney's fees may be higher, and more attorneys may have to be retained. It may be more costly to bring evidence to the forum selected. Procedural rules in one of the forums may protract the litigation. One intuitively expects that forums chosen for their recovery properties are unlikely to be the jurisdictions in which litigation can occur at lowest joint cost.[13]

Second, trade between the litigants regarding the forum for litigation must be costly.[14] The fact that litigation costs in K are higher than in J is not a sufficient condition for inefficiency. There must be limits on the ability of the parties to engage in *jurisdictional trade*. For example, if information regarding expected awards and the parties' expected litigation costs in forums J and K was common knowledge, there are substantial gains if the parties can agree to litigate in J. The gains arise from the costs saved. They will be divided between the parties according to their ability to bargain. Take the example we just referred to, and assume that Injurer and Victim expect to spend an extra $100,000 each if the matter proceeds in K. As before, both parties believe that the expected benefit to Victim from litigating in K is $675,000. Both parties will be better off if they agree to discontinue in K, in return for a payment by Injurer to Victim that is no less than $575,000 and no greater than $775,000. The former figure is the net benefit to Victim from litigating in K; the latter figure is the net cost to Injurer. The gains from trade are $200,000 less the costs of trade. Paying out a higher sum under K's law affects the distribution of wealth between Victim and Injurer. That might be inequitable, but it is not inefficient. Therefore, high variance choice of law rules may not be inefficient if the barriers to jurisdictional trade are not substantial.

Jurisdictional trade may only occur infrequently. It requires a degree of convergence in the party's beliefs about the expected outcomes from litigating in the forum, and some knowledge of how the other party's costs will change between forums. This may not occur until comparatively late in proceedings after discovery and interrogatories have taken place. By this stage, substantial costs may be incurred. In theory, there is no reason trade could not occur at this stage. However, it is an open question whether parties, having sunk substantial costs in a forum, will make fully rational decisions to discontinue there. Parties will depend greatly for advice on continuance from their lawyers who have a powerful interest in advising against discontinuance.[15] The underlying uncertainty about the *lex causae* resulting from erratic choice of law rules may also preclude settlement.

Strategic bargaining may be fatal to jurisdictional trade. Bargains may be possible, but they can be delayed or thwarted by parties who bargain strategically in order to secure the lion's share of gains from trade.[16] Strategic bargaining may be very intense in the context of jurisdictional trade. Parties may refuse to deal at this stage in order to establish their credentials as hard bargainers. Such a reputation will be valuable in later stages of litigation. Strategic bargaining is most severe when the parties' relation is bilaterally monopolistic, there are significant information asymmetries, and the size of gains from trade is substantial.[17] All of these conditions are typically present in jurisdictional trade: Victim and Injurer can only deal with each other, so bilateral monopoly is inevitable. We have already stated that information problems may be severe enough to hinder *cooperative* bargaining. Finally, gains from trade should rise proportionally to the variance of outcomes across forums. The larger the gains in forum K, the more parties will spend, and the greater the amounts of costs which can be saved by jurisdictional trade.

We must conclude that choice of law rules which increase variance in outcomes across forums are likely to be inefficient, given the possible failure of private ordering to accomplish efficient jurisdictional trade. This conclusion also applies to contract cases, but the parties are able to control that problem by choice of law and jurisdiction clauses. The latter solution is not viable for non-market torts. This inefficiency can be controlled in two complementary ways. One is to use jurisdictional rules which limit the amount of litigation in inefficient forums. This will be the subject of chapter 8, but some brief comments are important here. As we noted in chapter 3, the law regulates both the *establishment* and the *exercise* of jurisdiction.[18] These principles might be used to simulate the *result*, as regards forum, of jurisdictional trade.[19] However, jurisdictional challenges are a two-edged sword. Unless courts can verify the parties' expected litigation costs, applicants may use challenges to expand their strategic bargaining arsenal. Significant private gains accrue to the winner of a jurisdictional challenge if the forum the winner proposes as the appropriate forum applies his or her preferred *lex causae*. Jurisdictional challenges are important but may create inefficient incentives. The second means of controlling inefficient forum selection is by using choice of law rules that reduce the variance of outcomes between forums. The next part examines the form these should take.

The Optimal Choice of Law Rule for Discrete Non-market Torts

Chapter 5 described the principal tort choice of law rules and mentioned the recurring dilemmas associated with them.[20] There we rejected the usefulness of these rules, and advocated the use of contractual choices of law and transaction-based rules and presumptions. Contractual choices are irrelevant to discrete non-market torts. What then are the optimal rules?

Our analysis indicates that a rule should minimise the variance of outcomes across forums. This encourages the plaintiff to select a forum on cost minimising grounds. One cannot be sure that the jurisdiction that minimises the plaintiff's costs always minimises the parties' joint costs. However, the jurisdiction in which the plaintiff's costs are lowest is *more* likely to be the optimal forum than one selected to maximise the plaintiff's compensation. A variance minimising choice of law rule is as much as one can do if the plaintiff is permitted to select the forum.

A *lex fori* rule is deficient by this standard. The *lex loci delicti*'s merit depends on whether the criticisms in chapter 5 apply also to non-market torts.[21] We said there that the *locus delicti* is hard to define in the context of low transaction cost markets. Lower costs increase the ability for factors of production and products to move across extensive spatial distances. This makes isolating the *locus delicti* much harder. Non-market torts are much more narrowly defined in time and space. The *locus delicti* will often be the place accidents occur. Some cases will be complex, but most will be tractable. There may, however, be some cases where the conduct and the injury are separate, as they might be in a pollution case. Our preference is for the place of the injury, since defendants might otherwise rely on lax local tort laws. The risk that defendants will be subject to unforeseeable laws is mitigated substantially by the difficulty of asserting jurisdiction over defendants outside of their domicile.

Lex loci delicti is not the only conceivable rule that minimises variances in outcome. One might select the law of the place of domicile of one of the parties, as at the time of the accident. This is an inferior rule. A defendant-oriented rule might, in the case of corporations with significant tort exposures (e.g., a chemicals company), induce strategic domicile choice and the externalisation of costs. It would also preclude the other party from learning what liability rules were to apply, which would complicate decisions regarding activity levels, investments in care, and insurance. By contrast, *lex loci delicti* permits both parties to know what law will apply. This facilitates first party insurance decisions.

What of the rule in *Phillips v. Eyre*? As we explained in chapter 5, it has often been applied as a more confusing version of a *lex fori* rule, so the criticisms of the latter would equally apply. However, the rule could be improved, if the following interpretation was adopted:

> Once the forum court has ascertained the precise extent of the substantive claim allowed under the lex loci, the court must then give effect to its own law, even if, for instance, the operation of the local legislation cuts down the extent of the claim which could otherwise be maintained.[22]

The effect of this is to use the *lex fori* as a filter for rights recognised by the *lex loci delicti*. The use of the *lex fori* ceases to be problematic, because identity is required between the two laws as a precondition of liability.

Requiring this identity is the virtue of *Phillips v. Eyre*. It implies that the application by a forum of the foreign law of the *locus delicti* is likely to be beset by fewer judicial errors. Courts applying foreign law are likely to err, and will make more errors, the more different the foreign law is from local law. By controlling errors, the rule makes the application of choice of law rules more certain. Often the *locus delicti* will be an efficient forum where one of the parties is resident. Where one litigates there, the *lex fori* is also the *lex loci delicti*. The flaw in the rule is that where some other forum is cost-minimising, it may not recognise the rights in the *locus delicti*. In such cases, the rule impels the parties to litigate in an inefficient forum.

Phillips v. Eyre should not apply when the conflict arises within a federation.[23] The policy of error-control is much less significant within a federation, given judges' greater familiarity with the laws of other states or provinces and constitutional requirements for full faith and credit. The application by state courts of the *lex loci delicti* permits the plaintiff to choose the lowest cost jurisdiction in the federation as the forum. The use of a flexible exception, which permits a judge to apply a law other than that selected by the choice of law rule, should have no scope in discrete torts. It increases variance and uncertainty in outcomes across forums.

In chapter 3, we explained the substance/procedure distinction. It permits parties to assess the costs of proceeding in alternative forums, and to judge which forum will be cost-minimising. This implies a narrow definition of procedural laws. Until recently, the High Court of Australia held that limitation statutes and laws governing the heads of recoverable damage are procedural.[24] This approach is inefficient as it increases the scope of the *lex fori* and, therefore, variance between forums,[25] and unpragmatic given its basis in a tortuous metaphysical distinction between rules which destroy remedies and rules which destroy rights.[26] However, as chapter 5 notes, the High Court has at last recognised the inefficiency of its former approach, favouring both *lex loci delicti* and a narrow definition of procedure, at least for national torts. The increased convergence in choice of law is some evidence that, over time, the common law tends towards efficiency.

To conclude, the optimal choice of law rule for discrete, non-market torts would select the *lex loci delicti*, perhaps with a double actionability requirement in international cases. There would be no flexible exception and procedural laws would be limited to those regulating the conduct of litigation and proceedings.

The Optimal Choice of Law Rule for Relational Torts

Over the last forty years, a number of important tort choice of law cases have involved parties related by way of family, friendship, or common employment.[27] This factual configuration has placed significant pressure on courts to relax the *lex loci delicti* in cases where the *locus delicti* is of little relevance to the parties' relation.

A common explanation for this result is government interest analysis. Arguably, the state most interested in the tort has the best claim to apply its law. But that is not so. In a case where, for example, a married couple are driving in another jurisdiction, the expected costs of the driver's negligence are most likely to be borne by locals, not by residents of their state. It may be that the laws of the *locus delicti* most closely reflect the conditions in which the accident occurred.[28] The interests of states are too difficult to define tractably even in this paradigm case.

If party interests are our lodestar, can they justify a departure from the *locus delicti*? The fact that there is a relation between the parties provides a justification. Parties who live in J, and whose relation is based in J would be likely to contract in favour of its laws (we refer to these as *laws of the relation*). There are several reasons why this might be so. First, the typical parties to these sorts of cases, if they know any law at all, are most likely to be familiar with the laws of the relation. There is an information cost saving for plaintiff *and* defendant. Second, where the parties' relation is based in a particular jurisdiction, or both parties reside there, that jurisdiction is quite likely to be the cost-minimising forum for the case. Third, if that court is seised of jurisdiction in the matter it can resolve the choice of law issue by favouring the laws of the relation. This means that the matter becomes substantially a domestic case. Fourth, the parties may be insured in respect of the accident. If their policies are connected with the jurisdiction that provides the laws of the relation, application of those laws to the tort should make for greater consistency and predictability in their insurance coverage.[29] It is easy for the insurer and the parties to change the scope of the coverage if, contrary to our expectations, accidents abroad complicate insurance markets.

The 'trick' in supplying the optimal choice of law rule for relational torts lies in defining the cases in which it applies and the discretion a judge has to apply the exception. If the rule is implemented simply by way of a vague flexible exception, variance in outcomes across forums will increase. Consider *Boys v. Chaplin*.[30] In that case there was no relation between the parties. The only connection was that both were English servicemen in Malta. On the other hand, if relational torts can be sharply defined, and the laws of the relation apply to them as a matter of course, variance in outcomes would not increase. Sometimes recovery under the laws of the relation would exceed that under the *lex loci delicti*, sometimes not. The parties would know the *lex causae* at the time of litigation, and it would not vary with the forum selected.

We argue that relational torts are those where (a) there is a personal relation between the parties, (b) the parties and their relation have strong connections to the same jurisdiction, and (c) that jurisdiction is the forum. That jurisdiction would apply the *lex fori* to the tort between the related parties. The formulation would exclude the circumstances of *Boys v. Chaplin*, but not a common employment case where the parties were working together. Parties who have some form of relation such as a more distant family tie, but who come from different jurisdictions, would typically fall outside our concept of the relational tort. When there is a difficult choice between jurisdictions, one uses the *lex loci delicti* as a neutral, variance-minimising tiebreaker.

The problem is ascertaining the limits of the concept of a personal relation. If the concept is defined too widely, plaintiffs will seek to establish a relational tort where the laws of the alleged relation are more generous than the *locus delicti*. Rights become less predictable and litigation costs rise. If the concept is defined too narrowly, one creates unnecessary law costs, since the local forum will have to apply foreign law. One may also be applying a different law to the one the parties would have bargained for. Ultimately, much depends on the extent to which courts keep pragmatic considerations in mind when examining relational torts.

Choice of Law Behind a Veil of Ignorance

Our efficiency analysis advocates the use of the *lex loci delicti* as the general rule for non-market torts and the laws of the relation in relational torts that satisfy an appropriate formulation. As we said at the outset of this chapter, justice and equity may have cognisable claims. However, issues of justice have not often been considered rigorously in conflicts discourse.[31]

One difficulty is that the concept of justice is less well-defined than efficiency.[32] In a work such as ours, we need to specify a theory of justice. We rely on John Rawls' influential analysis.[33] Rawls' benchmark for justice is the distribution of rights and duties that rational individuals would agree to, if they lacked knowledge of what their individual status and attributes would be. Allocating rights and duties from behind this 'veil of ignorance' removes the bias of self interest.

Rawls also offers a more substantive analysis of justice. He argues that bargaining behind the veil of ignorance would produce two outcomes: equal liberty for all members of society, and distributional arrangements that maximise the welfare of the most disadvantaged members of society. This form of justice does not offer much insight into choice of law. Arguably, it might choose, in the context of a market tort, the law that maximised the plaintiff's recovery. But there is no strong evidence to believe that such plaintiffs are the most disadvantaged members of society. Moreover, choice of law rules are only a small part of a much larger welfare apparatus administered by modern states. It is doubtful that choice of law decisions make or break the delivery of substantive justice.

By contrast, the veil of ignorance is much more useful. It permits an instructive comparison to the Coasean bargains that would be reached by parties with full knowledge of bargaining circumstances. In cases of discrete torts, it is easy to see why parties would opt for a *lex loci delicti* choice of law rule. First, parties who do not know whether they will be Injurer or Victim will want rules that permit them to know the nature of the legal standards applicable to their conduct. Parties who know the rules will be in a position to make other judgments such as whether or not to go to certain places in the first instance, to change the manner in which they behave, or to effect insurance against loss. The *lex loci delicti* permits this. A rule based on attributes of the plaintiff or the defendant would not. Thus, inconsistency between the attributes and connections of the litigants would be resolved by a neutral, knowable factor, the place of the wrong.

Second, parties bargaining behind a veil of ignorance will prefer rules that are forum neutral.[34] The logic is substantially the same as in our efficiency analysis. Parties may individually prefer the luxury of selecting forum and *lex causae*. However, this is a prisoner's dilemma, because individual incentives do not align with the strategy that is in the interests of both parties collectively. The *lex fori* makes both parties worse off on average because greater costs will be incurred. *Lex fori* rules would also be rejected even if the Injurer is permitted to choose a forum by commencing an action for a negative declaration. The *lex fori* would then favour the better (speedy) litigator, which is inconsistent with a justice outcome.

Does this logic justify our relational tort approach? The problem is justifying an inequality of treatment between related and unrelated parties. Consider a hypothetical car crash in which the driver is subject to the *lex loci delicti* in respect of a suit by the other driver but is subject to the laws of domicile in respect of the suit by the passenger.[35] However, all conflicts of laws involve inequality. If we resolve a relational tort by applying the *lex loci delicti* we would create an inequality between the treatment of the parties when their accident occurs within the forum as opposed to when it occurs outside of it. This is because of a conflict between two factors relevant to justice — equality of treatment under the *lex loci delicti* and the application of the most suitable laws to a relation. If related parties would agree, behind a veil of ignorance, to apply the laws of the relation to their torts, as we have argued, a relational tort method would be just in a Rawlsian sense.

Choice of Law and Corrective Justice

The Rawlsian view of justice builds on the concept of the social contract, articulated originally in the works of Kant and Hobbes. In another wing of the justice stable is the Aristotelian notion that the law corrects wrongs done by Injurer to Victim. This has been intensely applied to the study of tort law. The application of corrective justice to choice of law problems is a difficult, speculative enquiry. Nonetheless a few comments can be made.

First, corrective justice should endorse the goal of variance minimisation across forums. A judgement about the need to correct any particular wrong should have a relative degree of stability across forums. Given the role of remedies in articulating the extent of a wrong, variable outcomes would erode a claim that the law gives effect to any coherent concept of justice. While moral standards naturally differ from place to place, there is something to be said for drawing primarily on the place the wrong is alleged to occur, since that is the context for correction. The further Victim must go, in terms of law and forum, to seek Victim's desert, the less convincing Victim's ethical claim to it.

Second, there can be no corrective justice if the law is not foreseeable. Consider the basic negligence principle which requires comparison between expected losses and the benefits from precautions. Injurers who do not adopt precautions justifiable by this comparison can be regarded as wrongful, because they prefer their own interests to others.[36] Strict liability can also be ethically justified given that it is most likely to apply in cases which the law regards as involving a high degree of risk to others.[37] Knowledge of which of these standards applies is a crucial guide to citizens who wish to conduct their behaviour ethically and in a way that respects the interests of others as much as their own interests.

Let us now think about the relational tort approach in corrective justice terms. A powerful criticism of the economic theory of tort law as deterrent is that it does not provide a compelling explanation of why only victims who have suffered harm have standing to litigate. Nor does it explain why injurers whose conduct is negligent are not subject to suit unless harm occurs *in fact*. Coleman argues that economic explanations of these aspects of torts litigation is 'fundamentally contingent and does not in any way depend on [the parties'] relationship to one another'.[38] Coleman goes on to say that tort law brings the parties together in a way that suggest a strongly relational, and therefore corrective, conception of justice. A relational approach to choice of law resonates with corrective justice. The notion of wrong done to Victim by Injurer should be referable to standards shared by the parties, where their relation is deeply implicated in the fabric of the tort. So, here, too, we find that efficiency analysis, social contract theory, and corrective justice all justify the approach we have recommended.

Reasonable Expectations in Choice of Law

Chapter 2 noted the theory that choices of law should give effect to the parties' reasonable expectations.[39] The merit of this approach is that its proponents recognise the importance of party interests. The primary problem is ascertaining the source of reasonable expectations. One author attributes it to intuitive understandings of territorial sovereignty, the relevance of which depends on the environment in which the tort occurs.[40] The problem with this approach lies in its normative content. It posits that parties have expectations about how the law is in fact applied which the law should reinforce. So far, so good. Everyone likes consistency. But apart from conflating normative and positive analysis, it offers no insight into whether the institutional practices it exhorts courts to perpetuate are just, efficient, or anything else.

As one of us has observed in a different context, reasonable expectations are analytical mush.[41] They do not tell us the time at which we should look for those expectations. They do not tell us whether a reasonable expectation is an actual expectation of one of the parties that happens to be reasonable, or an expectation imputed to the parties which a court thinks reasonable. If the former, it is not clear how one proceeds where the parties had different, but nonetheless reasonable expectations.

Peter Nygh offers a more sophisticated analysis of reasonable expectations.[42] Beginning with the law of contract, Nygh argues that reasonable expectations will be effectuated where the parties' agreed choice of law is enforced. Likewise, in market torts, Nygh argues that a choice of law in the contract should also govern tort law should a tort claim arise. This accords with our analysis. However, we disagree with Nygh's second claim (made essentially with respect to non-market torts) that the defendant should be entitled to select the *lex causae*, by selecting a forum, provided the result is not unjust. The proviso would be determined primarily by way of jurisdictional challenges. Nygh defends this approach by claiming an international consensus that plaintiffs should be able to choose the most favourable law available to them.

Here, too, we find a description of current practice being elevated to a prescription for current practice. The fact that courts permit forum shopping does not endorse the practice, because jurisdictional rules may reflect the self interest of the bar in attracting multistate litigation. We have shown why choice of law rules that increase the unpredictability and variance of outcomes across forums are inefficient, and that the inefficiency cannot be answered sufficiently by jurisdictional rules. We have also shown why justice concerns militate against *lex fori*. Nygh's second claim is inconsistent with his first claim. Contractual choices of law should be enforced because they express bilateral party agreement. Plaintiff choices of forum on an ex post basis should not be enforced because they are wholly unilateral and likely to be inconsistent with the law the parties might bargain for, either with full knowledge or veiled in ignorance.

To enforce the parties' reasonable expectations is just another way of saying that the law should economise on the parties' costs of determining the applicable laws. For example, a party driving in the jurisdiction in which he lives should be subject to the local law he can be expected to know most about. When abroad, he should be able to predict what law will apply. This is valid, but it adds nothing to our other arguments offered.

Conclusion

This chapter has shown, again, that a transactional approach to private international law is important. We have shown how the *lex loci delicti* is a deficient rule when applied to market torts, but that it is the optimal rule for non-market torts. Aggregating the two because they both apply to 'torts' is undesirable. The economic analysis of the two kinds of torts is fundamentally different, since the object of one is to facilitate markets and the object of the other is to facilitate settlement. Bridging the gap between market and non-market torts is the relational tort. We have shown how there is much to be said for adopting a different mode of analysis again, which emulates the bargain one can expect most parties would strike.

Notes

1. Cf. Posner (1997), G. Schwartz (1997). Jules Coleman (1992) regards efficiency as a valid objective in market torts such as products liability, but dismisses it in favour of corrective justice in the context of non-market torts. See generally Fletcher (1972), Epstein (1973), Weinrib (1983).
2. Rawls (1971).
3. Whincop and Keyes (1998b), borrowing terminology from Macneil (1978).
4. Landes and Posner (1987), Shavell (1987).
5. Shavell (1987).
6. See generally G. Schwartz (1994).
7. But it may not change them. Injurer is not a resident of J, and may have strong reasons for being there. The incremental cost of bearing accidents that occur even when Injurer exercises reasonable care may have no effect at all on Injurer.
8. Assume that Injurer must choose between two possible levels of care, namely the minimum levels of care that can be exercised in J and in K in order to avoid liability: call these c_j and c_k. Let $c_k = c_j m$, and $m > 1$. If Injurer chooses the lower care level, c_j, he risks being held liable for damages if the law of K is held to be the *lex causae*. Define Injurer's damages liability as the product of $l(c_i)$, which is a function of the care exercised (c_i), and p, which is the probability of the law of K being held to be the *lex causae*. The Injurer will seek to minimise the sum of the cost of care, and the expected value of a damages liability. If Injurer chooses care level c_j, his payoff is:

   $$= c_j + l(c_j)p$$

   If Injurer chooses care level c_k, his payoff is

   $$= c_j m + l(c_k)p$$

   $$= c_j m$$

($l(c_k) = 0$, since c_k is chosen so Injurer has no liability under the law of K.)
The Injurer will be indifferent between care levels where:
$c_j m = c_j + l(c_j)p$
It follows that we can derive the following inequalities, which describe the conditions when Injurer will choose to exercise the lower level of care:
$p \leq (c_j(m - 1))/l$
$m \leq 1 + (pl/c_j)$
If, as we posit, p is ordinarily very low in cases of torts between strangers, the extra care will very rarely be taken, unless the ratio of l to c_j is very high. Since l will be an index of the actual social costs of the accidents, the inefficiency of undercompensating rules will persist in the vast majority of cases.

9. Even this is not a sufficient condition. If K applies negligence principles, and Injurer has taken due care, Victim will still bear all losses. The Victim will only recover if K applies strict liability.
10. For example, the case could never be brought in K under the European Conventions on Jurisdiction and the Enforcement of Judgments in Civil and Commercial Matters.
11. See chapter 3, p. 50 *supra*.
12. $0.75 \times (1{,}000{,}000 - 100{,}000) = 675{,}000$. We assume Victim is risk neutral.
13. Strategic effects may also be significant. Perhaps each party's willingness to spend more at trial increases the likelihood of settlement.
14. These ideas draw from the classic works on the economics of settlement (Cooter and Rubinfeld 1989, Landes 1971, Posner 1973, Shavell 1982).
15. See generally Korobkin and Guthrie (1997).
16. Farrell (1987).
17. Crawford (1982).
18. See chapter 3, pp. 46-47 *supra*.
19. That is, they do not emulate the jurisdictional bribe the parties might have agreed. A plaintiff who loses a jurisdictional challenge is not compensated.
20. See chapter 5, pp. 73-74 *supra*.
21. See chapter 5, pp. 74-75 *supra*.
22. *Stevens v. Head* (1993) 176 C.L.R. 433, 441 per Mason C.J. A majority of the High Court rejected this approach.
23. Davies (1995). See generally chapter 10, *infra*. This is consistent with its recent rejection in *John Pfeiffer Pty Ltd v. Rogerson* [1998] H.C.A. 36 for intra-Australian torts.
24. *McKain v. R.W. Miller & Co. (S.A.) Pty Ltd* (1991) 174 C.L.R. 1, *Stevens v. Head* (1993) 176 C.L.R. 433. Even more extraordinary than these decisions was the initial cavalier response by state courts to legislative attempts to code statutory rules as substantive. In *Nalpantidis v. Stark* (1995) 65 S.A.S.R. 454 and *Martin v. Kelly* (1995) 22 M.V.R. 115, courts regarded *their* decision on what is or is not substantive as being final. In the High Court's most recent tort choice of law decision, *John Pfeiffer Pty Ltd v. Rogerson* [1998] H.C.A. 36, the

court makes it clear that it would yield to statutory language on the substance/procedure issue.

25. Cook (1933).
26. *Stevens v. Head* (1993) 176 C.L.R. 433, 452.
27. *Babcock v. Jackson* 12 N.Y.2d 473; 191 N.E.2d 279; 240 N.Y.S.2d 743 (1963), *Boys v. Chaplin* [1971] A.C. 356, *Breavington v. Godleman* (1988) 169 C.L.R. 41, *Tolofson v. Jensen* [1994] 3 S.C.R. 1022.
28. Posner (1998a, p. 646).
29. The reverse is also possible. It is not difficult to conceive of a case in which a husband and wife take out insurance coverage in relation to a driving holiday in a foreign country that is subject to the laws of that country. Such a contract arguably represents an ex ante choice of that country's tort laws. We are indebted to Vaughan Black for the example.
30. [1971] A.C. 356.
31. Kozyris (1981). Cf. Bliesener (1994), Fruehwald (1996). See now Whincop (2000c).
32. Easterbrook (1984, 1985).
33. Rawls (1971).
34. Dane (1987).
35. Cf. *Tolofson v. Jensen* [1994] 3 S.C.R. 1022.
36. Weinrib (1983), Owen (1992).
37. Epstein (1973), G. Schwartz (1981).
38. Coleman (1992, p. 380).
39. *Breavington v. Godleman* (1988) 169 C.L.R. 41, 77, Nygh (1995b), Kincaid (1996).
40. Kincaid (1996).
41. Whincop (1997b).
42. Nygh (1995b).

7 Property

Property Rights in Economics and Private International Law[1]

If tort choice of law has been the paradigm for interest analysis and contract choice of law the paradigm for economics, the private international law of property has remained the domain of vested rights theory. With the exception of critiques by interest analysts, the theory and the doctrine of multistate property law have remained frozen in time.

One cannot offer an economic theory of conflicts without an economic theory of property. Contract law facilitates voluntary transfers of property rights; tort law protects property rights against interference.[2] The object of this chapter is to show how conflicts affect the purposes served by property law, why conflictual doctrine takes the form it does, and some of the allocative consequences the law may have.

Property laws serve *definitive*, *exchange*, and *regulatory* functions. Property law's definitive function is to define how entitlements are allocated and the means by which they are protected against non-owners. Choice of law principles resolve which laws serve this definitive function. Because courts are involved in protecting property rights, either by making orders for compensation or by granting injunctive relief, jurisdiction principles identify which courts will protect rights.

Property law's exchange function specifies how parties may trade entitlements. Because choice of law principles define the property law that applies to exchanges they determine the transaction protocol parties must follow for trades to be effective, and the protections parties should take to ensure that others cannot set up inconsistent rights in priority to theirs. Finally, property laws regulate how property may be used. Choice of law and jurisdictional principles define the effectiveness of those regulations, and may limit or extend the freedom of parties to avoid those regulations.

In order to address the concerns of this chapter, we borrow from the economic theory on property law in general. That theory begins with Coase. The literature following Coase explores how impediments to trade should influence the allocation and protection of entitlements.[3] In domestic contexts, this economic theory assumes various things — that the allocation of entitlements is fixed (or at least determinate), that the procedure for trade is established, that there is only a single court of unlimited jurisdiction, and so on. But these things are not true in conflicts cases. Initially, we explore the exchange function of property law in conflicts cases. We unite the theory in chapter 3 with the idea that property choice of law rules function as focal points in a coordination game between strangers. Our analysis of property's definitive and regulatory functions concentrates on land and immovable property. This reflects the problems with these functions when a jurisdiction has a monopoly over property incapable of exit.

Property Rights in Multistate Exchanges

The Choice of Law Coordination Game

Where trade is a precondition to transfers of property, property law specifies how parties may trade entitlements. It will identify the minimum conditions (including form and procedure) for a state to recognise and enforce the trade. Additionally, the law describes how competing claims for the entitlement, each based on an apparently enforceable trade, are to be resolved. A party seeking to buy an entitlement must, first, ascertain its owner and the existence of any qualifications or encumbrances on that interest. Second, the party must determine what must be done in order to perfect title after the trade. Third, the party must negotiate and conclude a trade in recognised form with the owner, ideally negotiating an undertaking by the owner not to create competing interests and to do all things previously identified as necessary for the party to perfect the interest. Fourth, the party must take all steps needed to perfect title.

A party cannot do these things unless the party knows the applicable law. But neither can a party do these things if materially different legal rules are applied to the transaction to those expected. In other words, trade depends on the application of a determinate body of law, and thus on applicable choice of law rules.

Choice of law principles are receptive to the importance of transaction protocol. We showed in chapter 3 that choice of law principles applicable to contract formation respond to the need for the applicable procedural law to be clear. They typically select the domestic law of consumers and other transactors with relatively high information costs.[4]

These issues are also relevant to dealings with property, with a proviso. Transaction procedure must not only enable trade between *two* parties; it must permit *third* parties to ascertain what trades have occurred, so they can ascertain the persons with whom they must transact, and the rights those persons have to trade. Most obviously, this arises in a priorities case where two parties contend they have ownership rights to certain property, each having entered a separate transaction with the same person. No contract exists between them that might resolve the problem. Domestically, these problems are common, but, since no conflictual issue arises, the parties know the risks they face in perfecting their title. They can therefore take whatever protection is appropriate and effective under the law (expeditious registration, escrow, contractual undertakings from the owner, and so on). But in a multistate context, the parties may make conflicting assumptions about the applicable property laws. Unless the parties know which laws apply, they will be incapable of knowing the rights that are being traded, the alternative interests that might be asserted in priority, and the procedures they should follow to control these risks.

The parties are playing a *coordination* game. We examined the concept of coordination in chapter 2.[5] In a coordination game, parties do best if they make a common strategy choice. The selection from between two or more possible strategies, each of which (when mirrored by the other party's choice) forms a possible equilibrium, is the source of the problem. Parties may be able to coordinate because of the cognitive salience of one of the strategies — such equilibria are called *focal points*. In some coordination games, the parties may have diverging preferences between the possible equilibria.[6]

The transaction protocol followed by the two parties asserting rights to property in a conflictual situation raises coordination problems. Assume that there are two possible property law types. One is based on the time that interests are created, the other on time of registration. As between two parties who deal independently with a third, both are better off if their transaction protocol is based on the same premise — either that rights depend on registration-based law, or that rights depend on the creation-time law. That enables them to decide what protocol to follow and what protections to take. To be sure, their preferences between the conflicting laws will often diverge.[7] When, however, the parties do not coordinate and share different premises, they may not take the precautions they should take, and the actions they do take may be wasted. There will be higher transaction costs, more litigation, and potentially more fraud.

An Analysis of Property Choice of Law Rules

Two-party cases In those cases where the only dispute arises between parties regarding the effect of their contract, pro-party autonomy choice of law principles should apply.[8] The parties should have substantial autonomy to define the rights they are trading. Some property law systems may constrain party autonomy by prescribing mandatory rules. Since property law's exchange function is primarily procedural law, mandatory rules mostly affect transaction costs, not directly the substance of the exchange. English private international law reinforces the contractors' autonomy by assuming jurisdiction to enforce contracts and equities in personam relating to foreign property as discussed below.

In the absence of a choice, the default proper law should be the same as that applying to third party cases. Coordination between parties capable of communicating and contracting is not a serious problem. However, consistency between the default rules applying to *inter partes* cases and the choice of law rules applying in other cases is important, because there may be no way of telling that a third party will *not* become involved.

Three-party cases Party autonomy has no normative weight where the parties are *not* in privity of contract. Here, the function of the law is to facilitate coordination by using choice of law rules that select suitable focal points. It is implicit in characterising the situation as a coordination game that there may be several solutions, not one *correct* or *logical* one. However, particular choice of law rules may be preferred because that law is focal and thus increases the likelihood of coordination. We consider different property types below.

Land The *lex situs* has obvious claims as a choice of law rule for trade in land.[9] It has great intuitive appeal as a focal point, given its stability and salience. Markets for real estate are substantially territorial because land situated in one locality is a limited substitute for land in another. The *lex situs* reflects this. We will examine problems with the *lex situs* from regulatory and definitive perspectives below.

Tangible, movable property Tangible, movable property creates complexities because of the instability of the *lex situs*. The *lex situs* is unstable because, subject to transaction costs, movable resources gravitate to higher valuing uses. *Situs* is thus contingent on market valuations. From a two-party perspective, the contingency of *situs* is a good thing. The property's mobility enables the parties to choose the desired *lex situs*, even where there are constraints on party autonomy on choice of law.

However, mobility limits the coordinating properties of the *situs* in multi-party cases, since the apparent focal point may change between the times of the two transactions. Some of the problems of property mobility might be solved by equating the *situs* to a 'primary' *situs*. For example, highly mobile assets forming part of a business (e.g., aircraft) might be treated as situated in the principal place at which that business is conducted. This would solve some problems, although not those raised by highly portable or homogeneous goods.[10] Other alternatives to *situs* are inferior. For example, the law of the place of assignment is undermined by the fact that transactions may be entered in different places. Although the *situs* may also change, a *lex situs* rule encourages the party to the first transaction to control the movement of the asset. A place of assignment rule requires that party to control the movement of the assignor, which is much less feasible.

A common domicile rule, which may be implicit in a case such as *North Western Bank v. Poynter*,[11] is an inadequate focal point in multi-party cases, unless *all three* parties have a common domicile (which is quite unlikely in a conflicts case). Thus, assume that A and B, both domiciled in Iowa, deal separately with C, an English domiciliary in relation to the purchase of a Cézanne sketch. A and C deal and contract in London; B and C in Antwerp. Iowa law is not focal unless A has some reason to know of B.[12]

An alternative choice of law rule for tangible movable property would be to choose the principal place of business of the assignor.[13] The motivation for this rule is that it is likely to be a focal point that otherwise independent parties are capable of having in common. Compared to the *situs*, it provides better coordination where goods are mobile or portable, or where the location of goods is substantially irrelevant (as in the case of homogeneous commodities). On the other hand, it may be difficult to identify the principal place of business for multinational corporations. Place of business is also less flexible than *situs*. It locks an assignor into a particular law unless he relocates his business. *Situs* lets the assignor select efficient property rights regimes by taking the goods there.

The place of business rule is best suited to a case where an assignor enters separate transactions with two or more parties. It is not well suited to cases involving a chain of transactions. In the chain case, there are two or more sequential assignors, so the rule will not identify a focal point for third party litigants. It is in this sense similar to the problem that *situs* may change when the *lex situs* is the choice of law rule. A refinement is to use the law of the cause selected for the *last* transaction. If the first of the assignors wants to assert property rights, his costs of ensuring that he is able to do so ought to be lower than the costs of successors ascertaining the non-existence of a potentially unlimited number of predecessors in title.[14] A similar refinement is used by most treatise writers in their discussion of the *lex situs* in cases of changes of *situs*.[15]

To conclude this discussion of tangible movables, there can be no completely straightforward focal point that can be reflected in a choice of law rule. *Situs* is not a perfect rule for movable assets but some of these problems can be resolved by pragmatic interpretations of *situs*. The only alternative is to refer matters to the place of business of the assignor in priority cases, and of the last assignor in chain cases, a rule that requires similar adjustments to *situs* in chain cases, and may often be less flexible.

Choses in Action Many choses in action — probably those most likely to be traded — originate in a contract or exchange.[16] This is obviously true of debts. Corporations, and thus securities, arise from contracts between shareholders, managers, and creditors. Since the contract is the basis of the rights being traded, it provides a logical basis for coordination between parties trading rights created by that contract. This implies that, in general, the choice of law should be defined by express choice in the original contract. This enables parties to the original contract to choose the regime under which property rights are dealt with.[17] This approach is accepted in England based on its ratification of the Rome Convention.[18]

For debts, for example, an express choice of law in the contract of loan should govern not only the original parties but proprietary claims with respect to the debt (with the exception of two-party cases that we discussed above). Typically, a *lex situs* rule would select the place the debtor resides. In many cases, the choice and *situs* rules will coincide. However, the justifications of the place of residence rule (the debtor is subject to jurisdiction there and has assets there) are unconvincing.[19] A choice of law rule allows sophisticated debtors and creditors the ability to opt into a more efficient regime for future trading of rights in the debt. Where the debts constitute corporate bonds, investors will value liquidity in secondary markets for the bonds. Liquidity depends on the ability of assets to trade quickly, which in turn depends on the applicable property law.

The *situs* of shares is either the location of the register on which the shares appear or the place of incorporation.[20] The place of incorporation is an appropriate choice of law rule, given its consistency with the 'internal affairs' rule as regards corporate governance and members' rights. Both rules have desirable coordinating properties. The advantage of the share-register *situs* rule is that corporations whose shares are traded on stock exchanges in different jurisdictions are able to select the property law applicable to them in accordance with any differences in the business rules of the exchanges. Otherwise, the differences between a register-based rule and an incorporation state rule ought to be minor.[21]

Regulating and Defining Entitlements to Land

The last section argued that the *lex situs* — the principal choice of law rule for questions relating to foreign land[22] — is a superior rule for resolving exchange-related real property conflicts. Other justifications for the use of the *lex situs* are easy to find. Posner's comparative advantage theory, outlined in chapter 2, would support it. The *situs* jurisdiction knows most about local conditions affecting the property.[23] Its law enforcement apparatus is most likely to be called on to enforce any judgment. To the extent that a choice of law rule encourages parties to litigate in the jurisdiction that provides the *lex causae*, and the *situs* is the jurisdiction in which litigation costs are lowest, it can also be justified.

On the other hand, a *situs* rule can be dysfunctional in land cases. Land is the paradigm form of immovable property. Immovable property has two important economic features. First, it is always subject to a jurisdictional monopoly. The importance of this monopoly can be explained by an economic analogy. The transaction cost economics literature illustrates the contracting problems created by assets whose value depends on the continuance of the exchanges those assets support.[24] Parties investing in those assets are vulnerable to opportunistic threats by the other party to terminate the relationship. Land is a 'jurisdiction-specific' investment in a similar sense. A land owner makes a sunk-cost investment in the value of that jurisdiction's regulation.[25] The land can only be sold within the jurisdiction, which does not permit the parties to avoid the effect of suboptimal regulation.

Second, bargains between adjacent landowners may be affected by bilateral monopolies. Bargaining between owners of adjacent property is often bilaterally monopolistic because the ability of one property owner to exploit her land fully may require some or all of the entitlement belonging (only) to her neighbour. For both problems, we study the combined effect of the *lex situs* choice of law rule and the jurisdictional rules of English law regarding foreign land.

The Moçambique *Case and the Jurisdictional 'Cartel'*

In addition to the *lex situs*'s domination of choice of law issues involving land,[26] English law adds the *Moçambique* principle, which forms part of the law of most common law countries. It holds that courts have no jurisdiction to entertain an action for determination of title to, the right to possession of, or the recovery of damages for trespass to any immovable property located out of the jurisdiction.[27] The *Moçambique* principle has been criticised as either an arbitrary vestigial relic of medieval procedure,[28] or as being so riddled by evasions and exceptions as to be unrepresentative of the true extent of jurisdiction over foreign land.[29]

The practical effect of *Moçambique* is to intensify the jurisdictional monopoly over the land. Not only will the *lex situs* be the exclusive source of rights for choice of law purposes, but only the *situs* can be the forum for litigation. Private international law becomes practically irrelevant to the definition of rights and title to immovable property. The conventional justification for *Moçambique* is that only the court of the *situs* can make an effective decree in relation to the land.[30] This is unconvincing. First, the principle is not limited to cases where title is in dispute.[31] Second, a foreign court that can enforce judgments against the defendant can make orders *in personam* that simulate the effect of almost any decree from the *situs* court (apart from orders such as attachment and the other handful of claims based on jurisdiction *in rem*).[32] There are many cases involving contractual and equitable causes of action which require the adjudication of title to foreign land where a court has exercised jurisdiction in this way.[33]

How, then, can we explain this principle? *Moçambique* may have done the duty of a discretion to decline jurisdiction at times when English law used a very strict principle for granting stays of proceedings.[34] If the *situs* is the forum which minimises litigation costs in a majority of cases, *Moçambique* bars the cases a court would be likely to stay. However, the old law on stays has been relaxed in common law jurisdictions.[35] There are few instances of corresponding repeals of *Moçambique*.[36]

A better explanation lies in cost externalisation. Courts may be willing to exercise jurisdiction in respect of certain multistate cases on the basis that parties who repeatedly enter relevant transactions may move parts of their business to that forum. Substantive law and forum may be part of the attractions offered by jurisdictions competing for business. But if the subject matter of these transactions is immovable, there can be no competition for the primary business. For a court to accept jurisdiction would be for the state in which it sits to subsidise the litigation costs of resolving foreign land disputes, without any hope that the state might capture the primary business. However, local lawyers wanting to act for foreign plaintiffs would prefer fewer constraints on jurisdiction — relaxing *Moçambique* would be akin to an implicit subsidy paid by taxpayers to lawyers.

A related explanation recognises that *Moçambique* applies mainly to litigation brought by foreign plaintiffs against defendants with substantial forum connections. A plaintiff will not sue in the forum unless it can establish jurisdiction over the defendant, and it will usually need to prove those connections to do that. For the forum to exercise jurisdiction would most likely benefit out-of-state plaintiffs at the expense of in-state defendants.[37] *Moçambique* furthers the interests of in-state defendants.

A challenge to this theory is to understand why courts deny jurisdiction in foreign land title and torts cases on one hand, while asserting in contractual and equitable cases a jurisdiction virtually coterminous with what they otherwise profess not to have. The readiest answer is that in the second group of cases, a jurisdiction to enforce contracts involving foreign land is much more likely to be beneficial to in-state interests, and especially to those investing in foreign land. A justification of facilitating trade is clearly implicit in early authorities where the court accepted jurisdiction.[38] To hold otherwise may often increase the litigation costs of in-state residents. There are significant advantages for a jurisdiction competing for commercial business if it consistently enforces the parties' contracts.

Why do courts apply *Moçambique* to cases involving foreign intellectual property rights?[39] To recognise intellectual property rights is to grant a monopoly. Not recognising foreign intellectual property rights increases the wealth of in-state interests by permitting them greater property rights in the relevant idea, design (etc.). Alternatively, it transfers rents to intellectual property-based interest groups within the state (such as regulators, local lawyers, or collective rights organisations) by requiring the owner of the foreign right to transact with them for the rights to be recognised locally. It may often be efficient to recognise the foreign intellectual property right, in exchange for foreign recognition of local rights.[40] Thus, multilateral conventions often overrule the more parochial common law approach.[41]

Let us return to the game analogies. Earlier, we identified a coordination game between contractors, to which private international law contributes law-selecting principles that identify focal points. By moving from the exchange function of property law to the definitive and regulatory functions, the game becomes one between states. Here, the solution identified is not the multiple equilibria of a coordination game, but a single equilibrium consisting of a symmetric dominant strategy for each state — deny jurisdiction in cases involving foreign plaintiffs against defendants with local interests. The temptation to tag this game a prisoner's dilemma is strong, for a prisoner's dilemma involves symmetric dominant strategies.[42] But a prisoner's dilemma only exists — and *Moçambique* is only problematic — if the individually rational dominant strategy (deny jurisdiction) is inconsistent with the collectively rational strategy. In some cases, this is not so, because the *situs* court will be the cost minimising forum; to permit foreign litigation would be welfare-decreasing. But the spectre of the prisoner's dilemma is raised by the potentially dysfunctional effect of the jurisdictional monopoly of the *situs*.

The implication of our analysis is important. If there are inefficiencies in the jurisdictional monopoly over land, as may be attributable to rent-seeking, other states are unlikely to want to break that monopoly, except to the extent of contract enforcement and trade facilitation. There is otherwise no business worth competing for. Adherence to *Moçambique* thus represents an equilibrium legal rule for most states, unless lawyers are capable of securing the judicial or legislative repeal of *Moçambique*.

Harmful Externalities

Our analysis is relevant to suits brought by the residents of developing countries against multinational corporations in their 'home' jurisdictions, in which injury is alleged to have resulted from the harmful external effects of industrial activities. Examples include litigation in the U.S. regarding the gas disaster at the Union Carbide plant at Bhopal, India,[43] and the ejection of mine tailings and toxic substances into the Fly River system in Papua New Guinea by B.H.P. Ltd.[44]

A government seeking to maximise the wealth of in-state interests would favour laws encouraging the efficient use of property interests within the forum.[45] However, this result may be drastically changed by rent-seeking activity. Corporations looking to invest in the developing country may be prepared to pay the country's lawmakers for regulations that enable it to externalise its costs. A frightening example is the enactment of legislation in Papua New Guinea which makes the seeking of compensation in foreign courts a criminal offence.[46] B.H.P.'s lawyers apparently drafted the legislation. The likelihood of this occurring obviously depends on the extent to which institutional arrangements, including public law controls, constrain self-interested behaviour by regulators and politicians. Local residents have much higher costs of political organisation. Their capacity to resist laws limiting or extinguishing compensation rights may be minimal. In contrast to the coordination game examined above, the parties' interaction resembles a Hobbesian state of nature.[47]

Assume a scenario in which a multinational company procures legislation which eliminates the rights of residents to sue for compensation or seek injunctive relief against the defendant. Assume further that bargaining between polluter and resident is impossible. Two questions arise. First, is there is a case for relaxing *Moçambique*? Second, what choice of law principles should a forum court apply in determining these disputes? Environmentalists would urge foreign courts to accept jurisdiction, and hold the corporation liable for, at minimum, the damage it has done. Holding the corporation liable is the rule that lawyer-economists prefer. Louis Kaplow and Steven Shavell demonstrate that where transaction costs are substantial, the efficient rule imposes a damages liability on a polluter equal to the average harm the pollution causes.[48] Provided the court's estimate of average harm is unbiased (neither systematically too high or too low), liability will increase allocative efficiency. A law enabling the polluter to pollute without any obligation to compensate is equivalent to estimating the resident's damages as being equal to zero, which must be systematically too low.

Whether a pragmatist should agree with the environmentalist and the economist is more complex. Waiver of *Moçambique* would be efficient if it could be shown that the foreign forum was appropriate to the resolution of the dispute. Appropriateness would be referable not to issues of substantive law (which is a choice of law consideration), but to the forum's suitability to the litigation in question. Relevant here would be comparative costs of litigation in alternative forums, the cost of bringing evidence to the forum, the pendency of more advanced proceedings elsewhere, the amenability of defendants to the process of the court, judgment enforceability, and so on.[49] A court should accept jurisdiction if (a) it is able to enforce orders it may make in the case; and (b) the parties' joint costs of litigation are minimised in that forum compared to other forums satisfying condition (a).[50] There is no reason to believe these conditions *never* hold, on which a defence of *Moçambique* must depend.

On what legal basis would one apply forum law to such a case as this? Most conflicts theories would not favour the application of forum law to such a case. Vested rights arise in the *situs*. The *lex fori* theory, discussed in chapter 2, and interest analysis would probably hold that the matter was a false conflict and either stay the suit or apply foreign law.[51] If one follows Lea Brilmayer, it is unclear whether it infringes the political rights of a local corporation for its offshore activities to be subject to local law.[52]

To justify the application of forum law, one must resort to a theory alike choice of law tailoring. We reject this approach in other chapters. However, our reasoning may not hold in this case. The irrelevance of the choice of law in contract cases depends on low transaction costs, but this does not hold in property cases. Our defence of territorial rules in market torts is that they facilitate decisions to exit or enter a jurisdiction, and enable markets to price obligations of care and insurance. Exit is impossible when the asset is immovable, and facilitation of market pricing is irrelevant to regulatory issues. Our advocacy of *lex loci delicti* in non-market torts depends on the improbability that selecting more onerous care obligations affects investments in care. However, making first-order choices of law may improve allocative efficiency if the proprietary tort will continue where the foreign forum does not make an order. Inefficient continuing uses may be prevented. There is thus a case for non-application of the *lex situs*.

Thus far, few clear conclusions are possible. Applying compensatory forum law is arguably efficient, but can only be justified if one thinks it appropriate for judges to use efficiency to avoid law endorsed by virtually every choice of law theory. There is, however, another option that judges might employ which draws from the economic theory of property rights.

Calabresi and Melamed showed that polluter-resident litigation matters could be resolved in four possible ways. The entitlement can be allocated either to the polluter or to the resident. An entitlement can be protected by a *property rule*; the party not owning the entitlement must negotiate a consensual trade if she wishes to enjoy the benefit of it. Alternatively, that party may take it without consent on condition that she compensates the entitlement owner. This is described as *liability rule* protection. If, as we assume, the polluter gets the entitlement under the *lex situs*, the right might be protected by a property rule, so that abatement of pollution occurs only where the resident bribes the polluter to stop. Calabresi and Melamed's famous insight (often referred to as 'rule 4') was to show that the polluter's entitlement might only be protected by a liability rule. That would permit a resident to enjoin pollution provided the resident pays compensation for taking the polluter's entitlement.[53]

A judge unwilling to order the polluter to pay compensation, since the *lex situs* awards the entitlement to the polluter, might nonetheless use rule 4 injunctive relief against a defendant corporation.[54] The plaintiff would have to compensate the defendant for the loss arising from cessation. This rule is more likely to achieve an efficient result, since the plaintiff will only seek the injunction (which will require it to compensate the defendant) if it values the entitlement more than the defendant does. A court making such an order is not varying the *lex situs*'s allocation of the entitlement. It merely changes the manner of protection. Of course, this is manipulative. However, it is a manipulation with a long history, since courts have long regarded remedies as 'procedural'.[55] For once, the substance/procedure distinction can be used efficiently.

The economic merits of rule 4 depend on residents being able to make efficient decisions whether or not they value the entitlement more than the compensation payable. Even if we ignore the possibility that residents may have no money, suboptimal decisions may be made if the residents comprise a class.[56] Collective action problems may cause inefficiency, because some residents may not become adequately informed, or because residents may try to free ride by avoiding their share of the compensation liability. As James Krier and Stewart Schwab have pointed out, one would like to place the decision in the hands of the 'best chooser' (the party best placed to make a rational choice). In a resident class action, this is probably the polluter. This can be done by giving the polluter a put option over its entitlement.[57] This requires a court to estimate the damage residents suffer if the pollution continues, and then awarding these to the polluter *if* the polluter ceases the pollution, but not if it decides *not* to. A rational polluter will cease if the damage to the residents exceeds the cost to stop polluting (which is the efficiency condition). The polluter's decision is not affected by collective action problems.[58] An order relying on either rule 4 or a put option is a more efficient outcome than the one in which the polluter's right is protected by a property rule.

If foreign forums could be persuaded to assume jurisdiction in appropriate (efficient) cases, and to apply either the more radical option of awarding residents compensation, or the more conservative option of purchased injunctions or puts, they would increase allocative efficiency in the use of property entitlements. These options might also be more efficient in cases where trade between residents and polluters is possible.

Coasean Trade in Harmful Externalities Cases

Law and economics scholars originally thought that protecting entitlements with property rules was appropriate where transaction costs are low.[59] An entitlement protected by a property rule cannot be taken without the owner's consent. Liability rules require resort to the legal system in order to determine compensation. Courts and administrative processes are more prone to error in valuing the entitlement than its owner is.

A second generation of scholars questioned this analysis by examining the problem of strategic bargaining — the tendency to conceal and distort information, and to hold out from entering bargains as a means of capturing the majority of gains from trade.[60] For example, potential buyers understate their valuation of the entitlement. Potential sellers overstate their valuation. Despite the formal costs of bargaining being low, many trades may not be consummated, and the costs of reaching deals may rise substantially. Strategic bargaining is most problematic in bilateral monopolies.

A new generation of research argues property rules exacerbate strategic behaviour. They increase the capacity of an entitlement owner to hold out and the incentive to misrepresent his or her valuation. Seminal works by Jason Johnston, and by Ian Ayres and Eric Talley argue that strategic behaviour might best be addressed by dividing the entitlement between the parties.[61] Johnston's argument is that conditioning the rights of parties to an entitlement on an imprecise, standard-like contingent allocation of rights increases the likelihood that parties will agree to trade. The party wanting the entitlement is able to threaten to take the entitlement in a way not possible where the entitlement owner is protected by a property rule.

Ayres and Talley's analysis has two parts. First, they show that liability rules divide rights in an entitlement between its owner and a potential taker. The taker has a right practically resembling a call option — a right to buy for the amount of the compensation. The ability to take limits the incentive of the owner to bargain strategically. It gives him a choice — to bribe the taker not to take, or to sell his entitlement to the taker. The amount of compensation payable when a taking occurs caps the price agreed in a sale. Therefore, the owner will only attempt a sale when he values the asset *less* than the amount of compensation; it follows that the owner will consider bribing the taker — buying the call option — only when he values the asset *more* than the compensation.[62] The liability rule thus induces separation between high- and low-valuing owners, which reduces their ability to bargain strategically.[63] However, liability rules may increase strategic behaviour by low-valuing takers who try to extort a bribe by falsely threatening to take.

Second, the law may divide property between parties in other ways. An obvious example is a court order to partition the land of joint tenants. Ayres and Talley show that both parties' incentive for strategic bargaining may be reduced. The identity of the buyer and seller in the eventual transaction will not be obvious. The owner of a divided entitlement could buy the part she doesn't own, or sell the part she does own. The incentive to misrepresent valuation is reduced — one who claims a high valuation in the hope of making a sale might be asked to buy at that price.

Strategically, we have moved from a Hobbesian state of nature to a bargaining game in which private international law rules and foreign and *situs* property law define the 'pre-existing' entitlements.

Where *situs* courts alone resolve property conflicts, and apply their own law, constraints on strategic behaviour depend on the *lex situs*. If the *lex situs* allocates absolute entitlements protected by property rules, the level of strategic behaviour may be high. Consider the case where jurisdiction J allocates the right to 'air' to a polluter, P, and protects it by a property rule. A resident, R, living on adjacent land, must bribe P not to pollute. Coasean trade may be frustrated by strategic bargaining.

However, different jurisdiction and choice of law rules can convert a seemingly absolute entitlement into a conditional entitlement. The willingness of a foreign forum in state K, to accept jurisdiction over foreign land and to apply its different law has the potential to change an absolute entitlement into a conditional one. The plaintiff will litigate in a forum which has jurisdiction over the defendant, and which will, with nonzero probability, grant the entitlement to the plaintiff. The ultimate resolution of the matter depends on how the courts resolve their overlapping jurisdiction. One forum may either stay its own proceedings or attempt to issue an anti-suit injunction attempting to restrain a party from proceeding in the other forum. The likely result at the time the litigation commences cannot be known with certainty.

If parties are able to bargain during the pendency of the litigation, the ensuing bargaining game resembles what Ayres and Talley describe as a *probabilistic* division of the entitlement. Ayres and Talley conceive a case where only one court is involved but its decision regarding the allocation's entitlement involves uncertainty which is capable of description in terms of a probability density function.[64] The context described here is practically similar, since at the time litigation begins, the identity of the forum whose law and orders will ultimately prevail is uncertain and can only be described in probabilistic terms. Ayres and Talley show that the ability of probabilistic divisions to facilitate trade is highest when the chances of the two parties succeeding is equal. Intuitive appreciation of this is easy — where one party is certain to get the entitlement, that party can only be the seller. The other party, certain *not* to get it, can only be the buyer — this is the same result as the case where the domestic law of the *situs* awards the entitlement to the polluter and protects it with a property rule.

It seems that the possibility of more active exercise of jurisdiction in respect of foreign land and the application of conflicting law may overcome strategic behaviour. This result does not depend on foreign law being more just (or more efficient), but on the fractured entitlements caused by the conflict. However, various factors qualify this conclusion. First, the costs of bargaining must be relatively low. This may not be so in pollution cases where there are multiple residents, as we have observed above.[65] If bargaining cannot occur, parallel foreign proceedings can only be justified if they result in the transfer of the entitlement to the higher valuing user.

Second, property rules may be necessary to encourage an entitlement owner to make asset-specific investments increasing the value of the entitlement.[66] The incentive to do that may be weakened if one has, at most, a fractional interest in an entitlement. Perhaps corporations will only invest in countries with underdeveloped systems of law and property rights if ownership of relevant entitlements is clarified by legislation.

To conclude, recall that our initial discussion identified two potential problems with the primacy of *situs* in proprietary conflicts — jurisdictional monopoly and bilateral monopoly. This section has shown the relation between the two. The availability of competing forums for the litigation of the case may mitigate the problems associated with bilaterally monopolistic bargaining situations which arise from the property law of the *situs*. However, this may not happen because the incentives for forums to depart from *Moçambique* in foreign torts cases is weak.

Conclusion

This chapter demonstrates the importance of a pragmatic approach to policy in choice of law. The analysis of property law's exchange function shows how party autonomy and private ordering cannot be a complete theory of choice of law in contract cases. Coordination in the multistate world is logically prior to the facilitation of trade. Likewise, we showed how our preference for territorial approaches to torts needs some qualification, and that 'crystalline' choice of law rules may not always facilitate trade, at least in bilateral monopoly cases.

Notes

1. This chapter is based on Whincop (2000a).
2. Posner (1998a, p. 35).
3. The seminal article is Calabresi and Melamed (1972). We shall refer to a 'first generation' of scholarship on this issue of which the premier examples are Kaplow and Shavell (1996) and Polinsky (1980). See generally Krier and Schwab (1995). The second generation of scholarship draws on bargaining and game theory: Ayres (1998), Ayres and Talley (1995a, 1995b), Ayres and Balkin (1996), Johnston (1995).
4. See chapter 3, pp. 39-40 *supra*.
5. See chapter 2, p. 28 *supra*.
6. This is the basic distinction between the stag hunt (both parties prefer a single equilibrium to another) and the battle of the sexes (players prefer different equilibria) paradigms: see chapter 2, note 67 *supra*.
7. This suggests the battle of the sexes may be a more persuasive analogy.
8. One treatise favours the resolution of two-party cases in this way (Sykes and Pryles 1991, pp. 666-667). Others differentiate contractual and proprietary issues in assignments, only the former of which may be governed by the proper law of the contract: see, e.g., Collins (1993, p. 967), Clarkson and Hill (1997, pp. 451-454), Castel (1994, pp. 453-454). Our approach is more pragmatic because the property/contract distinction is more conceptual and metaphysical.
9. *Nelson v. Bridport* (1846) 8 Beav. 547; 50 E.R. 215, *Adams v. Clutterbuck* (1883) 10 Q.B.D. 403, *Gregg v. Perpetual Trustee Co.* (1918) 18 S.R. (N.S.W.) 252, *Duke v. Andler* [1932] S.C.R. 734. Textbook writers treat these propositions as orthodox: see Collins (1993, pp. 960-964) (rule 117), Castel (1994, pp. 437-438), Sykes and Pryles (1991, p. 704).
10. See *Winkworth v. Christie, Mason and Woods Ltd* [1980] Ch. 496.
11. [1895] A.C. 56. This case involved a question as to the title of certain immovable property, located in Scotland, the subject of a security transaction between two parties domiciled and carrying on business in England. Although not strictly necessary to the decision, the House of Lords held that English law applied to such a transaction.
12. Some early cases imply that the validity of transfers depends on the owner's domicile: see, e.g., *Re Ewin* (1830) 1 Cr. & J. 151, 148 E.R. 1371. Dicey and Morris reject this rule as being based on the assumption that chattels followed

changes in the domicile of the owner, which they say is no longer accurate as a statement of fact (Collins 1993, p. 966). However, linking business assets to the principal place of a business seems a much more defensible rule. In any event, the consequential merits of the rule depend less on its approximation of reality as its ability to induce coordination and reduce transaction costs.

13. Such a rule has similarities to the use of characteristic performance in contract cases: *Contracts (Applicable Law) Act* c. 36 sch 1, art 4(2).
14. Accord, Staughton L.J. in *MacMillan Inc. v. Bishopsgate Investment Trust plc.* [1996] 1 All E.R. 585, 597.
15. Collins (1993, pp. 970-976), Castel (1994, p. 442), Cheshire and North (1992, p. 801).
16. One important category of intangible property that does not originate in exchange is intellectual property rights. Registration-based rights such as patents are easily assimilated with the proper law approach suggested in the text because one can rely on the law of the place of registration.
17. Parties should have strong incentives to make optimal choices of the property law regime since the returns to those parties are inversely related to the transaction costs of trading rights under the contract, which is influenced by their choice of proper law. This argument is similar to the economic defence of the internal affairs rule: see pp. 39, 85 *supra*. The usual provisos concerning status quo biases and learning and network externalities apply.
18. *Contracts (Applicable Law) Act 1990* (U.K.), sch. 1 art. 12. See Collins (1993, p. 979), Clarkson and Hill (1997, pp. 450-454).
19. Rogerson (1990) criticises the use of the place of residence rule. As he argues, an assumption that it is appropriate because the debtor will have his or her assets there is naive. Moreover, the rule cannot be justified on the ground that the court of the place of residence will have jurisdiction over the defendant since residence is not the only basis for jurisdiction. The changeability of the *situs* raises difficult questions about when one is to assess it. He favours the use of the proper law of the debt contract.
20. *MacMillan Inc. v. Bishopsgate Investment Trust plc. (No. 3)* [1996] 1 All E.R. 585. Staughton L.J. proposes the place of incorporation but says that there 'may be cases where it is arguably the law of the place where the share register is kept' (ibid., 602). Aldous L.J. takes a similar view (ibid., 616). Auld L.J. proposes the place of the share register (ibid., 608).
21. Benjamin (1998, p. 608).
22. *Coppin v. Coppin* (1725) P. Wms. 291; 24 E.R. 735, *Nelson v. Bridport* (1846) 8 Beav. 547; 50 E.R. 215, *Adams v. Clutterbuck* (1883) 10 Q.B.D. 403.
23. *Kaczmarek v. Allied Chem Corp.*, 836 F.2d 1055, 1058 (7th Cir. 1987), Posner (1998a, p. 646).
24. See generally Williamson (1985, 1996).
25. Alchian (1975).

26. The *lex situs* will also apply to torts affecting land since the *situs* is the *locus delicti*, and, if foreign courts refuse jurisdiction in these cases, the forum.
27. *British South Africa Co. v. Companhia de Moçambique* [1893] A.C. 602. Affirmed in *Hesperides Hotels Ltd v. Muftizade* [1979] A.C. 508.
28. Welling and Heakes (1980).
29. Lee (1995, 1997a, 1997b).
30. See, e.g., Sykes and Pryles (1991, p. 60).
31. *Hesperides Hotels Ltd v. Muftizade* [1979] A.C. 508.
32. Nygh (1995b, p. 418).
33. Lee (1997a, pp. 274-275, 279-283).
34. *St. Pierre v. South American Stores (Gath & Chaves) Ltd* [1936] 1 K.B. 382. See *Hesperides Hotel Ltd v. Muftizade* [1979] A.C. 508, 537.
35. *Voth v. Manildra Flour Mills Pty Ltd* (1990) 171 C.L.R. 538, *Spiliada Maritime Corp. v. Cansulex Ltd* [1987] 1 A.C. 460, *Amchem Products, Inc. v. British Columbia (Workers Compensation Board)* [1993] 1 S.C.R. 897.
36. *Jurisdiction of Courts (Foreign Land) Act 1989* (N.S.W.) s. 3. In the United States, see *Restatement (Second) of Conflict of Laws* (1971) § 87. In England, *Moçambique* has been superseded by statute but much of it remains intact: *Civil Jurisdiction and Judgments Act* 1982 (UK) ss. 2, 3A, 30, sch. 1, arts. 2, 15, 16, 19, 28.
37. Contrast the Canadian *Uniform Transboundary Pollution Reciprocal Access Act* (1982) 64 Proc. Unif. L. Conf. Can. 504, which enables courts to exercise jurisdiction in respect of pollution affecting foreign land in cases where the polluter-defendant is an in-state resident. Jurisdiction is only extended where the state in which the plaintiff resides has enacted the legislation. In the United States, see *Restatement (Second) of Conflict of Laws* § 87 cmt. c (1971).
38. See, e.g., *Lord Cranstown v. Johnston* (1796) 3 Ves. 170, 171, cited with approval *British South Africa Co. v. Companhia de Moçambique* [1893] A.C. 602, 626. See Lee (1995, pp. 622-626).
39. See *Potter v. Broken Hill Pty. Ltd* (1906) 3 C.L.R. 479, *Def Lepp Music v. Stuart-Brown* [1986] R.P.C. 273, *Tyburn Productions Ltd v. Conan Doyle* [1991] Ch. 75, *Pearce v. Ove Arup Partnership Ltd* [1997] 3 All E.R. 31. Cf. Lee (1995, pp. 630-631).
40. Kramer (1990, pp. 341-344).
41. *Civil Jurisdiction and Judgments Act* 1982 (U.K.), sch. 1, arts. 2, 6(1). Cf. *Pearce v. Ove Arup Partnership Ltd*, [1997] 3 All E.R. 31.
42. See generally Baird et al (1994, pp. 31-35).
43. *In re Union Carbide Corp. Gas Plant Disaster at Bhopal, India,* 634 F. Supp. 842 (S.D.N.Y. 1986), 809 F.2d 195 (2d Cir.), 484 U.S. 871 (1987).
44. *Dagi v. B.H.P. Ltd (No. 2)* [1997] 1 V.R. 428.
45. See generally Trachtman (1997).
46. *Compensation (Prohibition of Foreign Legal Proceedings) Act* 1995 (P.N.G.).
47. Calabresi and Melamed (1972, pp. 1090-1091).

48. Kaplow and Shavell (1995, pp. 727-728).
49. Welling and Heakes (1980).
50. There are two other cases where a court should accept jurisdiction even if condition (b) is not satisfied. First, where trade is possible between the parties, accepting jurisdiction may attenuate strategic bargaining. We discuss this below. Second, where the alleged tort is or may be a *continuing* one, the social benefits of a more allocatively efficient division of property rights between the resident and the polluter may outweigh the higher costs of litigation. The ability to enforce orders remains an essential condition.
51. Ehrenzweig (1960), Currie (1963).
52. Brilmayer (1989).
53. Calabresi and Melamed (1972, p. 1116). See *Spur Industries, Inc. v. Del E Webb Development Co.*, 108 Ariz. 178, 494 P.2d 700 (1972).
54. We assume that the court is willing to ignore *Moçambique* and exercise jurisdiction as the *forum conveniens.* One might fairly think this more radical than departing from a choice of law rule.
55. See *Stevens v. Head* (1993) 176 C.L.R. 433. Cf. Cook (1933).
56. Polinsky (1980).
57. Krier and Schwab (1995, pp. 470-475). A holder of a put option has the right but not the obligation to sell an asset to another person for a specified price.
58. Ayres (1998).
59. Posner (1998a).
60. Farrell (1987).
61. Ayres and Talley (1995a), Johnston (1995).
62. The ability of liability rules to have these effects depends on the compensation amount being known at the time of the taking, that is, it cannot be 'tailored' to the circumstances of the litigant: Ayres and Talley (1995a, pp. 1065-1072).
63. Cf. Kaplow and Shavell (1995), *contra* Ayres and Talley (1995b).
64. Ayres and Talley (1995a, pp. 1073-1078).
65. Polinsky (1980, p. 1107).
66. Ayres and Talley (1995a, pp. 1083-1090).

8 Jurisdiction and Procedure

The Significance of Jurisdiction

We have anticipated jurisdictional issues in earlier chapters. Chapter 2 stated that economising on litigation costs should be a priority of private international law. Chapters 3 and 4 discuss forum defaults and their relation to mandatory rules. Chapter 5 notes that the existence of multiple jurisdictions favours a passive approach to the enforcement of choice of law clauses in market torts. Chapter 6 advocates a choice of law rule applicable to market torts on the ground that it induces cost-minimising jurisdictional choices. Chapter 7 describes the relevance of jurisdictional monopolies to immovable property. This chapter extends the earlier work by theorising the assertion of jurisdiction and multistate civil procedure.

The law on jurisdiction and multistate civil procedure is important economically for two reasons. First, it affects the efficiency or inefficiency of any nation's choice of law rule. As chapter 2 indicates, objections to *lex fori* as a choice of law rule might be overcome if a jurisdiction restricts the cases in which it will accept jurisdiction. Conversely, an efficient choice of law rule, such as the enforcement of the parties' agreed choice of law, presupposes that the parties can establish jurisdiction in a forum that offers that choice of law rule *and* can restrain litigation in a jurisdiction that would thwart their choice. We have shown how parties might achieve these things by the enforcement of jurisdiction clauses, but this presupposes that transaction costs are low enough to permit an ex ante agreement. This is not true in cases involving discrete torts and third party property assignments.

Second, jurisdictional rules affect litigation costs. They do this in two ways. Obviously, they select the forum for litigation. Forums are likely to differ in the litigation costs that parties (and the state in which the forum sits) incur. It is likely to cost less to litigate an automobile accident occurring in Sydney between an Indian and an Australian in the State of New South Wales than in Brazoria County, Texas. Jurisdictional principles also affect the *distribution* of litigation costs. A plaintiff will choose to litigate in a forum that minimises her costs, other things being equal, and in a multistate case her advantage may come at the defendant's expense.

Jurisdictional principles also affect costs by altering the sequence of civil procedure. This affects the nature of strategic behaviour during the litigation process. For example, parties litigating a multistate case are obliged to consider offers to settle, as well as opportunities to resolve jurisdictional disputes out of court. We refer to this as *jurisdictional trade*, a possibility hitherto ignored in conflicts scholarship. Jurisdictional procedures designed to control the selection of excessively costly forums (such as applications to stay proceedings on *forum non conveniens* grounds) may themselves affect the level of strategic behaviour, including the nature of bargaining in jurisdictional trade.

Initially, we return to a basic theoretical issue: what interests are relevant to jurisdictional principles? We then extend the existing economic analysis of litigation and civil procedure to conflicts cases. We use these insights to analyse a range of relevant legal issues, including *forum non conveniens*, anti-suit injunctions, and the recognition of judgments.

Interests Relevant to Jurisdictional Principles

We have argued that party interests should be paramount. The relevance of party interests to jurisdiction is obvious. The historic concern to limit 'long-arm' statutes reflects the need to ensure plaintiffs do not choose forums that impose high costs on the defendant, a concern which goes simultaneously to fairness and efficiency concerns.[1] Even though long arm statutes have, over time, widened in scope, courts have over a similar period expanded the grounds on which they decline to exercise jurisdiction. The willingness of most modern legal systems to enforce jurisdiction agreements treats party interests as sovereign.

States also have 'interests' in the exercise of jurisdiction. It is possible to argue that these interests are legitimate. Exercising jurisdiction imposes costs on a state through its court system. As chapter 7 shows, states may be unwilling to exercise jurisdiction when litigation does not involve either the citizens of the state or any aspect of its economy or polity.[2] Why would the taxpayers of jurisdiction J subsidise the production of private goods for litigants of jurisdiction K? Although, in theory, states could impose a tax on litigants, jurisdictional principles can also serve to ration scarce judicial resources.

The sorts of government interests we examined in chapter 2, such as the furtherance of domestic policy, might also be asserted in jurisdictional contexts. Cases such as *The Hollandia*[3] and *Akai*,[4] discussed in chapter 4, imply that jurisdiction should be accepted when declining it would thwart a remedial purpose of forum legislation. Legislatures may instruct local courts not to enforce jurisdiction clauses. For reasons we have previously offered, where legislatures have not done so, these government interests should not serve as bases for jurisdictional decisions.

Besides states and parties, lawyers are the other interested constituency. Lawyers are direct beneficiaries of expanded jurisdiction. Even where a court checks expanded rules for the establishment of jurisdiction with a wide discretion to decline jurisdiction, lawyers will benefit. They will have the opportunity to take at least those steps in the litigation process up to and including the stay application. Lawyers have an incentive to limit the enforcement of foreign jurisdiction agreements by parties in order to prevent leakage of cases out of the jurisdiction. Likewise, they can be expected to advocate other jurisdiction-expanding arguments, such as those based in 'justice'. The next section analyses in more detail how jurisdictional principles affect the parties in their conduct of litigation.

The Economics of Jurisdiction

The economic literature analysing civil procedure stylises the litigation process as one with a small number of discrete steps involving choices for one or both of the parties.[5] Following Cooter and Rubinfeld, we assume that domestic litigation has four relevant stages.[6] The first concerns the underlying primary behaviour of the parties, such as the performance of a contract or the taking of care. Second, a party must decide whether or not to bring suit. Third, the parties negotiate in respect of a settlement offer. Parties must decide whether or not to make an offer and what offer to make, and the other party must decide whether or not to accept it. Fourth, if the parties do not conclude a settlement, parties must decide how much effort to make at trial.

Most of the attention in these models of domestic litigation has been directed, first, to why some, but not all, cases settle? The answers are either that the parties' expectations about the case differ (in particular, where the plaintiff is relatively optimistic), or that there are information asymmetries. Second, what influence do regimes for the allocation of legal costs have? Theoretical analysis has compared the 'American rule' (each party bears its own costs) to the 'British rule' (the loser pays the winner's costs).[7]

These issues also arise, with some twists, in conflicts cases. We discuss these in the context of three unique issues that arise in conflicts cases. First, a party must decide the forum in which to bring suit. This must be resolved at the time of the decision whether or not to bring suit. Second, a defendant must decide whether or not to object to the exercise of jurisdiction by the plaintiff's preferred forum. Third, the parties may engage in jurisdictional trade. That is, a plaintiff may agree to discontinue in a particular forum, perhaps on receiving a side payment.

As regards timing, an objection to jurisdiction typically must be made around the time at which suit begins. The timing of an offer of jurisdictional trade is less clear. It might occur at any time before trial. However, it is unlikely to occur too close to trial. Since jurisdictional trade involves discontinuance, parties will prefer to discontinue earlier rather than later, since parties will prefer not to sink deadweight costs in a jurisdiction to be abandoned. Although not strictly rational, parties may resist jurisdictional trade *because* they have sunk significant costs into a jurisdiction. There is a documented 'endowment effect', by which an individual places a higher value on a thing she owns than she would be willing to pay for it.[8] A plaintiff's decisions relating to a jurisdiction which he has chosen, and incurred legal costs in, may be similarly affected. We assume that an offer of jurisdictional trade is in most cases accepted or rejected before the resolution of a jurisdictional challenge.

Our analysis of jurisdiction equates it to an entitlement. One's right to sue for damages for injunctive relief is conventionally analysed in these terms, since that entitlement is a second-order aspect of a more fundamental recognition of a right, such as freedom from trespass. Calabresi and Melamed note that the recognition and protection of entitlements depend on some measure of state enforcement.[9] A choice of jurisdiction reflects the fact that there is often a choice as to the state by which an entitlement is recognised and protected. Because domestic cases do not question the jurisdiction of a court or its capacity to make certain orders, there is little to be gained by viewing this entitlement to sue separately from the substantive right. But since the entitlement to sue in a particular court is contingent in a conflicts case, its separate recognition is important. Not only does it enable us to see that there may be trade in jurisdictional entitlements, but we may be able to apply the economic theory of entitlements to evaluate the efficiency of the law on jurisdiction.[10]

Choice of Forum

Initially, we assume that parties bear their own costs. To illustrate how parties make choices of forum, we define two functions. These are: F_n, which yields the payoff to the plaintiff from commencing litigation in forum n, and F_l, which yields the payoff from commencing in an 'efficient' forum. The variables used in F_n are defined in Table 8.1.

Table 8.1 Definition of variables used in this chapter

e_{pn} (e_{dn})	cost to plaintiff (defendant) of litigating in jurisdiction n up to the time of a jurisdictional challenge
j_{pn} (j_{dn})	cost to plaintiff (defendant) of contesting a challenge to jurisdiction in n
t_{pn} (t_{dn})	cost to plaintiff (defendant) to try the case in jurisdiction n^*
c_{pn} (c_{dn})	total cost to plaintiff (defendant) of litigating a claim in jurisdiction n
D_{pfn} (D_{dfn})	plaintiff's (defendant's) estimate of expected damages awarded by a court in n if it applies forum law
D_{px} (D_{dx})	plaintiff's (defendant's) estimate of expected damages awarded by a court applying the efficient second-order choice of law rule.
p_{pjn} (p_{djn})	plaintiff's (defendant's) subjective probability that jurisdiction n will exercise jurisdiction
p_{pfn} (p_{dfn})	plaintiff's (defendant's) subjective probability that jurisdiction n will apply forum law
p_{pvn} (p_{dvn})	plaintiff's (defendant's) subjective probability of victory at trial where the court applies the law of n.

* Excludes all costs incurred prior to and including a jurisdictional challenge.

The efficient forum is the forum that minimises litigation costs. We presently assume the defendant will be unable to challenge its jurisdiction successfully. If the plaintiff chooses to litigate in n, it will accept jurisdiction with probability p_{jn} (p_{pjn} as perceived by the plaintiff), and apply forum law with probability p_{fn} (p_{pfn} as perceived by the plaintiff). Should forum law be applied, the expected damages for the plaintiff are denoted by D_{pfn}.[11] We make the further assumption that a court that does not apply forum law applies the same *lex causae* as the efficient forum. Should that law be applied, the expected damages are D_x.[12]

We also assume that the costs of litigation differ between forums. A plaintiff litigating in the efficient forum can expect to pay costs of t_{pl} from the time of commencing the litigation until its resolution in a trial. A plaintiff litigating in another jurisdiction, n, incurs costs in two parts. The first part, e_{pn}, is the costs of establishing jurisdiction in that forum incurred up to and including the time of any jurisdictional challenge. If that challenge succeeds, those costs are a deadweight loss. If that challenge does not succeed, the plaintiff continues to trial, and incurs t_{pn}. Our assumption is that if the defendant successfully challenges jurisdiction in n, the plaintiff will proceed in the efficient forum.

Given the above description, a plaintiff commencing in n always incurs costs of e_n. The plaintiff's probability of getting the damages based on the law of n, D_{pfn}, equals the product of the probabilities that the court will exercise jurisdiction *and* apply forum law. If the court doesn't accept jurisdiction or apply forum law, the plaintiff only gets damages of D_{px}, either from forum n, if it accepts jurisdiction, or from the efficient forum if n declines jurisdiction. The plaintiff therefore incurs the costs of t_{pn} if the court accepts jurisdiction, and t_{p1}, if the court does not. Thus, F_n and F_1 can be derived as follows:

$$\begin{aligned} F_n &= p_{pjn}(D_{pfn}p_{pfn} - t_{pn}) + D_{px}(1 - p_{pjn}p_{pfn}) - (1 - p_{pjn})t_{p1} - e_{pn} \\ &= p_{pjn}p_{pfn}(D_{pfn} - D_{px}) - p_{pjn}(t_{pn} - t_{p1}) + D_{px} - t_{p1} - e_{pn} \\ F_1 &= D_{px} - t_{p1} \end{aligned}$$

By subtraction one gets:

$$F_n - F_1 = \{p_{pjn}p_{pfn}(D_{pfn} - D_{px})\} - [p_{pjn}(t_{pn} - t_{p1})] - e_{pn} \qquad (1)$$

A risk-neutral plaintiff will not litigate in jurisdiction 1 if $F_n - F_1$ is negative, and will choose n to maximise F_n. Equation (1) establishes many of the propositions we have advanced intuitively in this book. First, the primary spur to forum shopping is the scale of the advantages from application of local law and the willingness of the court to apply it. This is reflected in the term in brackets.

Second, the term in brackets indicates that the higher the costs of a forum, the less attractive it is. If all possible forums apply the same multilateral choice of law rule, plaintiffs would select the jurisdiction that minimised their costs. The willingness of a court to exercise jurisdiction and apply forum law can distort this incentive, since the greater expected award may dominate substantially higher costs. In these cases, the term in braces will be greater than the term in square brackets. This is inefficient. The plaintiff's private benefit from the damages payment sums to zero when added to the defendant's private cost, but the costs are genuine social costs. Except for the case in which the plaintiff's higher costs are offset by the defendant's lower costs, the choice of forum will be inefficient.

Third, the final term in equation (1) indicates that the higher the litigation costs that must be incurred in the forum prior to the resolution of jurisdictional challenges, the less likely a plaintiff is to sue there. The plaintiff must sink this cost whatever decision is made. Although these costs will not affect decisions that the plaintiff makes after the jurisdiction challenge is resolved, they influence the initial forum choice.

F_n has been constructed on the basis that the matter goes to trial in each forum. In fact, many cases will settle. The settlement dynamic, however, suggests a further source of inefficiency. The literature refers to the phenomenon of the 'nuisance suit', brought by a plaintiff who could never expect to win at trial (i.e. $D_{pfn} = 0$), on the basis that a settlement offer might be made.[13] One explanation for nuisance suits is an asymmetry between the costs of the plaintiff and the defendant. A defendant may have to pay to the plaintiff some of his cost savings if the action does not proceed. This is especially likely in multistate litigation if the plaintiff can locate a jurisdiction in which the defendant would find it very costly to litigate, perhaps in consequence of the locus or mobility of evidence.

Objections to Jurisdiction

The inefficiencies created by the divergence between the plaintiff's private costs and the social costs of forum choice may be controlled either by limiting the circumstances in which a plaintiff can establish jurisdiction, or by enabling the court to stay litigation by not exercising jurisdiction in appropriate cases. To the extent that establishment rules rely on second-order standards whose content is only ascertainable by adjudication, they would be practically quite similar to the stay-based method.[14] We will return below to the possibility of ex ante certain establishment rules.

The law on stays should endow the defendant with a credible threat if and only if the plaintiff makes an inefficient forum choice, and not otherwise. The threat (bringing the stay application) is only credible if the defendant is better off carrying it out, and the plaintiff worse off where the plaintiff has made an inefficient forum choice, and not otherwise. Two examples are illustrated in extensive form in Figure 8.1.

Figure 8.1 Objections to jurisdiction

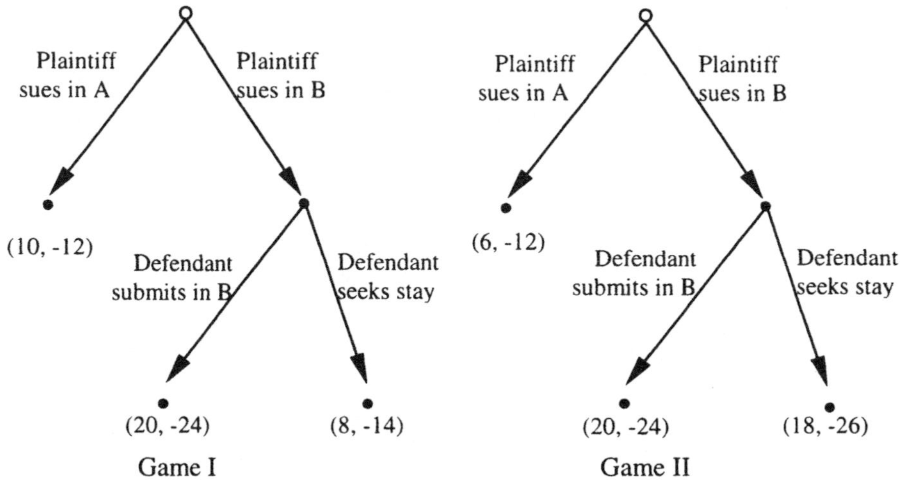

Payoffs: Plaintiff, Defendant

The social costs of litigation are minimised where the (negative) sum of the payoffs is lowest.[15] The plaintiff will maximise his payoff (the left component of the pair). In both games in Figure 8.1, the plaintiff would like to litigate in B ($20 is better than $6 or $10). This is the efficient choice in Game II (the sum of the payoffs is –$4 in B, and –$6 in A), but not in Game I (–$4 in B; –$2 in A). If this is to be disciplined, the defendant must have a credible threat to deter inefficient forum choices. If invoked, the threat must (a) decrease the plaintiff's payoff so that a plaintiff is better off commencing suit in the efficient forum than anywhere else; and (b) increase the defendant's payoff so that the defendant is better off seeking a stay in an inefficient forum than submitting to jurisdiction there. Thus, in Game I, this is done by an order for stay of proceedings in B, which forces the defendant to litigate in A. Thus, in Game I, suit in A is the Nash equilibrium, since the defendant's best strategy is to seek a stay if suit is brought in B. In Game II, the choice of forum is efficient, so the defendant should be worse off by seeking a stay. The costs of the jurisdictional challenge are the source of this penalty. The plaintiff does best by suing in B, and the defendant does best by submitting to jurisdiction.

In *neither* game is there actually a jurisdictional challenge. In Game I, a jurisdictional challenge is a credible threat which deters the inefficient forum choice. In Game II, the jurisdictional challenge is not a credible threat. The threat is only credible if the defendant is better off carrying the threat out. Consider a case where litigation in A gives the plaintiff a payoff of \$10 and the defendant a payoff of –\$12. Litigation in B gives payoffs of \$14 and –\$18. However, the making of a jurisdictional challenge depends on its cost to the defendant. If it costs more than \$6, the defendant is better off submitting; he cannot credibly threaten to challenge if he would be worse off in consequence. The plaintiff may choose a forum in which it is costly for the defendant to make a challenge.

The social benefit of jurisdictional challenges may exceed their social cost. In the examples in Figure 8.1, the implicit assumption was that a jurisdictional challenge would cost each party \$2, so the social cost of the challenge is \$4. But the social benefit of the challenge in Game I was in fact only \$2, being the difference between the sums of the outcomes in A (–\$2) and B (–\$4). In the situation we have examined, the credibility of the jurisdictional challenge permitted the socially optimal result to obtain. But that was because the game was one of complete information — each party knew all relevant facts about the payoffs of all strategy combinations, and it is both common knowledge and certain when a court would uphold the stay. If information is not complete, the result is more problematic. If the plaintiff commenced in B, the defendant would seek a stay, despite its social cost outweighing its social benefit. To the defendant, the private benefit of the stay is \$10 — the difference between a loss of \$14 and \$24. Thus, as with choice of forum, the social benefits of the grant a stay may be dominated by private benefits where there are significant substantive conflicts allied to choice of law rules that increase variance.

The social benefit of a jurisdictional challenge is equal to the *future* costs of litigation in the actual forum, less the costs of the challenge plus the costs of litigation in the forum the defendant proposes. Thus, it will be efficient for a jurisdictional challenge to be made only where:[16]

$$(t_{pn} + t_{dn}) - (t_{p1} + t_{d1}) - (j_{pn} + j_{dn}) > 0 \quad (2)$$

The private benefit of a stay application continues to include the terms t_{dn}, t_{dl}, and j_{dn}. However, the plaintiff's terms are replaced by the saving achieved if the forum does not apply its law, discounted by the probability of it doing so. Thus, the defendant will seek a stay where:

$$(1 - p_{djn})[(t_{dn} - t_{d1}) + p_{dfn}(D_{dfn} - D_{dx})] - j_{dn} > 0 \quad (3)$$

If the inequality in (2) does not hold, but that in (3) does, the defendant's application for a stay appears to be inefficient. The only device open to a court to address this is by affecting the probability that the stay will be granted (so affecting p_{pjn} and p_{djn}). This will affect both the forum the plaintiff chooses initially and the willingness of the defendant to seek a stay.[17] Below, we discuss some of the factors that influence courts when exercising jurisdiction in applications for stays.

Even if a court can use the resolution of the stay to ensure that the inequality in equation (3) holds when the inequality in equation (2) holds, it will be very difficult for it to equate the actual private and social benefits of jurisdictional challenges. This has an important implication. We have so far assumed that the cost of a jurisdictional challenge is fixed and exogenous to the model. In practice, there may be a range of strategies which parties take in contesting jurisdictional challenges. The strategy a party chooses will depend on the stakes (private benefits) available and the choices that other parties are expected to make. Rational *plaintiffs and defendants* will seek to equate at the margin the cost and (private) benefit of jurisdictional challenges. Higher variation in substantive outcomes may lead to an inefficiently high level of spending on jurisdictional challenges, when lower expenditure would in fact be efficient. That can only be addressed by consistency in choice of law rules.

Jurisdictional Trade

A doctrinal focus on private international law leads one to think about jurisdiction in strictly noncooperative terms. However, as the earlier chapters argue, jurisdictional disputes arising between contracting parties are often resolved by jurisdiction agreements. This is an example of jurisdictional trade. When negotiating jurisdiction agreements, parties should make efficient jurisdiction choices. As per the Coase theorem, social costs and private costs should be equated when transaction costs are low. This would imply that where the expected costs of legal liability are higher in one jurisdiction than another, and this favoured a seller of goods, the buyer would react by demanding a lower contract price.

Ex ante choices of jurisdiction will sometimes be impossible, for example in non-market torts. However, parties might be able to agree to a forum *after* the dispute arises. Given our earlier analysis, a rational plaintiff will expect to be worse off if she desists in her preferred jurisdiction, since jurisdiction is chosen to maximise F_n. However, the defendant may be even worse off litigating in jurisdiction *n*, compared to some other forum. Remembering that the payment of damages is a zero sum outcome, this would occur where the parties' joint litigation costs are higher in *n* than in some other forum. Since the plaintiff is worse off by discontinuing, post-litigation jurisdictional trade would need *either* a side payment by the defendant, which we shall refer to as a *jurisdictional bribe*, or an undertaking by the defendant not to traverse the plaintiff's plea that the *lex causae* is that of the jurisdiction in which they are discontinuing.

The former arrangement resembles the sale of the plaintiff's entitlement to proceed in the chosen forum. That entitlement has the quality of an alienable property right. A *lex causae* undertaking resembles an ex post choice of law. Its ability to lubricate jurisdictional trade depends on the extent to which the new court enforces it. Courts may take a dysfunctional approach to enforcing their own procedural law, or of course, their mandatory rules. Such undertakings are sometimes offered during jurisdictional challenges. For example, a party resisting the grant by a Brunei court of an anti-suit injunction directed to proceedings in Texas offered an undertaking that it would not rely on relevant aspects of Texan law if the injunction was not granted.[18] Of course, a choice of law other than that of the agreed forum requires the proof of foreign law, a procedure which is cumbersome, costly, and difficult for the parties to control contractually.[19]

To illustrate, take the situation in Game I of Figure 8.1. There, if litigation occurs in A, the payoffs are \$10 and –\$12 for the plaintiff and defendant. In B, the payoffs are \$20 and –\$24. Litigation costs must be higher in B for the sum of the payoffs to be lower. Even if there is no procedure for the defendant to seek a stay in B, jurisdictional trade is possible. The defendant would be prepared to pay up to \$12 (\$24 – 12) for litigation to be discontinued in B and transferred to A. The plaintiff will demand at least \$10 (\$20 – 10). There are \$2 of gains from trade that the parties may share, although the trade will involve transaction costs. How the parties share the net gains from trade depends on their bargaining abilities.

Our analysis resembles John Donohue's claim that parties who would be better off under a rule for the allocation of legal costs other than the one the law imposes by default can achieve those gains by Coasean trade.[20] Donohue, however, envisages cases where the trade may not require a side payment since a change is Pareto superior. It is hard to perceive cases where a jurisdictional bribe might be dispensed with, excepting the case of a choice of law undertaking.[21]

The literature ignores jurisdictional trade. Why might jurisdictional trade be infrequent? Answers are suggested by the reasons domestic cases do not settle. The conventional economic reasons are that the plaintiff is relatively optimistic about his prospects of success compared to the defendant, and the existence of asymmetric information.[22] Both may be pervasive in jurisdiction cases. A plaintiff's outcome depends on choice of law rules which may often be uncertain. A plaintiff's lawyer's self interest may lie in boosting the plaintiff's expectations at least in the initial stages of litigation. Asymmetric information is also pervasive in conflicts cases, especially since the stages at which jurisdictional issues are disputed precede discovery, interrogatories, and the like. Information asymmetries may be high in multistate cases where evidence is scattered around the globe.

Barriers to jurisdictional trade will also be barriers to settlement in general. However, once these barriers are overcome, as will occur as civil procedure progresses, jurisdictional trade may not occur because settlement itself is possible. Offers of jurisdictional trade grow less likely over time, as the cost savings from discontinuing may be offset by the costs of having to start anew in another jurisdiction.

So far, we have examined barriers to jurisdictional trade which apply to cooperative negotiations for jurisdictional trade. The parties may act irrationally or strategically. A possible endowment effect or status quo bias may decrease the plaintiff's willingness to agree to discontinue in her chosen jurisdiction. The plaintiff's lawyer may have a self interest in advising the plaintiff not to agree to the trade unless the lawyer will also act for the plaintiff in the other jurisdiction.

Strategic considerations are difficult to generalise about. They turn on the structure of the bargaining game and its relation to steps in litigation.[23] These steps may affect greatly the willingness to engage in trade and to reveal information. In general, strategic considerations may counsel caution in agreeing to jurisdictional trade. Both parties may forego profitable opportunities for trade in an effort to stake claims as hard bargainers. A reputation for toughness is important because parties considering an offer of jurisdictional trade will contemplate the need for a further round of bargaining in the substantive settlement. Some defendants may be engaged in similar types of cases and the outcome of any particular trade may have implications for other negotiations.

Strategic bargaining is facilitated by the fact that parties have imperfect knowledge of the other parties' valuation of the tradeable entitlement. In these circumstances, each has an incentive to misstate the valuation as a means of engrossing a larger share of the gains from trade.[24] We discussed a similar problem in chapter 7 when discussing Coasean trade in pollution cases. As regards jurisdictional trade, a plaintiff may overstate her marginal costs of litigating in the defendant's proposed forums, just as the defendant will overstate his marginal costs from litigating in the forum the plaintiff has chosen.[25] The extent to which this confines the ability of the parties to achieve jurisdictional trade depends on how the law defines a plaintiff's entitlement to insist on the exercise of jurisdiction. It may be most severe when the plaintiff's right to the exercise of jurisdiction is absolute and unchallengeable. We return to this topic below.

Primary Behaviour

We have touched on the effect of conflicts on the primary behaviour of the parties, such as precautions against harm or breach of contract.[26] Little needs to be said where transaction costs are low, since the parties typically are able to contract around inefficient rules. The expected costs of failing to take due care in a torts case are arguably higher in a multistate case because of the risk of being sued in a high-cost jurisdiction. This might increase the optimal level of care, which may or may not be inefficiently high. However, as chapter 6 argues, an effect on the level of care depends on the plaintiff's expectations of conflicts arising. In discrete non-market torts, we doubt that the plaintiff will normally expect such a possibility. The only parties likely to do so are those who repeatedly engage in particular types of activities which cause harm, such as trucking companies causing road accidents. Even then, special fact situations (such as an unusually large concentration of out-of-state residents in particular places) would seem to be necessary for the law of the place of the wrong *not* to be the primary law affecting the behaviour of the injurer. Conflicts in products liability cases present greater risks of affecting primary behaviour as we saw in chapter 6. Not unlike the choice of law literature, lawyer-economists have argued in favour of clear second-order jurisdiction rules, so that manufacturers can make decisions concerning entering or exiting markets.[27]

Costs

The effect of litigation cost allocation regimes has been an object of fascination to lawyer-economists. Three issues arise in the intersection of costs regimes and multistate litigation.

Effect on settlement of litigation The most keenly scrutinised issue has been which cost allocation regime makes settlement most likely. If parties settle whenever settlement is possible, the same number of cases should settle under the U.S. and British rules if the parties' expectations of the plaintiff's victory are the same. There will be an even wider 'settlement range' where the plaintiff is relatively pessimistic.[28] The plaintiff's relative optimism makes settlements less likely under the British rule. The logic is that the saving of litigation eosts is an inducement to settle. At the limit, however, under the British rule, neither party values that saving if each is positive he or she will win.[29] However, if risk aversion is considered, the British rule may in fact increase the number of settlements, since it raises the stakes of the trial.[30]

These models of settlement assume that the higher the level of costs the parties will incur to try the matter, the more likely settlement is. The gains from trade (the cost savings) are higher. Thus, plaintiffs whose choice of forum increases the parties' joint costs may ironically make settlement more likely. If, however, the gains from trade are high, the negotiation required to divide the gains may also be longer and more costly.[31] The British rule may make some plaintiffs more likely to settle. To the extent that plaintiffs choose jurisdictions which are inconvenient and costly for the defendant to sue in, plaintiffs faced with the risk of bearing these costs if they lose may be more willing to settle than under the U.S. rule. This result will hold *a fortiori* where the plaintiff's own costs are significantly higher than in some other forum, the plaintiff having been attracted by a higher damages award. These factors are also likely to influence choice of forum.

Effect on choice of forum The plaintiff's choice of forum is particularly influenced by the applicable regime for cost allocation. We have referred to the nuisance suit phenomenon, in which $p_{pvn} = 0$ but the plaintiff expects a settlement offer. A threat to bring a nuisance suit is only credible under the U.S rule. Under the British rule, the defendant rationally expects the plaintiff to bear the costs of litigation, and therefore has no incentive to settle — assuming any costs order can be enforced. By contrast, the British rule creates certain dysfunctionalities where the plaintiff's probability of victory differs between forums. Under the U.S. rule, the plaintiff always experiences a disincentive at the margin from choosing a higher cost forum because the plaintiff always bears these costs. However, under the British rule, the plaintiff's expected litigation costs may be lower in a higher cost forum because of the 'cross-effect' of the decreased probability of victory. The result is possible if choice of law rules are not multilateral. Thus, although the British rule discourages nuisance suits it can also encourage inefficient forum selection.

Effect on jurisdictional trade Litigation costs provide a positive incentive for resolving jurisdictional disputes contractually, just as they do for substantive disputes. Ayres and Talley have shown that the litigation costs associated with the invocation of a court resolution process can encourage contracting. As one of us shows in more detail elsewhere, the existence of litigation costs for the resolution of an objection to jurisdiction can actually increase the gains from jurisdictional trade.[32] Litigation costs similarly increase the scope of cases in which trade is possible, compared to a model in which objections to jurisdiction are costlessly determined.

Establishing Jurisdiction: Second-order Rules Revisited

In earlier chapters, we have advocated the use of second-order choice of law principles. These are rule-like; their content is specified ex ante. The application of this conclusion to jurisdiction depends on the heterogeneity of the population of cases raising conflicts issues. The extent to which particular factors have a systematic relation to the cost-minimising forum is an empirical question. We can however venture a few relevant comments.

The traditional common law jurisdictional rule permitted a plaintiff to establish jurisdiction over a defendant who is present in the forum.[33] Perhaps that was a useful rule when people travelled infrequently. But when travel costs are low for natural persons, and an increasing number of businesses have multistate operations, the rule's efficiency deteriorates. The litigation costs of 'ordinary' citizens will probably be minimised in their place of domicile.[34] But where the citizen has committed torts abroad, it is less likely that joint litigation costs are minimised in the forum in which the defendant is domiciled. The defendant's cost savings will probably be offset by the plaintiff's higher costs, and evidence will probably be located in the *locus delicti*. In Chapter 9, we argue that applying the 'presence' criterion to a corporate defendant is not just dysfunctional but often meaningless.

Common law jurisdiction is typically supplemented by a long arm statute, which permits defendants to be served *ex iuris*. The statute typically specifies subject matters where this is permitted. The European Conventions on Jurisdiction (the Brussels and Lugano Conventions), are good examples. However, other provisions may not be true jurisdictional *rules*, in the sense that the content of the law is determined ex ante, since the right to invoke them may depend on the court's permission.[35] Permission is usually discretionary, one consideration being the appropriateness of the forum.[36] This inquiry is similar to the inquiry raised when a defendant seeks a stay on *forum non conveniens* grounds.[37] Thus, the long arm statute may partake of the nature of a standard. This may be explicit, or it may be indirect. For an example of the latter, in the U.S. courts, a defendant may claim that in light of her 'contacts' with the state, suit violates constitutional due process constraints.[38] These approaches move away from rules to a first-order approach, in which content is given to the legal norm after litigation begins.

Can we explain these methods? Maybe fairness explains why common law jurisdiction was traditionally narrow and exceptions reviewable ex post. However, why would local courts prefer to be fair to foreign defendants than amenable to local plaintiffs, when most policy analysis of choice of law assumes the opposite?[39] Another explanation is that jurisdictional principles are better administered ex post than formulated ex ante, as the locus of the cost-minimising forum may be heavily case-specific, as we have proposed. Rules would be both underinclusive and overinclusive.[40] A related explanation is that the utility of a legal rule, like a contract, requires that the matters on which the rule depends be verifiable.[41] Party costs, the most important variable, may not be verifiable. Perhaps a court employing a balancing test stands a better chance of working out the *relative* magnitude of each party's costs if litigation occurred in alternative forums.[42]

If a court uses similar principles in service-out cases and *forum non conveniens* cases, why bother with rules for establishment of jurisdiction? Would it not be simpler to resolve everything at the exercise stage? The value of jurisdictions using rules to constrain the establishment of jurisdiction probably limits the plaintiff's ability to select jurisdictions which involve much higher costs for the defendant, and, if expected awards are higher, higher costs for the plaintiff. In this situation, unless jurisdictional challenges are effective in controlling inefficient forum choices, the parties are thrown back to jurisdictional trade. While high cost savings ought to make trade more likely, transaction costs will also be high. Both parties will want to capture the lion's share of those gains, making negotiations more costly. Thus, limits on the jurisdictions in which one can commence should cap the gains from trade, making trade less necessary or less demanding and placing less pressure on jurisdictional challenges.

It is thus interesting to compare the rule-based approach of the Brussels and Lugano Conventions regulating jurisdiction in the European Union. They allocate jurisdiction over a defendant domiciled in a Convention state to the courts of that state; however, they also provide for special jurisdiction which increases the scope of forum choice.[43] In contracts cases, a defendant may be sued in another convention state where the obligation in question was to be performed there.[44] In torts cases, a defendant may be sued in another Convention state where that is the place of the tort.

These are clearly jurisdictional rules but the plaintiff still has an option to sue the defendant in his or her place of domicile. Jurisdictional rules which provide for limited choice mitigate some of the risk that precise jurisdictional rules will be overinclusive or underinclusive. However, the Conventions go a step further by eliminating discretionary aspects of the exercise of jurisdiction. They do this by requiring in cases of parallel proceedings the court first seised of jurisdiction to proceed, and all others to stay their proceedings. Otherwise, a court has no discretion to decline jurisdiction.[45] This intensifies the rule-like qualities of the treaty's jurisdictional principles. Nonetheless, the Conventions preserve scope for jurisdictional trade, since they enforce jurisdictional agreements,[46] and since parties may litigate in another forum once they have agreed to discontinue in the one first seised of jurisdiction.[47]

A rule-like approach to jurisdiction may be especially possible in a federation or a regional economic community where there are similarities in substantive and procedural law. The marginal cost for a defendant to litigate out of his preferred jurisdiction is probably lower when the court that accepts jurisdiction is within that group of countries, than outside of it. Compare, however, the approach to jurisdiction between the Australian states. Legislation allows the initiating process of all courts to be served anywhere within Australia. The contacts between the court issuing the proceedings and the parties and subject matter are irrelevant. Principles similar to *forum non conveniens* are used to resolve jurisdictional disputes.[48]

The superiority of the two approaches is an empirical question. One may ultimately find that discretion-based systems produce results that could be closely approximated by systems using rules. This would be a powerful argument for the latter given the higher adjudication costs of a discretion-based system. Much depends on the appropriate degree of rule complexity. Our analysis in chapters 5 and 6 illustrates the undesirability of a single rule for torts, a conclusion which seems equally applicable to jurisdiction.

One unattractive aspect of the European Conventions is the 'first-mover' principle as the resolution to *lis pendens* cases. By making the sequence of steps in litigation dispositive, it gives parties an incentive to litigate. This is especially so since no distinction is made between a normal action and an action for a declaration of negative liability.[49] Thus, the person who would normally be the defendant can choose the forum if his action for a negative declaration precedes that of the party applying for substantive relief. In chapter 6, we suggested that parties bargaining behind a veil of ignorance would not choose such a rule.[50] Although the rules themselves constrain forum shopping by limiting the available forums, plaintiffs (especially in negative declaration actions) may still be attracted by substantive or procedural law advantages, such as limitations periods and recoverable heads of damages. The ability to control these inefficiencies depends on jurisdictional trade. Yet, as we see in the next section, jurisdictional trade may be facilitated by wider grounds for stays.

Declining Jurisdiction

Our analysis of the economics of jurisdiction shows how the likelihood that a court may not accept jurisdiction plays a crucial role in every important decision taken in conflicts cases. It affects the plaintiff's choice of forum, the defendant's decision to challenge jurisdiction by seeking a stay, the parties' inclination to engage in jurisdictional trade, and the terms of that trade. Where the parties have complete information about their own and each other's payoffs, the cost of the jurisdictional challenge is not excessive, and the court is known to grant a stay whenever it is not the cost-minimising forum, the plaintiff should normally make efficient forum choices. In practice, those assumptions will often not hold. The application for the stay remains an opportunity to correct inefficient forum choices, but the defendant making the application will be motivated by private advantage which may not coincide with social welfare. Seeking a stay may also be used as a delay tactic which enables defendants to screen impatient plaintiffs. Such information has private value to the defendant for settlement negotiations.

A Short Doctrinal History

Historically, England, Canada, Australia, and to a lesser extent, the United States adopted very restrictive approaches to the grant of stays. The first three jurisdictions ascribed to the principle in *St. Pierre v. South American Stores (Gath and Chaves) Ltd.*[51] Where jurisdiction had been invoked regularly, a stay would only be granted if the continuance of the action was oppressive, vexatious, or an abuse of process, and the stay would not cause injustice to the plaintiff. A balance of convenience was by itself an insufficient ground. The efficiency of that rule depends on the overinclusiveness of the common law rules on establishment of jurisdiction. A wider jurisdiction to grant stays is needed to the extent that the rules permit a substantial number of inefficient actions to be brought in the forum. The overinclusiveness of the common law rule may increase over time, as we have suggested may occur in consequence of greater mobility of people and capital. If so, stays should be granted more often.

Thus, we have seen liberalisation of the principles on stays and the emergence in England, Canada and the United States of a *forum non conveniens* doctrine.[52] Although there are local differences, the essence of the inquiry is whether there is some other forum which, having jurisdiction over the parties, is the appropriate forum for the trial of the action, based on the interests of the parties and the ends of justice. Australia has not gone so far. Oppression and vexation continue to apply, but their meaning has been softened. It is now sufficient that the applicant show that 'there is an available and appropriate tribunal in some other country and that the local court is a clearly inappropriate forum in all the circumstances'.[53] Since adopting the test, the High Court of Australia has decided four cases under this test, and upheld the grant of a stay in three of them.[54] On the other hand, lower courts have sometimes exercised jurisdiction under this test where a stay under the English test was likely.[55]

A Theory of Forum non Conveniens

It is possible to view *forum non conveniens* in two ways. The first is that moving from oppression to *forum non conveniens* as the basis for the grant of stays is a movement from second-order rules to first-order standards (or from untailored to tailored forum defaults). Although oppression may operate flexibly from case to case, it makes it clear that in a majority of cases stays will not be awarded. Thus, there is a rule *not* to award a stay in most cases. *Forum non conveniens* substantially changes this by making the award of a stay a marginal proposition in each case, to be assessed on the basis of a wide range of relevant considerations.

Second, *forum non conveniens* defines the allocation of property rights. We have shown how a party's right to litigate in a forum can be treated as a property-like entitlement, which is susceptible of jurisdictional trade. Moving from oppression to *forum non conveniens* as the basis for the grant of stays changes the nature of the plaintiff's property interest vis-à-vis the defendant.

In chapter 7, we discussed the distinction between entitlements protected by property rules and liability rules. Entitlements protected by the former cannot be taken unless the entitlement owner consents to trade. Liability rules permit takings at the option of another person, but that person must compensate the owner for the taking. Mitchell Polinsky first observed that entitlements may not be absolute but *divided*.[56] That is, the entitlement is effectively divided between the parties across some relevant range. For example, in a pollution context, a factory might have an entitlement that permits it to emit a certain volume of pollution a day. Beyond that point, the entitlement reverts to the resident. Chapter 7 noted theories claiming that divided entitlements may facilitate Coasean trade between parties in bilaterally monopolistic relations. Divided entitlements weaken the incentive of a party to hold out from trade and to falsify the value he places on trade in the entitlement.[57]

Jurisdictional disputes involve competing claims to an entitlement. One party claims an entitlement to sue in the forum. The other party either claims that entitlement does not exist (i.e., the forum has no right to proceed) or that the entitlement is his (i.e., the forum should stay its proceedings in favour of the forum the defendant proposes).[58] The forum's rules on establishment and exercise of jurisdiction define the extent and protection of the parties' entitlements.

An oppression test defines jurisdictional entitlements simply — the plaintiff has the jurisdictional entitlement apart from exceptional cases of oppression. The entitlement is not wholly absolute, but is close to it. *Forum non conveniens*, however, creates a more even division of the entitlement. The plaintiff's entitlement is limited to those cases where another more appropriate forum does not exist. The precise division between the parties depends, of course, on the matters which the forum regards as relevant. As is implicit in our analysis, costs burdens should be relevant.[59] Other relevant issues, such as delay, can also be treated commensurably with costs. Although these seem to give the doctrine an algorithmic quality, this is offset by the difficulties a court will have in verifying this information at the interlocutory stage, the limits on judicial competence, and the relevance of 'justice' to most formulations of the doctrine.[60] It is likely that the calculus of appropriateness tracks that of the efficient forum only with a sizable standard error. This makes the division similar to the probabilistically divided entitlements described in chapter 7.

How then are these entitlements protected? The apparent answer is 'by property rules'. If a court decides not to grant a stay, or lacks a procedure for granting stays, the defendant must proceed in the plaintiff's chosen jurisdiction unless the parties agree to jurisdictional trade. A court ruling on a jurisdictional challenge makes the entitlement of the winner difficult to challenge. There is no recognised domestic procedure by which the defendant might 'take' the plaintiff's choice of forum without consent.

However, jurisdictional disputes may be resolved in a court other than the one whose jurisdiction is in dispute. Consider a case where a plaintiff has commenced suit in forum F. The defendant would prefer to litigate in forum G. If F resolves the jurisdictional dispute alone, its grant of a stay to the defendant would allocate the entitlement to the defendant. A rejection of the stay motion allocates the entitlement to the plaintiff. However, G might resolve the matter if it is capable of enforcing an order that a party not litigate in F. Such an order is an anti-suit injunction, which operates *in personam* against the respondent. Its grant resembles the taking of the plaintiff's entitlement to litigate in F. If the applicant is required to give an undertaking to the other party in order to obtain the injunction, the undertaking resembles the compensation. As we show below, the test used for the grant of anti-suit injunctions is restrictive, using the language of oppression, in the manner of traditional formulations of the test for stays of proceedings.[61] The fact that an anti-suit injunction is not available as of right prevents the order from functioning in the manner of a classical liability rule, although the analogy remains suitable. Table 8.2 describes the permutations of entitlement allocation and protection.

Table 8.2 Allocation and protection of jurisdictional entitlement

		Entitlement protected by: Property Rule	Entitlement protected by: Liability Rule
Entitlement allocated to:	Plaintiff	F rejects stay	G grants anti-suit injunction against plaintiff
	Defendant	F grants stay	F grants anti-suit injunction against defendant

The allocation and protection of entitlements are important for two reasons. First, if we ignore jurisdictional trade, the law on jurisdictional entitlements determines the forum for litigation. Because legal rules may select inefficient forums, which the parties do not contract around, the conventional economic argument is that liability rules may be preferable since they dispense with the need for consent as the precondition for transfer.[62] Does this imply that there should be an expanded basis for anti-suit injunctions? The problem with this argument is the difficulty of calculating the compensation the grantee should pay.[63] Setting the appropriate amount of compensation is vital to most accounts of the superiority of liability rules.[64]

Second, the allocation and protection of entitlements may affect the likelihood of jurisdictional trade. Above, we have suggested that there may be substantial impediments to jurisdictional trade — endowment effects and status quo biases on one hand, and a range of strategic behaviour problems characteristic of bilateral monopoly situations. Assume a bargaining game is played by a plaintiff and a defendant. Each has imperfect knowledge of the cost burden the other bears in the respective forums. Neither can be trusted to reveal that cost burden credibly, since to do so would increase the ability of the other to capture more of the gains from trade. The defendant will apply for a stay and must choose whether or not to make an offer of jurisdictional trade by paying a bribe as consideration for proceeding in another forum. The plaintiff must choose whether or not to accept it or to proceed to the resolution of the jurisdictional challenge.

If the plaintiff's entitlement to proceed in his chosen jurisdiction is absolute, the plaintiff is less likely to accept (or to accept *immediately*) an offer of trade. Strategic behaviour is most problematic in these cases. In contrast, making the plaintiff's jurisdiction entitlement dependent on a standard-based adjudication may limit the plaintiff's capacity to engage in hold out behaviour during the anticipated jurisdictional trade. The defendant's stay application is a potentially credible threat to take the plaintiff's entitlement without compensation that may stimulate jurisdictional trade prior to the jurisdictional challenge.[65] Jason Johnston points out that the threat of uncompensated harm stimulates ex ante trade where the balancing test used by the court is imprecise.[66] Thus, imperfections associated with comparing costs at the interlocutory stage are not an insuperable objection.

Trade may also be stimulated by *forum non conveniens* in other ways. If jurisdictional trade does not occur, and a jurisdictional challenge proceeds, the use of *forum non conveniens* as the legal standard forces both plaintiff and defendant to disclose significant aspects of their cases, including their expected cost burdens, their causes of action, and the locus of their evidence. The oppression standard forces information only from the defendant. The defendant is placed in an unenviable position — seek a stay and reveal important information relevant to his valuation of the jurisdictional entitlement and the underlying legal right, or submit to jurisdiction and make the plaintiff's entitlement (and ability to act strategically) absolute. The *forum non conveniens* standard's compulsion to release information thus may function not only to make jurisdictional trade more likely, but it may endow parties with significant information that facilitates the parallel process of settlement bargaining. The standard therefore creates efficient litigation incentives.

Declining Jurisdiction in the Courts

In light of this theory, we now examine judicial approaches to stays of proceedings. Should a court to whose jurisdiction the parties have submitted by a jurisdiction clause ever stay its own proceedings?[67] Chapter 4 argued that a court should enforce a jurisdiction clause specifically unless local legislation explicitly instructed it not to do so. This is an example of jurisdictional trade, which is entitled to a presumption of enforceability.

There may be a theoretical justification for not enforcing jurisdiction clauses. Jurisdiction clauses are not usually obligationally incomplete since they typically apply to all litigation under the contract, but they may be contingently incomplete. Fully informed parties negotiating at no cost might not agree to submit all of their litigation to a single court. Their agreements might reflect the nature of the dispute, locus of evidence, and so on. In fact, parties may not enter contingently complete contracts, because negotiation is costly, foresight is limited, parties strategically withhold information, and because the information needed to make such a contract (such as the parties' costs) is unverifiable by a court.[68] The last reason makes ex post attempts by the courts to 'complete' the jurisdiction clause highly problematic. Given the parties typically have better information than courts, the jurisdiction clause should normally be enforced passively.

Where no jurisdiction clause exists, what factors should be relevant to the decision to stay? The current edition of *Jaffey* extracts six factors English courts consider when determining the *forum conveniens*.[69] The first is the parties' territorial connections with the forum and the locus of the evidence. These are obvious influences on party costs. The second factor, the existence of another forum in which proceedings are significantly further advanced, also has an economic basis in relevant (avoidable) costs, provided one looks at *future* costs in the other forum, not costs already incurred. Third, courts will lean towards a stay where a suit is a part of complex multi-party litigation which is most expeditiously resolved in another forum. This contemplates wealth maximisation as the object of the stay, since it seems to condone the grant of a stay that makes the parties to the suit before it worse off, if parties to other suits were made sufficiently better off to be able to compensate the former litigants. The fourth factor is similar. It recognises the economies of litigating, in a single forum, two or more cases which are related not in terms of parties but in terms of subject matter and legal representatives. The sixth factor is that it is desirable to stay proceedings in a forum whose language is not that of a majority of the relevant documents. Judicial error and litigation costs will be minimised if the need for translation is minimised.

Jaffey's fifth factor refers to choice of law issues. *Jaffey* states that it may often be preferable for the legal system whose law applies to provide the forum.[70] This is consistent with comments we have made elsewhere in the book — the proof of foreign law has positive costs, including expected judicial errors. However, the legitimacy of choice of law concerns depends on choice of law rules. The sorts of choice of law rules we have proposed, which are as likely to select local law as foreign law, would be legitimate considerations. However, using first- or second-order methods biased to the *lex fori* would be inappropriate, since the choice of law would become a self-generating source of authority to exercise jurisdiction.

Choice of law is related to the so-called 'second stage' of *forum non conveniens* in English law — justice requires that the plaintiff be permitted to litigate in her chosen forum, despite its inappropriateness.[71] Here, we return to the ambiguity of multistate justice.[72] If, following Rawls,[73] justice is equated with equality, an approach must be unjust if it favours plaintiffs by *refusing* a stay when the local forum is *non conveniens* but will not *grant* a stay to a defendant when the local forum is *conveniens*. Yet the defendant is more in need of procedural protection than the plaintiff, since the plaintiff chooses the forum. We would argue that it can *only* be unjust to grant a stay if the foreign law is unjust when viewed behind a veil of ignorance — not when the court is endowed with knowledge of the plaintiff's case. Laws discriminating against particular types of defendants are an example.[74] Laws which provide for larger damages awards, longer limitations periods, and different regimes for costs are not of the same kind and should not normally support a decision not to grant a stay.[75]

Consider this issue in the context of two specific case types. One is where the parties' contract would not be enforced in the *forum conveniens* but would be enforced elsewhere. This is likely to be rare. Parties normally can control this by a jurisdiction clause and most courts lean towards enforcing contracts. Second, what if the *forum conveniens* applies inefficient choice of law rules?[76] This is doubtful as a basis for the grant of stays. By the time cases come to be litigated, that decision may have only minimal effect on social welfare, although of course it will affect the distribution of wealth. The cases of continuing externalities examined in chapter 7 are a possible but limited exception.

Some considerations thought relevant to justice are actually more relevant to efficiency. For example, delay in one of the legal systems may be significant.[77] Long delays in hearing a case affect the probative value of evidence. They also impose a cost on the plaintiff who must discount the expected award for the time value of the money. Similar comments might apply to inadequate procedures for, say, discovery of documents, as these intensify information asymmetries.

The Anti-suit Injunction

We described the nature of an anti-suit injunction above.[78] Like the stay, it functions in the manner of a jurisdictional challenge. Unlike a stay, it is not an act of self-denial in favour of another forum. Rather it is an act of self-elevation in spite of another forum. This aggressive aspect of the order naturally provokes conservative judicial responses as to its proper role.

A recurring theme in expositions of the law on anti-suit injunctions is 'comity' or the maintenance of mutual respect between forums. An anti-suit injunction is supposed to be offensive to the jurisdiction affected. There are instances where this is the case, such as the *Laker Airlines* litigation.[79] But that case involved a significant question of competition law in an inter-continental market, and it is unlikely that other cases will have anything like that political quality. Posner has made a similar point judicially that the impairment of comity is not something that should be presumed.[80] This argument also accords with our rejection of the normative relevance of state interests to the conflict of laws. An interest positivist approach would mean that comity would rarely justify the rejection of an anti-suit injunction when other grounds favour it.[81]

Comity aside, the exercise of the jurisdiction to grant anti-suit injunctions largely conforms to what one would expect if party interests are to be paramount and analysed in efficiency terms.[82] The clearest case for the grant of an anti-suit injunction is where it enforces an existing contractual obligation, such as a jurisdiction or arbitration agreement, or a covenant not to sue agreed in a settlement. The enforcement of jurisdictional trade accords fully with our theoretical analysis. English courts are coming to regard this as a straightforward case for granting an injunction to which comity is irrelevant.[83] There seems little reason to permit a court an opportunity to stay its own process, especially where the parties have agreed to litigate in the forum asked to grant the injunction.

The second case type may be called 'single forum' cases. These divide into two groups. The first is where the foreign forum exercises a jurisdiction which the local forum will regard as sound in terms of its private international law. Typically, an anti-suit injunction will be inappropriate, because the soundness of the foreign court's jurisdiction raises a presumption that it is an efficient forum for the litigation, and often one that is cost-minimising for the defendant. The only conceivable case where an anti-suit injunction might be justified is where the foreign forum does not respect a choice of law agreement by the parties. However, in most of these cases, the parties should be able to make a jurisdiction agreement, in which event, they will fall into the first category of case.

The other type of single forum case is where the plaintiff seeks to invoke an exorbitant, extraterritorial jurisdiction. The paradigm example is reliance on the extraterritorial operation of American antitrust law.[84]

Courts have been more willing to give relief where the behaviour on which the plaintiff relies is not connected with that jurisdiction, and the forum is *non conveniens*. The logic is unarguable. The injunction prevents litigation in a high cost forum and quells the incentive of plaintiffs to shop for an award-maximising forum. Further, it limits the domain of (and thus preserves scope for exit from) statutes taking effect as mandatory rules. Chapter 4 observed that a legislature is competent to compel local courts to assume jurisdiction to apply its laws in any cases it specifies, but that foreign courts are not so obliged. An anti-suit injunction enables a court to restrain a party from opportunistic invocation of an exorbitant jurisdiction, and to enforce bilateral agreement that such jurisdictions not be invoked.

In the third case type, the plaintiff's cause of action is available in both the foreign forum and the forum in which the defendant seeks the injunction. The defendant will allege that litigation should proceed in the latter forum. English and Australian authority states that demonstrating that the local forum is the appropriate forum is a necessary but not sufficient condition for the injunction. The defendant must demonstrate that litigation in the foreign forum would be oppressive or vexatious (which is of course the language of *St. Pierre*).[85]

There are few attempts to define 'oppression' and 'vexation'. In theoretical terms, is there any justification for a court to adopt a different test in anti-suit injunction cases to the one it adopts in stay cases? We contend that the answer depends on the principles the foreign forum adopts in resolving challenges to its jurisdiction. Where the foreign forum has a liberal stay procedure, based on a *forum non conveniens* principle, the case for requiring a heavy onus of proof is not immediately apparent. A court's ability to judge itself inappropriate is neither less nor greater than its ability to judge the foreign forum inappropriate. Appropriateness should be judged at the margin — that is, by comparing the parties' future joint costs in the two forums. A forum is only inappropriate because party costs are higher in it than somewhere else (or its jurisdiction is exorbitant). So the rationale for different tests cannot be attributed to a higher propensity for errors in anti-suit injunction cases than in stay cases.

On the other hand, judicial caution may in fact enable judicial trade. According to our earlier analysis, a first challenge, brought as the defendant's application for a jurisdictional challenge, requires both parties to reveal information in order to succeed. Blatant cases of forum shopping will be restrained; more evenly weighted cases go onto the second round stay application in the forum the plaintiff has chosen with (by hypothesis) jurisdictional entitlements evenly divided by the *forum non conveniens* standard. Parties will be able to update their estimates of the other party's valuation of the jurisdictional entitlement. This, together with the effect of the divided, imprecise allocation entitlement makes jurisdictional trade more likely — although two sets of hearings are obviously more costly than one, and some plaintiffs will prefer to defer acceptance of jurisdictional trade until just before the second hearing.[86]

Where the foreign forum adopts a restrictive stay procedure,[87] the case for a more restrictive anti-suit injunction test is less justifiable. Restrictive stay procedures substantially allocate the jurisdictional entitlement to the plaintiff. This inhibits jurisdictional trade and makes litigation in an inappropriate jurisdiction more likely.

Much depends on how courts evaluate the concept of oppression. As for stay cases, courts should emphasise the parties' costs. They should not normally permit the plaintiff to argue that she will be disadvantaged by an injunction because awards of damages are lower locally than in the forum she has chosen. Since a court asked to stay its own proceedings will be disinclined to take a potential overcompensation bias or any other distortion in its own law into account, it is important that a court asked to enjoin foreign proceedings not reinforce this local bias by legitimating the plaintiff's advantage.

How close do courts come to our reasoning?[88] The English courts display some variation but often approximate it quite closely. The availability of higher damages in the foreign forum was regarded as a legitimate advantage which did not justify the grant of an injunction in the House of Lords decision in *Castanho v. Brown & Root (U.K.) Ltd.*[89] This was surely inefficient, since the foreign forum, in Texas, did not have a *forum non conveniens* test applicable to stays of jurisdiction, and since the parties were very close to settlement in England (so the parties' future marginal costs were negligible). By contrast, a plaintiff's attempt to claim triple or punitive damages under the exorbitant jurisdiction provisions of American legislation such as the *Sherman Act*[90] has met with hostility, as we saw in the single forum cases.[91] The decision in *Lee Kui Jak* enjoining the plaintiff from litigation in Texas, in favour of Brunei, was an efficient decision, since the defendant's claim for contribution against a third party could not have been litigated in Texas.[92] Brunei minimised total litigation costs. The courts have been more willing to grant anti-suit injunctions in cases in which their claim to be the *forum conveniens* is strong.[93]

The Australian High Court decision, *C.S.R. Ltd v. Cigna*, has aspects of all three categories of anti-suit injunction cases.[94] The case involved a contract of products liability insurance, written by the respondent insurer, in favour of the appellant. The proper law of the contract was Australian, and Australia was in every respect the jurisdiction most closely connected to the contract. The respondent disclaimed certain liability, asserting that the claims which related to asbestosis were not insured risks. The insurers told C.S.R. that if it continued to press its claim, they would rescind the insurance policy for non-disclosure and misrepresentation. After negotiation, C.S.R. sent a letter withdrawing all of the asbestosis claims notified and acknowledging that its cover did not extend to asbestos-related claims. Subsequently, C.S.R. commenced suit in New Jersey for rights to indemnity and triple damages under the *Sherman Act* on the basis of a conspiracy by Cigna and its holding company to pressure insurers to refuse to write new insurance for C.S.R. Cigna sought a declaration in Australian courts to the effect that it had no liability to C.S.R. and an anti-suit injunction restraining the U.S. proceedings. C.S.R. sought to stay the Australian proceedings. Failing at first instance, and on appeal, C.S.R. succeeded in the High Court.

The case is arguably one in which there was a contract not to sue, contained in C.S.R.'s withdrawal of claims, which appeared to constitute a settlement. Brennan C.J., who dissented, argued that the injunction should give effect to this contract. Brennan C.J. thought an injunction was also warranted on grounds that, for the indemnity claims, Australia was the natural forum; the other claims were not recognised by Australian law, and could only succeed by the exercise of an exorbitant extraterritorial jurisdiction inconsistent with Australian competition law. This follows our earlier analysis that Australia was the cost-minimising forum and that the scope of extraterritorial legislation should be confined, especially where it will distort forum choice. Dawson, Toohey, Gaudron, McHugh, Gummow, and Kirby JJ. considered that the anti-suit injunction might have been granted but for the *Sherman Act* claim. However, the U.S. proceedings were not oppressive since they sought a remedy the defendants could not obtain in an Australian court. The exorbitance of the jurisdiction and its inconsistency with Australian law were not discussed.

There are strange relations between *C.S.R.* and the High Court's decision in *Akai*, which we discussed in chapter 4. In *Akai*, the court refused to enforce a contract that attempted to choose a foreign jurisdiction on the ground that it might not have applied an Australian statute to an

Australian contract. In *C.S.R.*, the court refused to enjoin foreign proceedings that would have enforced foreign law (the policy of which is radically at odds with local law) notwithstanding that Australian law was the proper law of the contract and Australia the natural forum. Indeed, in similar litigation with another insurer, C.S.R. had commenced suit in Australia.[95] Both cases refused to enforce contracts between the parties — a pre-contractual jurisdictional trade in *Akai* and a post-dispute settlement in *C.S.R.*

Equally perplexing is the reconciliation of *C.S.R.* with Australian authorities on the test to be applied in applications for stays. Australian authorities, as we have seen, hold that a court should not decline jurisdiction unless it is a clearly inappropriate forum, not simply because another forum is more appropriate. The test has been criticised as making Australia more amenable to forum shopping.[96] It is therefore ironic that in *C.S.R.*, the party who lost had brought suit in Australia, which was the natural forum for the primary liability issue, and the party doing the forum shopping *overseas* won.

In the final category of anti-suit injunction, no-one seeks to bring suit in the court asked for the anti-suit injunction. The court is a 'non-combatant'. In *Airbus Industrie G.I.E. v. Patel*,[97] litigation commenced in India in relation to an air crash. An Indian court had granted an anti-suit injunction. However, the plaintiffs (who included some British citizens) commenced proceedings in Texas. The House of Lords refused to grant an anti-suit injunction. Lord Goff said that an English court must have a sufficient interest in the matter before it can grant an anti-suit injunction.[98]

We have rejected the relevance of state interests to these suits. There are, however, two economic explanations for this reference to 'interest'. One is based on the concept of judicial error. Recall that we said above that where the court from whom an injunction is sought is a 'combatant', it is in just as good a position to rule on its appropriateness as a foreign court, as it is in a good position to weigh claims made about the cost of local litigation. In the non-combatant case, its judgments are more likely to be in error. The other explanation recognises state incentives. Courts from whom anti-suit injunctions are sought in non-combatant cases are likely to sit in the jurisdiction in which the plaintiffs in the impeached legislation are domiciled. Courts may have a narrow self-interest in eschewing jurisdiction in these cases, since it will typically be to the advantage of in-state interests, and to the disadvantage of out-of-state interests. As with

Moçambique, the state refuses to subsidise litigation by foreigners against locals.

It is probably inconsistent with social welfare for courts never to exercise jurisdiction in these cases. Although courts will often make errors, the efficiency of one forum may be plain in some cases.[99] *Airbus* is one of those cases. Since the anti-suit injunction can only operate *in personam*, the ability of the plaintiff to avoid the jurisdiction of the natural forum sets the efficiency claims of the anti-suit injunction at naught.

Recognition of Judgments

Chapter 2 notes the relation between the recognition of judgments and jurisdiction.[100] Non-recognition limits the incentives of states to encourage forum shopping by excessive jurisdictional rules. However, this presupposes a fundamental issue — that states have incentives to recognise in cases where efficient forum choices are made. Is this so?

Generally, recognition raises similar issues to the application of forum law and the stay of local proceedings — action may often be welfare-maximising, but, for strategic reasons, may not be taken. Every state would like to be in a position where its judgments were widely recognised in order to give litigants every incentive to choose to litigate there. There are other systemic gains to wide recognition, such as chilling the dysfunctional incentive to shift assets. The wider choice of forums enables a plaintiff to choose the cost-minimising forum. However, there are several reasons why a state would like to refuse recognition of other states' judgments.

First, recognition is likely to transfer wealth from in-state residents to out-of-state residents, analogously to *Moçambique*. The judgment debtor is likely to be a resident of, or have substantial economic interests in the state, or both. If the judgment creditor were also a resident there, it would be unlikely the judgment would have been entered elsewhere, since the forum would often be mutually suitable. Second, a non-recognition policy may encourage potential defendants to move their assets to the jurisdiction. Third, a non-recognition policy may benefit lawyers through an increased number of local instructions, since that policy encourages plaintiffs to choose that state as the forum. The second and third reasons are mutually exclusive — potential defendants would be foolish to move assets to a jurisdiction where lawyers expected increased local instructions.

This prisoner's dilemma explanation may be contrasted with a claim that recognition is often a weakly dominant strategy for the recognising state (i.e., the state is sometimes better off, and never worse off). To refuse recognition will do two things. It will encourage the plaintiff to seek recognition in other jurisdictions where the defendant has assets (in which case recognition would make the defendant no worse off). Or it will encourage local litigation, which the state must subsidise by funding the court system. The state would often bear a lower cost and potentially save both parties some deadweight litigation costs by recognising. Additionally, the instructions that lawyers gain from local litigation will be offset by the instructions they lose where other states do not recognise local judgments, as part of the defensive strategy in a prisoner's dilemma. They win only if there is net movement of assets *into* the jurisdiction, but as we have already argued, this can hardly ever be sequentially rational.

We might expect the law on judgment recognition to shed light on which hypothesis is true. If non-recognition is dominant, recognition will only occur because of the threat of future retaliation for non-recognition. That is not true for the hypothesis that recognition is weakly dominant. The law in this respect is indecisive. Two factors point in opposite directions. First, most states do not impose a reciprocity requirement, which would function as a tit-for-tat threat to non-recognition. Second, the common law on recognition preserved an opportunity for punishment, by requiring the plaintiff to sue on the judgment, and denying full faith and credit in the absence of convention or constitution.

However, the enquiries courts make when the plaintiff sues on the judgment do not seem to be directed to non-recognition,[101] but to a further strategic problem arising from the commitment to recognise. That is the problem of 'cheating', through dilation of the judgment court's jurisdictional competence, and the use of the recognition mechanism to give it effect. Expanding jurisdictional competence has clear appeal to local lawyers, because it widens the scope of cases that can be heard locally. The inefficiency of dilated competence should be obvious from earlier in the book. It encourages socially costly forum shopping and inefficient regulatory spillovers. A jurisdictional competence requirement does two things — it punishes expansionist, 'unilateral' states seeking to externalise the costs of their laws, and it punishes plaintiffs for inefficient forum shopping. We can see that the latter effect is very similar to the operation of an anti-suit injunction, without its apparently strong-arm overtones.[102]

The traditional jurisdictional competence requirement in English law is that the defendant was a resident of the forum giving judgment, submitted contractually to the forum's jurisdiction, or voluntarily appeared in the forum.[103] In some ways, the competence requirements are narrow. They would not permit a defendant to be sued for torts committed while present in the forum. As such, they may be inefficient, because they discourage litigation in a potentially efficient forum. It is notable — and in accord with our thesis in this book — that the parties can indirectly contract for recognition through the expedient of a jurisdiction clause. This enables the parties in contract cases to avoid the inefficiencies that may arise in tort. We may also note the irrelevance of choice of law to judgment recognition, even strongly unilateral methods. Presumably, this is attributable to a likely relation between jurisdictional incompetence and unilateralism, and the ease of evading apparently harmless choice of law rules.

The historical requirements for jurisdictional competence are evidently verifiable. Verifiability is a requirement of recognition rules adopted in any international convention. As observed several times in this book, parties will not contract on the basis of unverifiable terms. This should apply equally to conventions. The truth of this proposition is evident in the clear tendencies of established conventions, such as Brussels and Lugano, and proposed conventions, such as the one under consideration by the Hague Conference,[104] to adopt rule-like jurisdictional bases which are used for expedited recognition. Expedited recognition is only possible where states credibly commit not to exercise particular forms of jurisdiction, and the commitment can only be credible if compliance with it can be verified.

What this suggests is that standard-like principles, such as *forum conveniens*, are unlikely to form the basis of white-listed jurisdictional grounds. They are unverifiable and create a strong incentive for the judgment court to cheat. However, this does not mean that such principles can have no role. We have already seen that they may encourage jurisdictional trade. They could still be used by a court to decline jurisdiction conferred by verifiable white-listed rules, in favour of another court which also has jurisdiction.[105] This would operate in the manner of a transfer mechanism.

The use of rules in a convention creates the usual problem of overinclusivity and underinclusivity. Following our earlier arguments, this risk is best addressed by greater rule complexity and differentiation, especially for tort cases.[106] A discretion to stay proceedings along the lines mentioned would decrease the costs of overinclusive jurisdictional rules.

Do interest groups favour recognition or not? There are two conflicting incentives. First, interest groups capable of cutting political deals in which their interests are favoured by mandatory rules will favour recognition. Although the jurisdictional rules in a recognition convention will often limit the capacity of a state to externalise the costs of mandatory rules to the residents of other states, they increase the value of local judgments, based on the mandatory rule, and thus the scope of those rules. Parties are less able to avoid the mandatory rule by shifting assets out of the jurisdiction. Second, what of interest groups who have been ineffective in gaining legislative protection in particular states? Where the members of the group expect to be defendants, these interest groups would like to minimise their expected liability in these states. This counsels in favour of lobbying for narrower recognition. Which effect prevails will be uncertain, and depends on relative effectiveness in the political process.

Conclusion

This chapter treads uncharted territory in theorising jurisdictional issues. We have retained our focus on party interests, but our approach to first- and second-order adjudication is more varied than our choice of law analysis, consistently with the different allocative effects of jurisdiction. Here, too, we have emphasised a transactional approach to jurisdiction, by emphasising the possibility of jurisdictional trade both at the time of contracting and the time of litigation. Rather than justifying changes in jurisdictional doctrine as the modern understanding of comity, we have shown how treating jurisdiction in economic terms explains the historic move from absolutism to contingency and standards.

Notes

1. Brilmayer (1989), Dane (1987), Kogan (1987).
2. *James Hardie Industries Pty Ltd v. Grigor* (1998) 45 N.S.W.L.R. 20, 40-41, 43. Chapter 7 also observes that courts may reasonably take a wide view of the litigation a forum should entertain, especially if it facilitates trade by in-state interests: see chapter 7, p. 115 *supra*. Courts might also take the view that accepting jurisdiction in cases in which the forum has no real interest has two further benefits. First, it contributes to a richer, more dynamic body of case law, which is beneficial for commercial litigation. Second, accepting cases

from other jurisdictions may be part of an implicit contract with other jurisdictions which enables in-state interests a broader choice of forums.

3. [1983] 1 A.C. 565.
4. (1996) 188 C.L.R. 418.
5. This literature is extensive. Representative works include Bebchuk (1984, 1988), Donohue (1991), Katz (1987), Landes (1971), Posner (1973), Priest and Klein (1984), and Shavell (1982). Cooter and Rubinfeld (1989) is a valuable review article. Baird, Gertner and Picker (1994, pp. 244-266) provide an accessible game theoretic analysis of these issues.
6. Cooter and Rubinfeld (1989).
7. Compare Posner (1973), Shavell (1982) and Donohue (1991).
8. See, e.g., Kahneman et al. (1990). One might alternatively refer to a status quo bias: see chapter 3, p. 37 *supra* and Korobkin (1998).
9. Calabresi and Melamed (1972, p. 1090).
10. For references to that theory, see chapter 7 note 3 *supra*.
11. This figure is an expected damages figure, not an actual damages figure, adjusted for the probability of the award. For example, if there is a probability of 0.8 that damages of \$1,250,000 will be awarded, the expected damages are the product of those amounts (\$1,000,000).
12. For most interesting cases, $D_{fn} > D_x$. However, that does not mean that the probability of damages being awarded is necessarily higher: it might be lower. Thus, there may be a 0.5 probability of damages of \$4,000,000 being awarded (expected damages \$2,000,000). A plaintiff would need to be highly risk averse in order not to prefer this award of damages to the award referred to in note 11.
13. See, e.g., Bebchuk (1988), Cooter and Rubinfeld (1989), Rosenberg and Shavell (1985).
14. Kaplow (1992).
15. Lawyers unused to game theory may wonder where the numbers 'come from'. The essence of the exercise is to show how payoffs for the strategy in which the defendant seeks a stay affect the plaintiff's choice of forum, and how this can be used to reduce the litigation costs. The joint costs of litigation in A are –\$2 in Game I and –\$6 in Game II, and the social costs in B are –\$4. We assume that where the defendant seeks a stay, it costs each party \$2. Thus in Game I, the plaintiff who litigates in B gets the payoff he would have got in A, minus \$2. In Game II, the defendant who seeks a stay of litigation in B (the efficient forum) is \$2 worse off than he would have been had he not sought a stay.
16. A court's decision on the stay should, not, however include the costs of the jurisdictional challenge (the terms in the last set of parentheses). By that time, those costs have been sunk and are irrelevant. Thus, the court may have to grant motions for stays which should never have been brought.
17. By rearranging equation (1), we can see that the plaintiff will choose the natural (cost-minimising) forum where:

$$p_{pjn} < \frac{e_{pn}}{p_{pfn}(D_{pfn} - D_{px}) - (t_{pn} - t_{p1})}$$

18. *Société Nationale Industrielle Aerospatiale v. Lee Kui Jak* [1987] A.C. 871.
19. The defendant might raise a *renvoi*, and so seek to reinstate foreign law inconsistently with the purport of his undertaking. The contract could deal with this, but drafting the appropriate agreement is obviously costly. As to renvoi, see chapter 2, pp. 15, 31 *supra*.
20. Donohue (1991). Ian Ayres brought the similarity to our attention.
21. Assume that if litigation occurs in A, the parties expect damages of $10. Each party faces costs of $2. In B, the parties expect damages of $20, and face costs of $4 each. The plaintiff will choose forum B. If the defendant gives an undertaking that she will concede the application of B's law in litigation in A, the plaintiff does not require a side payment, since in these circumstances he should be better off litigating in B since his costs are lower.
22. See, e.g., Bebchuk (1984), Landes (1971), Posner (1973).
23. Baird et al. (1994, p. 245).
24. Ayres and Talley (1995a), Farrell (1987), Johnston (1995).
25. Accurate and credible statements of this information would be especially useful for the other party in relation to settlement bargaining.
26. Cooter and Rubinfeld (1989, pp. 1084-1086), Polinsky and Rubinfeld (1988).
27. Rubin et al. (1997).
28. Shavell (1982), Posner (1973).
29. Hence, the adjective 'relative'. The parties are as likely to settle under either rule where both believe the plaintiff's victory is certain. The defendant will have to offer a higher sum under the British rule but the probability of settlement should not change.
30. Cooter and Rubinfeld (1989, pp. 1077-1078).
31. Crawford (1982). Parties are likely to incur litigation costs in the high-cost forum until a settlement is agreed.
32. Whincop (2000b).
33. *Laurie v. Carroll* (1958) 98 C.L.R. 310, *Pennoyer v. Neff*, 95 U.S. 714 (1877). *Pennoyer* is no longer good law in the U.S.: *International Shoe Company v. Washington*, 326 U.S. 310 (1945).
34. Domicile is very important in the European Conventions on Jurisdiction and the Enforcement of Judgments: *Convention on Jurisdiction and the Enforcement of Judgments in Civil and Commercial Matters*, opened for signature 26 May 1990, O.J. No. C. 189, 1, 29 I.L.M. 1413 (entered into force 28 July 1990) ('*Brussels Convention*'), consolidated and updated version of an original convention by the same name, opened for signature 27 September 1968, O.J. No. L. 299, 32, 8 I.L.M. 229 (entered into force 31 December 1972), *Convention on Jurisdiction and the Enforcement of Judgments in Civil and Commercial Matters*, opened for signature 16 September 1988, O.J. No. L.

319, 9, 28 I.L.M. 620 (entered into force 25 November 1988) ('*Lugano Convention*') . These are enacted in English law in the *Civil Jurisdiction and Judgments Act* 1982.

35. Greater variety in approaches to service are observed today. In some courts, the plaintiff may have to obtain leave prior to service *ex iuris* (e.g., *High Court Rules* (High Court of Australia), O. 10 r. 1), or the plaintiff may have to obtain leave to continue if the defendant does not enter an appearance (e.g., *Supreme Court Rules 1996* (Vic.), r. 7.04). The latter probably saves costs if there is a positive probability that defendants will enter an appearance.
36. *The Hagen* [1908] P. 189, 201, *Cordova Land Co. v. Victor Bros Inc.* [1966] 1 W.L.R. 793, *Voth v. Manildra Flour Mills Pty Ltd* (1990) 171 C.L.R. 538.
37. *Spiliada Maritime Corp. v. Cansulex Ltd* [1987] 1 A.C. 460, *Voth v. Manildra Flour Mills Pty Ltd* (1990) 171 C.L.R. 538. Historically, the tests were *not* similar, since stays of proceedings commenced regularly were infrequently granted: *Maritime Insurance Co. Ltd v. Geelong Harbour Trust Commissioners* (1908) 6 C.L.R. 194 and *St Pierre v. South American Stores (Gath & Chaves) Ltd* [1936] 1 K.B. 382.
38. Brilmayer (1980b). See, e.g., *International Shoe Company v. Washington*, 326 U.S. 310, 316 (1945), *World-Wide Volkswagen Corp. v. Woodson*, 444 U.S. 286 (1980), *Burger King Corp. v. Rudzewicz*, 471 U.S. 462 (1985).
39. Compare our argument regarding *Moçambique*: chapter 7, p. 115 *supra*.
40. A rule is overinclusive if it permits an action to be brought in the forum despite its inefficiency. A rule is underinclusive if it does not permit an action to be brought in the forum despite its efficiency. Of course, inefficient jurisdictional rules could be overcome if jurisdictional trade was possible.
41. A. Schwartz (1992).
42. This argument enjoys some theoretical support from Hadfield (1994).
43. Arts. 5(1) and (3).
44. This is subject to certain limits for consumer, insurance and employment contracts: arts. 7-15, 17.
45. The *Civil Jurisdiction and Judgments Act* 1982 s. 49 provides that the Conventions do not prevent English courts from staying proceedings on *forum non conveniens* grounds where a stay would not be inconsistent with the Conventions. The Court of Appeal has held that it might grant a stay where the court of a non-Convention state is the *forum conveniens*: *Re Harrods (Buenos Aires) Ltd* [1992] Ch. 72.
46. Art. 17. The Conventions specify formal requirements, which would serve cautionary purposes (Fuller 1941, Ayres and Gertner 1989).
47. *Internationale Nederlanden Aviation Lease B.V. v. Civil Aviation Authority* [1997] 1 Lloyd's Rep. 80.
48. *Service and Execution of Process Act 1992* (Cth) s. 15. As to resolving jurisdictional overlaps, see *Jurisdiction of Courts (Cross-Vesting) Act 1987*

(Cth) s. 5, *Service and Execution of Process Act 1992* s. 20, *Bankinvest A.G. v. Seabrook* (1988) 14 N.S.W.L.R. 711.

49. *Owners of the cargo lately laden on board the ship Tatry v. Owners of the ship Maciej Rataj* [1995] All E.R. 229. See Bell (1995) and Collins (1992).
50. See chapter 6, p. 100 *supra*.
51. [1936] 1 K.B. 382, 398. As to former U.S. law, see *Restatement (Second) of Conflict of Laws* § 84 (1971) (stating a test alike Australia's current standard).
52. *Piper Aircraft Co. v. Reyno*, 454 U.S. 235 (1981), *Spiliada Maritime Corp. v. Cansulex Ltd* [1987] 1 A.C. 460, *Amchem Products, Inc.* v. *British Columbia (Workers Compensation Board)* [1993] 1 S.C.R. 897.
53. *Voth v. Manildra Flour Mills Pty Ltd* (1990) 171 C.L.R. 538.
54. *Voth v. Manildra Flour Mills Pty Ltd* (1990) 171 C.L.R. 538 (stay granted), *Henry v. Henry* (1996) 185 C.L.R. 571 (stay granted), *Akai Pty Ltd v. The People's Insurance Company Ltd* (1996) 188 C.L.R. 418 (stay not granted because exclusive jurisdiction clause inconsistent with a mandatory rule), *C.S.R. Ltd v. Cigna Insurance Australia Ltd* (1997) 146 A.L.R. 402 (stay granted).
55. Garnett (1999).
56. Polinsky (1980, pp. 1086-1088).
57. Ayres (1998), Ayres and Talley (1995a, 1995b), Ayres and Balkin (1996), Johnston (1995).
58. We will focus in this section on the case where the forum in which litigation is commenced has jurisdiction to hear the plaintiff's case.
59. Costs are relevant even under the oppression test: *Logan v. Bank of Scotland (No. 2)* [1906] 1 K.B. 141, 150, *Egbert v. Short* [1907] 2 Ch. 205, 213, *Maritime Insurance Co. Ltd v. Geelong Harbor Trust Commissioners* (1908) 6 C.L.R. 194, 198.
60. The Australian High Court has referred to verification difficulties at interlocutory hearings as a reason to adopt an approach somewhat biased against stays: *Voth v. Manildra Flour Mills Pty Ltd* (1990) 171 C.L.R. 538, 558.
61. *Société Nationale Industrielle Aerospatiale v. Lee Kui Jak* [1987] A.C. 871, *C.S.R. Ltd v. Cigna Insurance Australia Ltd* (1997) 146 A.L.R. 402.
62. See, e.g., Posner (1998a, pp. 72-81). Cf. Krier and Schwab (1995).
63. Presumably, it should equal the sum of the enjoined party's additional costs in the new forum, plus the difference between the expected value of that party's judgments in the two forums. Expected value should take into consideration the size of possible awards and the probability that they would be awarded. These decisions are almost impossible to make in the interlocutory stages of a case.
64. Epstein (1997), Kaplow and Shavell (1996), Polinsky (1980).
65. Johnston (1995). See also Ayres and Talley (1995a).
66. Johnston (1995).
67. There may be procedural grounds. These are discussed in chapters 3 and 4.

68. A. Schwartz (1992).
69. Clarkson and Hill (1997, pp. 116-119).
70. Clarkson and Hill (1997, p. 118).
71. *Spiliada Maritime Corp. v. Cansulex Ltd* [1987] 1 A.C. 460.
72. See chapter 6, pp. 99-102 *supra*.
73. Rawls (1971).
74. *Oppenheimer v. Louis Rosenthal & Co. A.G.* [1937] 1 All E.R. 23.
75. *Spiliada Maritime Corp. v. Cansulex Ltd* [1987] 1 A.C. 460, 478. Cf. *The Vishva Abha* [1990] 2 Lloyd's Rep. 312 (differences in damages), *Roneleigh Ltd v. MII Exports Inc.* [1989] 1 W.L.R. 619.
76. Cf. *Irish Shipping Ltd v. Commercial Union Assurance Co. plc.* [1991] 2 Q.B. 206. The second problem is a more general description of the first.
77. *The Vishva Ajay* [1989] 2 Lloyd's Rep. 558.
78. See generally Bermann (1990), Bell and Gleeson (1997), Wilson (1997).
79. See Bermann (1990, pp. 591-593).
80. *Allendale Mutual Insurance Co. v. Bull Data Systems Inc.*, 10 F.3d 425 (7th Cir. 1993).
81. *China Trade and Development v. M.V. Choong Yong*, 837 F.2d 33, 40 (2d Cir. 1987) ('no comity principles ... are at stake in resolving a piece of commercial litigation').
82. We adopt Wilson's (1997) classification schemata although we will not analyse cases arising under the Brussels and Lugano Conventions.
83. *Aggeliki Charis Compania Naviera Maritima S.A. v. Pagnan S.p.A. (The Angelic Grace)* [1995] 1 Lloyd's Rep. 87, 96, *Akai Pty Ltd v. People's Insurance Co. Ltd* [1998] 1 Lloyd's Rep. 90, *Apple Corps Ltd v. Apple Computer Inc.* [1992] R.P.C. 70, *Continental Bank v. Aeakos S.A.* [1994] 1 W.L.R. 588.
84. For examples, see *Midland Bank plc. v. Laker Airways Ltd* [1986] Q.B. 689, *C.S.R. Ltd v. Cigna Insurance Australia Ltd* (1997) 146 A.L.R. 402.
85. *Société Nationale Industrielle Aerospatiale v. Lee Kui Jak* [1987] A.C. 871, *Bank of Tokyo Ltd v. Karoon* [1987] A.C. 45, *C.S.R. Ltd v. Cigna Insurance Australia Ltd* (1997) 146 A.L.R. 402.
86. For a discussion of this 'skimming' property, see Fudenberg and Tirole (1991, pp. 407-408).
87. Bell and Gleeson (1997, pp. 968-969). The different international approaches to declining jurisdiction are described in Fawcett (1995).
88. The U.S. approach is susceptible of few generalities, there being differences between Federal circuit courts (Bell and Gleeson 1997, pp. 965-967).
89. [1981] A.C. 557.
90. 15 U.S.C. § 1 (2000).
91. See also *Maxwell Communications Corp. plc. (No. 2), Barclays plc. v. Homan* [1992] B.C.C. 757.
92. [1987] A.C. 871.

93. See *Smith Kline and French Laboratories Ltd v. Bloch* [1983] 1 W.L.R. 730, *Bank of Tokyo Ltd v. Karoon* [1987] AC 45.
94. *C.S.R. Ltd v. Cigna Insurance Australia Ltd* (1997) 146 A.L.R. 402. For analysis, see Whincop (1998b).
95. *C.S.R. Ltd v. New Zealand Insurance* (1994) 36 N.S.W.L.R. 138.
96. Pryles (1988), Garnett (1999).
97. [1998] 2 W.L.R. 686.
98. Ibid, 698-699.
99. Briggs (1997).
100. Other theoretical issues regarding recognition are discussed in Whincop (1999b).
101. And so, perhaps, supportive of the second hypothesis.
102. Cf. Harris (1997).
103. *Emanuel v. Symon* [1908] 1 K.B. 302, *Adams v. Cape Industries plc.* [1990] 1 Ch. 433.
104. See the Preliminary Draft Convention on Jurisdiction and the Effects of Judgments in Civil and Commercial Matters, adopted provisionally by the Special Commission of the Hague Conference on Private International Law, 18 June 1999 (hereinafter '*Preliminary Draft*').
105. The proposed Hague convention adopts such a provision: see *Preliminary Draft* art. 24.
106. Kessedjian (1997, §§ 120, 122).

9 Corporations as Subjects of Jurisdiction

In chapter 8, we discussed how jurisdictional principles affect the conduct of litigation in multistate disputes. The simplifying assumption made there was that the parties were autonomous economic actors. However, most reported conflicts cases involve corporations, and some involve multinational corporations ('MNCs'). Much literature addresses the aptitude of MNCs in reinventing themselves to avoid the exercise of authority by sovereign states, becoming, in effect, a law unto themselves.[1] This is, *au fond*, a statement about the subjection of MNCs to jurisdiction. Some of the dilemmas associated with MNCs reflect a larger problem — corporations do not easily fit into the framework in which states determine when their courts should exercise jurisdiction. That framework assumes that defaults are autonomous economic actors. But almost a century of corporate law scholarship warns us to reify or 'thingify' the corporation at our peril. The better view is that corporations are accorded legal personality for pragmatic reasons, not ontological ones.[2]

In this chapter, we develop the pragmatic and economic case against assimilating the treatment of corporations with other types of defendants. The questions we must ask if assimilation occurs are difficult to answer and may give perverse results. Assimilation also blinds us to the fact that jurisdictional issues play a part in defining the contracts and property rights that comprise corporations. Thus, the redefinition of jurisdictional rules may be desirable on substantive grounds. After dealing with these issues in general terms, we consider a unique conflictual problem the corporation poses — the choice of law and jurisdictional issues raised by international insolvency.

The Corporation and the Theory of the Firm: Coase Again

The firm was long regarded as simply a production function by economists.[3] Modern theories of the firm derive from R.H. Coase's classic 1937 article.[4] Coase observed that decisions made within firms allocated resources managerially. In so doing, the firm superseded the basic allocative functions markets were thought to perform. Coase ascribed this to the fact that market transactions were costly. Firms permitted those costs to be reduced. Firms could do this by decreasing the number of contracts by substituting longer-term contracts based on fiat rather than short term spot exchanges, and by the intermediation of the firm itself in the contracting process. Since these things themselves were costly, the integration of transactions within firms would be limited. The boundary of a firm would be referable to an equilibrium between the marginal costs of organising a transaction hierarchically and transacting for the same in the market.

Decades later these ideas were embraced by two schools of economists. One school sought to explain the ownership, management, and governance of corporations in contractual terms.[5] The diverging interests of a range of constituencies were brought into equilibrium by processes of contracting — the corporation was described as a nexus of contracts.[6] Legal scholars embraced these ideas, which cut against the long-standing premise that regulation was needed to control conflicts of interest by managers.[7] Law and economics scholars argued that these conflicts were limited by both contracts and markets. With the Coase theorem in mind, corporate law was reconceived as a means of decreasing transaction costs by providing the rules that contracting parties would typically agree to themselves. These rules should be susceptible of private ordering in Coasean trade between shareholders and managers.[8]

Whereas the first school focused on ex ante contractual control of contracting problems, the second school emphasised the ongoing need for governance in most complex contracts and corporations (especially relations supported by transaction-specific assets).[9] Corporate lawyers used the theory to examine various phenomena, such as the structure of corporate governance and competitions for control.[10] Theorists doubted that courts were able to deal competently with governance problems in complex contracts or corporations, given the unverifiability of relevant information and the tendency for dispute resolution mechanisms to develop endogenously to relations.[11]

The point to be gleaned from these theories is the danger of applying jurisdictional rules to the corporation as one would to a natural person. Corporations are best analysed in terms of a dynamic contracting process. The contracts and contractors change as economic circumstances alter. The personified corporation is a convenience which facilitates synthesis with other parts of the legal system (such as regimes of property rights). Thus, great care is needed in attempting to identify relevant attributes of a corporation and using them as a basis for legal intervention.

The Corporation in Private International Law

Given our comments in chapter 2, it is not greatly surprising that neither judges nor scholars have developed clear consequential models of the corporation for jurisdictional purposes. Most analysis treats the corporation as a natural or artificial entity.[12] This is likely to be a consequence of the law's use of spatio-territorial factors in defining the persons over whom a court may assert jurisdiction. As we saw in chapter 8, the common law required that the defendant be present in the jurisdiction when served with process.[13] We argued there that the rule was problematic because of the greater mobility of persons and resources in the modern age. This is true for natural persons, but there is a greater problem for corporations. Only a tangible thing can reliably be said to be present in space. A corporation is not a tangible thing. Therefore, an approach to jurisdiction which remains spatial in nature must take one of two possible approaches.

One is to seek a formal correspondence between the corporation's juristic status and some territory. The most obvious way is to rely on the state in which the corporation is incorporated: that state would be the only one in which jurisdiction might be regularly established. This is the basis for choice of law in the internal affairs of the corporation.

This approach would restrict the forums in which jurisdiction might be established. An approach which restricts jurisdictions is unlikely to minimise litigation costs if the efficient forum varies between cases. The jurisdiction of incorporation might be chosen *because* its courts apply rules which minimise the corporation's liability to plaintiffs. This may permit the corporation to externalise the costs of its operations, especially as regards involuntary creditors such as tort victims.[14] This would decrease social welfare. Those plaintiffs whose claims are based in contract might contract around the rule by agreeing to a jurisdiction clause. However, transaction costs are incurred to reach this solution. For those contracts where the gains from trade are low, agreement may never occur. The difference between endorsing such an approach in the case of internal affairs is that the choice of state of incorporation only affects shareholders, who presumably choose to invest in the securities of a corporation, out of a huge range of alternatives, where the chosen law is desirable.[15] Creditors and other third parties are unaffected.

The alternative method is more empirical. We will call it the contacts approach, since it relies on apparently observable characteristics of the corporation. Methods may differ as to the number and sufficiency of characteristics necessary for jurisdiction to be established. The method most like the juristic approach is to look for the state in which the corporation has its closest contact. Sometimes this is put in terms of the corporation's place of central management and control; sometimes the civilian concept of *siege real* is used.[16] This approach is used to establish general jurisdiction over a corporation in the Brussels and Lugano Conventions.[17] Like the juristic approach, it tends to reduce the number of possible jurisdictions. Whether it permits externalisation depends on the costs shareholders and managers bear in transferring its *siege real*, compared to the place of incorporation.[18]

Both methods have difficulty in dealing with corporate groups. The proper defendant may be a subsidiary, the *siege real* of which is located in one place. However, the unit in the corporate group which holds assets against which a judgment might be enforced may be located elsewhere, making suit against the former nugatory. This is a persistent problem for any approach to jurisdiction over the corporation which relies on observable characteristics of a putative corporate defendant. Although a corporation may be a nexus of contracts, the terms of which should be respected and enforced, the topology of a corporate group often results from the unilateral acts of managers. We discuss potential solutions to the problems of groups below.

The empirical contacts approach can be broadened in a way that selects characteristics which need not be exclusive to a single jurisdiction. An approach used in English and Australian law is to have regard to whether or not the corporation carries on business in the relevant state. Before examining how this method works in practice, we examine its theoretical merit in light of economic theories of the firm.

We said above that Coase referred to the boundary of the firm as the point at which transacting in markets becomes a more economical means for the firm to give effect to its production-investment decisions than attempting to organise particular types of transactions hierarchically. The firm boundary seems to be a means by which to ascertain what the corporation's 'business' is, and where it is conducted.

Unfortunately, this approach is not of much use. First, even if one can establish the 'marginal' transaction, the theory does not provide any useful means of mapping transactions or stages of production onto jurisdictions. For example, where a firm chooses to forward integrate into a downstream stage of production, rather than transacting in the market place, it is unclear what characteristics of the new production stage should be identified as the basis for allocating jurisdiction.

Second, by which dimensions do we define the firm's boundary? The theory works well with production and distribution decisions. But other corporate transactions are harder to analyse. For example, are we to define the firm's boundary to include its sources of finance? Williamson argues that equity financing is like an intra-firm transaction, whereas debt financing is market-like.[19] If that is so, would the firm's boundary include all places where it distributed a prospectus or registration statement? Or all places from which offers for shares were made? Or all places where shareholders live?

Third, it is doubtful whether use of the firm boundary for jurisdictional purposes is sound even if the above two problems could be solved. Economists consider that intra-firm transactions are primarily subject to internal governance and dispute resolution. Market transactions often do not contemplate enduring relations, which makes legal enforcement more important to the performance of those obligations. Yet, if the firm boundary was used for jurisdictional purposes, it would limit the entitlement of a party to use court-ordered enforcement. This would be internally contradictory. It seems strange to say that because a corporation transacts in the market in jurisdiction A, rather than integrating that transaction within the firm, counterparties to that transaction should, *ipso facto*, be unable to assert jurisdiction against it in the place where the transaction occurred. So defining the firm economically would use theory in a context where it is not sound or useful.

Corporations legislation often requires foreign corporations which carry on business within the jurisdiction to arrange a place that could accept service of process. Although this avoids the conceptual questions about the corporate boundary, it still tells us relatively little about what is or is not the conduct of business. The common law requirement that there be a fixed place of business is antiquated, given advances in communication technology and changes in distributional arrangements.[20]

The most general method is the approach analysing contacts and interests developed by the United States Supreme Court.[21] Corporations might be subjected to jurisdiction in a number of jurisdictions, based on its interests in those places. The attempts made by the United States Supreme Court, for example, to define contacts are undoubtedly vague. *International Shoe Co. v. Washington* speaks of 'minimum contacts ... such that the maintenance of [a] suit [in the forum] does not offend "traditional notions of fair play and substantial justice"'.[22] Later cases added circularity to generality by asking whether the defendant's contacts were such that he 'should reasonably anticipate being haled into' the forum.[23] Chapter 8 indicates that vague jurisdictional principles are not necessarily bad. However, it would be better for the establishment rule, at least, to be clear, even if it is coupled with fuzzy grounds for a stay. The defendant objecting to jurisdiction established under a contacts approach will rely on information which sheds less light on its valuation of the jurisdiction entitlement or the cause of action, unlike the stay.

Asking the Right Questions

If there are flaws in conventional doctrinal methods for determining the forums in which a corporation might be sued, how might we improve them? If the corporation is a network of contracts and other obligations imposed by law, jurisdictional principles define how those contractual rights and other obligations can be enforced. As chapter 8 shows, jurisdictional rules should try to select efficient forums for the enforcement of those entitlements. For example, courts of the state of incorporation have a powerful claim as the forum for matters of internal affairs and securities cases, which arises from the optimal choice of law rule for these contracts. The appropriate court for other claims depends on their nature. The fact that the efficient forum depends on the nature of the suit may not be fatal to the use of rule-like jurisdictional principles. However, those rules are likely to be relatively complex, since they will be linked to the nature of the claim asserted.

The notion that a forum should have general jurisdiction over a corporation is something we find of limited use. Rather, we favour more attention being directed to potential bases for special or subject-matter jurisdiction.[24] In the case of a corporation whose activities are substantially domestic, most of the bases for jurisdiction would point to that jurisdiction. However, other corporations may represent a fluid network of contracts having international elements to them. It is the international element *to the contract* which states the potential case for subjecting the corporation to suit in a particular jurisdiction, not the international element to the corporation. Furthermore, the lack of an element required to establish jurisdiction in a particular forum in *one* contract should not be supplied by its presence in *another* contract constituting the corporation. For example, a corporation which sells products in jurisdiction J, having neither an agent or a permanent establishment there, might be subject to J's jurisdiction in a products liability suit.[25] Those issues should be irrelevant to the jurisdictional issues arising in a case where a defendant seeks damages in J for personal injury sustained when injured in K by a truck-driver of the same corporation.

Thus, our claim is that using empirical characteristics of a subset of the contracts of which the corporation is nexus is likely to be overinclusive if used as a basis for general jurisdiction. The overinclusivity problem is not adequately dealt with by imposing more onerous requirements for jurisdiction since that leads back to underinclusivity and the inability to assert jurisdiction as of right in what may be an efficient forum. A special jurisdiction approach moves towards (relatively) complex rules, which enables us to ask better questions about how jurisdiction should be allocated.

An approach that regards state interests as relevant to private international law will tend to analyse the corporation in terms of general jurisdiction. These approaches will examine the relation between the state and the corporation, and ask whether the exercise of jurisdiction over the corporation can be justified, either in terms of state policy or political rights.[26] But the state does not bring the suit, so the justification of the forum should be found in the contract or other circumstances from which the obligations arise.

Political defences of the defendant's subjection to suit in a particular forum cannot sustain a strong argument for general jurisdiction. First, corporations do not cast votes.[27] They may be active politically, but it would be more common to be active as part of a larger interest group, which makes attribution of political responsibility difficult. Second, the exercise of jurisdiction might be defended as politically legitimate on the grounds that the corporation's contacts with a forum were voluntary. A corporation not wanting to be liable is capable of exiting the jurisdiction.[28] However, legitimacy does not tell us much when choices must be made between forums as is inevitably the case for MNCs. For that, one must consult the interests of parties.

That is not to say that there should not be a particular court in which any suit could be brought against the corporation. However, the choice of a forum with general jurisdiction over the corporation could be justified on the ground that the jurisdiction is consistently likely to minimise the corporation's costs across a wide number of claims. The tendency to limit that to the place of incorporation or domicile seems a plausible guess of the jurisdiction that satisfies this criterion.

Our analysis implies that the approach of the common law to establishing jurisdiction by relying on a limited basis for general jurisdiction was sensible, but that its equation of special jurisdiction with the rules on service *ex iuris*, which it was cautious in exercising, was likely to be underinclusive. The American approach may have the opposite faults. Its definition of contacts is unclear. Since contacts are not defined in terms of the efficiency of the forum to the particular litigation, they may also be overinclusive. However, very few American cases rely on general jurisdiction. The approach of the European conventions is preferable, since it uses domicile as a limited basis for general jurisdiction, and has straightforward grounds for special jurisdiction in particular cases. Whether these latter grounds are suitable is a question we turn to now.

A Contractual Theory of Jurisdiction

Our analysis points strongly towards a special jurisdiction approach to the contracts and obligations comprising a corporation. What would the legal principles of such an approach look like? The first rule would simply be that a jurisdiction agreement, struck either at the time of a contract or during litigation, would be enforced specifically by stays or injunctive relief. The harder question is to know what form rules for the establishment of jurisdiction should take in the absence of an express jurisdiction agreement.

Contract Cases

On what basis should forum defaults be set for contract cases? If we aspire to find a rule that anticipates the efficient forum, rules restricting litigation to a single forum may be problematic if the efficient forum varies between cases. However, single forum rules are not problematic if transaction costs are low or if parties do not usually litigate their disputes. This suggests that forum defaults may be most important where parties infrequently transact multistate business (the parties' standard forms may not be adapted to these contexts), and do not expect to transact with each other in the future (litigation is important to enforcing contracts).

In chapter 3, we outlined the instrumental purposes a default rule might serve. A default that attempted to anticipate the efficient forum is similar to a majoritarian rationale. In chapter 3, we also referred to defaults which compel parties to contract explicitly to avoid terms that are not preferred.[29] Might forum defaults be set in this penal form? A possible argument for penalty defaults is that the difficulty of determining the efficient forum ex post makes an ex ante jurisdiction agreement desirable. But a suitable means by which to penalise a failure to contract is hard to find. Three possibilities come to mind — non-enforcement of the contract,[30] requiring the parties to litigate in a forum which both will dislike, or permitting the plaintiff to choose any jurisdiction. The first two have little appeal. They may increase the amount of opportunistic behaviour, such as threats to breach, since plaintiffs will be unable to litigate or will only be able to do so at high costs. Barring an estoppel defence, these two penalties encourage a corporation offering to contract on standard terms to *exclude* a jurisdiction clause, where it expected that it would not be the plaintiff, but that it might be the defendant. The penalty default would *encourage* incomplete contracts, not discourage them.

An unrestrained choice for the plaintiff does not raise the same problems if the corporation is the probable defendant and the term-giver. The corporation will recognise the legal risks it faces if it is sued in a forum where its costs will be high. It will therefore insist on a formal provision. However, recall that we said that forum defaults matter most for infrequent multistate transacting between parties who do not envisage repeated dealings. These parties are less likely to know the penalty default exists and may not contract around the term. Parties would depend on jurisdictional trade after the dispute has arisen or the willingness of the forum chosen by the plaintiff to stay proceedings. Trade is complicated by the factors mentioned in the last chapter. Stays of proceedings may be impossible if the plaintiff has chosen a forum that does not readily grant stays (which the plaintiff will prefer to do). In these situations, where the default matters most, its efficiency claims seem weak.[31]

The most efficient forum default seems therefore to lie midway between single forum defaults and unrestricted forum defaults. That is, a plaintiff should have a limited choice. Limited choice overcomes the difficulty of consistently selecting the efficient forum in a range of heterogeneous cases, and of the problem of opportunistic nuisance suits in inefficient forums. Selecting the forums that are most likely to be efficient caps the surplus the parties have to bargain over in jurisdictional trade, in the event that the rule does not itself induce a choice of the optimal forum. The European jurisdiction conventions do something like this. They offer a choice between the court of the defendant's domicile (which has general jurisdiction) and the court of the place where the obligation was to be performed. Parties aware of the default options have an incentive to contract in order to reduce the need for jurisdictional challenges. Risk averse parties will prefer to contract over forum to decrease variance of possible outcomes arising from differences in costs, laws and choice of law rules.

The question of how much choice and how to define the choices are purely pragmatic questions. Greater complexity, in the form of differentiating rules by contract type, may be appropriate, just as we argued for market tort choice of law rules. Thus, the forums for breach of an insurance contract may be (a) the place of the defendant's domicile; (b) the *locus contractus*; (c) the locus of the insured risk; and (d) the place whose law the parties have agreed to govern the contract. Fairness may justify extending the list by adding the place of the insured's domicile in cases of household risks.[32] Alternative options are possible, but the point is that a list of four choices is likely to include the efficient forum or a forum where joint costs are close enough to the minimum to make interference welfare-decreasing. Adding extra choices is not likely to substantially increase the probability that the efficient forum is a member of the set. We have explained the use of domicile. The second and third choices are justified as the places most likely to coincide with the locus of evidence, which is crucial to the forum's efficiency. We explain (d) below.

Thus, a plaintiff in a contracts case should be able to choose any of these jurisdictions, without the need to seek special leave. A defendant who did not enter an appearance could be sued to a default judgment. Since this approach does not eliminate the risk that the plaintiff will choose an inappropriate forum to maximise the expected award, the defendant should be entitled to object to the exercise of jurisdiction on *forum non conveniens* grounds, preferably by application for a stay where the procedure exists, or by application for anti-suit injunction. Either party should be entitled to seek the transfer of proceedings to some other forum in which related litigation is taking place.

Torts Cases

As in chapter 5, we would assimilate most market torts with contract rules. As to non-market torts, the choices seem clear: (a) the place of the defendant's domicile; and (b) the place the accident occurred — which are similar to the provisions of the European conventions. Again, these choices anticipate the place where the parties' costs will be minimised, or the locus of most of the relevant evidence. The choice might be expanded to include the place where managerial decisions are made to engage in the relevant behaviour in question. This would be of value where the defendant is a MNC, for reasons chapter 7 addresses.

Related Issues

Effect of choice of law agreements Courts often hold that choice of law clauses do not constitute a submission to jurisdiction.[33] This seems reasonable. If the parties are capable of agreeing to a choice of law, and embodying the agreement in a written term, the marginal cost of agreeing to and drafting a jurisdiction clause would also seem low. But there is no reason to believe that the cost is zero. Although it is an empirical question, we suspect that a majority of persons who have agreed to choice of law *and* jurisdiction terms will choose the same ones. The probability of errors in the application of a court's own law are likely to be substantially lower than the probability of errors in the application of foreign law. The exercise of jurisdiction by that court will also save the costs of proving foreign law. If these premises are correct, it is logical to reverse the current presumption by recasting the default so that a choice of law also operates as an exclusive choice of jurisdiction. Those who want a different jurisdiction must contract for it.

Natural persons The rules we have advocated are easy to apply to natural persons, since they do not predicate on any fact unique to corporations. However, if natural persons are sued by corporations, litigation outside their place of domicile may place an unfair burden on the defendant. There are two ways by which this might be dealt with. First, one might limit jurisdiction to the place of the domicile of the defendant. The European conventions do this. Domicile, however, may not minimise the parties' joint costs. Second, one might retain the existing rules but provide a more far reaching costs indemnity for natural person defendants who fall into a 'deserving' category and are the subject of suit outside their place of domicile. Thus, one might adopt what Steven Shavell calls the costs regime favourable to the defendant.[34] Under this regime, the defendant bears his costs only when he loses. The plaintiff always bears its own costs and, when the plaintiff loses, the defendant's costs. The logic is simple — wider rules permit the selection of a more efficient regime, but the costs regime redistributes wealth from the plaintiff to defendant.

Corporate groups Conventional approaches to jurisdiction have difficulty with the corporate group. Approaches treating the corporation as an entity make it difficult to assert jurisdiction against corporations other than local subsidiaries if all of the group's business there is conducted through them. It may be valuable to sue a parent. In Anglo-Australian law, however, a corporation, even within a corporate group, is treated as a separate legal entity, supposedly on the basis of the House of Lords decision in *Salomon v. Salomon & Co. Ltd.*[35]

One proposed solution to the problem of asserting jurisdiction over the parent is the use of enterprise theory.[36] This asks whether the subsidiary and the parent comprise a single economic entity. This has two problems. First, it is unclear why a subsidiary managed more or less independently of the foreign parent should always preclude the parent from being sued locally. These sorts of managerial decisions are taken internally, as part of corporate governance decisions. Managerial autonomy in a jurisdiction is most likely when information relevant to management is costly to transfer. It is unclear why these decisions should bind those, besides managers and shareholders, who are not party to them, since they can obviously create an externality. Second, the enterprise approach encourages the maintenance of a façade of subsidiary independence. Judges are not consistently astute in recognising evasion.[37]

Corporate groups are structured by unilateral acts of corporate managers, or by bilateral contract with shareholders. Those against whom the corporate group is asserted are rarely parties to those acts. The usual law on corporate groups resembles a default rule that precludes claims against other companies in the group. Why not simply reverse the default rule by permitting the parent to be sued as a party to the proceedings, and put the onus on the subsidiary to contract for immunity for the remainder of the group? The alternative default rule implicit in the current law places the burden of being informed about group arrangements on the counterparty. This is both unfair and inefficient, since the 'subsidiary's' costs of communicating that information are likely to be lower than the counterparty's search costs.

An argument for the status quo is that subsidiaries enable companies to control the forums in which they will be liable, and the laws to which they will be subject.[38] Maybe that's true, but a better way to do the same thing is by jurisdiction and choice of law agreements notified to the counterparty at the time of the contract. The alternative permits the defendant to decide these issues unilaterally, or by asserting the subsidiary's existence against parties who have not had a chance to contract. Judges and scholars have recognised the strength of the case for permitting liability to be asserted beyond the unit in the group formally liable.[39]

Jurisdiction and Choice of Law in International Insolvency

The division of responsibility of states for insolvent corporations with assets and claims in multiple countries is highly controversial.[40] This problem allows us to see several practical illustrations of points made in this book. The two paradigms for resolving these problems are universalism and territorialism, although there are discrete points between. Universalism holds that the courts and law of a single jurisdiction should dominate the insolvency process. If the cooperation of other courts is required, they will apply the law of the selected state and function purely to assist the primary forum. The law of other states has at best a minor role, which might include the specification of requirements of formal validity for instruments creating a creditor's interest.

Territorialism holds that each state should have jurisdiction over the assets of the insolvent corporation present in its borders. Until a recent but compelling defence of territorialism by Lynn LoPucki, scholars deprecated territorialism as a manifestation of uncooperative state self-interest.[41] The advantages of universalism are supposed to include the fact that only a single administrator is empowered, who is able to make decisions about the assets as a whole. This decreases administration costs as well as the need for cooperation in making or implementing decisions to reorganise or liquidate the firm. It is argued to be more predictable, so facilitating the pricing of debt.

In practice, the arguments break down. In the same way as we argued that choice of law rules applicable to products liability other than the place of sale would complicate the operation of markets, universalism would create confusion in the pricing of goods and services. There are significant variations in international insolvency regimes, and a large range of these regimes could be operative in any one market depending on the regimes corporations come under. The rule would significantly increase information costs. It is quite likely that the effects of particular insolvency rules would not be reflected in prices in domestic markets given those high costs. We have argued that choice of law rules should select domestic law in substantially domestic transactions, but a universalist system may regularly fail to do this.

Conventional approaches to universalism find it difficult to identify the primary law. As we argued earlier in this chapter, incorporation-based approaches are easily manipulable. As LoPucki points out, jurisdictions may react to manipulation by providing incentives to attract corporations, as indeed the American states do now in insolvency cases, notwithstanding the apparent uniformity of the substantive bankruptcy law.[42] Reacting to this dilemma by allowing local courts to refuse to cooperate with the administrator appointed under a substantially unfair system[43] creates uncertainty about the applicable law, and undermines the advantages of coordination and cooperation. Identifying the home country is particularly difficult in the insolvency of a corporate group, since each unit may have a different home state, and hence private law. If so, the advantages of universalism (especially those of ex ante predictability) collapse.

Robert Rasmussen makes a serious attempt to address problems of identifying the applicable law by permitting it to be specified in the corporation's constitution.[44] The home state would be the subject of contractual choice. Change would require the consent of all creditors. The choice, unless unreasonable, determines both the applicable bankruptcy law and the forum. Rasmussen argues that the choice will be made to maximise the value of the firm, provided lenders are capable of ascertaining the effects of bankruptcy regimes on the probability of default and expected payouts. However, as we acknowledged for choice of law in market tort cases, the cost of making these assessments may be high. In a share market, the fungibility of equity permits a degree of free riding by uninformed investors on informed valuations in efficient markets. Such effects may be minimal in bankruptcy cases, since the uninformed debtors, such as employees and trade creditors, are unlikely to extend credit in efficient markets for debt. Creditors arising from non-market torts are especially at risk, a problem which forces Rasmussen to make an ad hoc exception to his approach.

LoPucki's defence of territorialism envisages bankruptcy proceedings in each jurisdiction in which the corporation has assets administered under local law. To the extent that national law discriminates against foreigners, a territorial system limits discrimination to local property. In the upshot, there may be differences between the payouts creditors get, given different local priorities. However, the difference is only relevant to the distribution of wealth, not to efficiency.

Like our prescriptions for market torts, the system gives less informed parties the benefit of local law, with which they are most familiar, so minimising their information costs. Since the law of the place where assets are located will be the applicable law, the creditor only needs to know the *situs* of the assets and the law in effect in that place.[45] In the event of insolvency, creditors employ local procedures, advice in respect of which should be readily available locally, compared to the necessity to file a single claim under foreign law in the universalist system. Territoriality also fits well with our treatment of choice of law in property. We argued in favour of the *lex situs* compared to other alternatives, because *situs* is a focal point for coordination. Similar logic supports the use of local law in dealings in the property of an insolvent corporation. The other advantage of territorialism is that claims arising from the operation of local law (such as non-market torts), which are recognised by efficient choice of law rules, will not be annihilated, whereas the primary universalist law for the insolvency may accord low or no priority to such claims.

Does territoriality minimise litigation costs? Universalism might be superior if a single court was capable of resolving all claims to all assets. But in practice, the assistance of other courts where assets are located is needed. The inclination of foreign courts to compromise local interests for foreign ones probably makes for longer and more protracted proceedings. If a local court is the most appropriate (lowest cost) forum for the resolution of claims to assets over which the court has power, territoriality should result in lower litigation costs. The exception to this is in cases where trials are needed to establish the amount of claims, such as unliquidated tort damages. Unless there is a system by which courts can accept the liquidation of a claim in a foreign court, multiple trials may overwhelm the territorialist system. But, as LoPucki points out, universalism only does better if the primary forum grants full credit to the foreign judgment — which is often unlikely for reasons discussed in chapter 8.

LoPucki's claim is that territorialism can be made cooperative, rather than competitive. An obvious example is a convention resolving the multiple trials problem. Conventions can also address the repatriation of assets moved between countries in anticipation of bankruptcy. Under a territorialist system, countries share a common interest in preventing asset flight. Conventions might also minimise the need for multiple filings by creditors.[46]

Universalism subjects the corporation to jurisdiction in a single state, which may not often be the efficient forum for some of the contracts comprising the corporation. From a choice of law perspective, the ex ante specification of a single choice of law and forum may be contingently incomplete — as the corporation's business changes, and new opportunities arise, the need to vary or differentiate a single choice of law will arise. Individual creditors can vary the terms on which they lend, but the corporation cannot agree to change the applicable law in an individual case. Rasmussen would require unanimous consent (in effect, a refinancing of its debt). Cooperative territorialism would be more likely to reduce the cost of financing. For any given production-investment opportunity, managers will prefer to borrow money in, and shift corporate assets to, a jurisdiction whose commercial and bankruptcy laws minimise the cost of capital. By borrowing money and shifting assets to a jurisdiction, the corporation and the creditor effectively make a choice of law and jurisdiction. For example, an enterprise which is labour intensive might minimise its cost of labour if it located its assets in a jurisdiction whose bankruptcy laws assigned a higher priority to employee claims.

Posner's comparative advantage argument may be persuasive here, since local jurisdictions may have an advantage in formulating laws suited to local conditions and markets. We have already referred to the appeal of territorialism in non-market torts cases where creditors lack any opportunity of contracting with the firm. To permit the firm a choice of bankruptcy law in these cases may not only be inefficient because it permits costs to be externalised, but also unfair, since parties would not agree to permit a party to make a unilateral choice behind a veil of ignorance. Territorialism may also follow from Ayres and Gertner's claim that it is desirable for the default rule to reflect the preferences of parties, such as involuntary creditors, whose contracting costs are high. Those with low contracting costs, such as financial institutions, have a greater ability to contract around inefficiencies of local law by requiring particular covenants or security.[47]

Conclusion

Our analysis of jurisdiction over the corporation in general and in insolvency cases demonstrates the need for a transactional approach to private international law. Recognising the corporation as a nexus of contracts favours limited general jurisdiction but more expansive special jurisdiction. We have advocated a limited choice model as best trading off the problems of heterogeneity in forum appropriateness and opportunism in forum selection. Likewise, forums with power over local assets state the best claim to resolve claims against those assets in insolvency. There are also strong choice of law reasons for a territorial approach to insolvency, which accord with our analysis of contracts, torts, and property. Throughout, the transactional approach dominates a more metaphysical approach designed to ascertain contacts or characteristics of the corporation. The pragmatic appeal of our analysis is clear — the approach is less conceptual, more predictable, capable of incremental adjustment in the light of experience, economically efficient, and fair.

Notes

1. A valuable summary of the literature is found in Orts (1997).
2. Whincop (1997d).
3. Bratton (1989) summarises the development of economic analysis of the firm and its influence on legal scholarship.
4. Coase (1937).
5. Jensen and Meckling (1976), Fama (1980), Fama and Jensen (1983a, 1983b).
6. Jensen and Meckling (1976, pp. 311-312).
7. Berle and Means (1937).
8. Easterbrook and Fischel (1991) is the definitive reference.
9. Williamson (1985, 1996). See chapter 7, p. 113 *supra*.
10. The literature is reviewed in Romano (1996).
11. Williamson (1996, pp. 98-100).
12. See, e.g., *Adams v. Cape Industries plc.* [1990] 1 Ch. 433, *Dunlop Pneumatic Tyre Co. Ltd v. A.G. Cudell & Co.* [1902] 1 K.B. 342, *Okura and Co. Ltd v. Forsbacka Jernverks Aktiebolag* [1914] 1 K.B. 715, Fawcett (1988), Goldsmith (1989, p. 614).
13. See, e.g., *Laurie v. Carroll* (1958) 98 C.L.R. 310, Pryles (1972).
14. Hansmann and Kraakman (1991).
15. LoPucki (1994).
16. Charny (1991), Drury (1998).
17. *Civil Jurisdiction and Judgments Act* 1982 s. 42(3).
18. See generally Kobayashi and Ribstein (1999).
19. Williamson (1988).

20. *Dunlop Pneumatic Tyre Co. Ltd v. A.G. Cudell & Co.* [1902] 1 K.B. 342.
21. See, e.g., *International Shoe Company v. Washington*, 326 U.S. 310 (1945), *World-Wide Volkswagen Corp. v. Woodson*, 444 U.S. 286 (1980), *Burger King Corp. v. Rudzewicz*, 471 U.S. 462 (1985), *Asahi Metal Industry Co. Ltd v. Superior Court*, 480 U.S. 102 (1987).
22. 326 U.S. 310, 316 (1945).
23. *World-Wide Volkswagen Corp. v. Woodson*, 444 U.S. 286 (1980).
24. Special jurisdiction is the term the Brussels and Lugano Conventions use when they formulate rules on jurisdiction for particular subject matters: see chapter 8, p. 143 *supra*. U.S. courts speak of 'general' and 'specific' jurisdiction: *Helicopteros Nacionales de Colombia v. Hall*, 466 U.S. 408, 414 (1984). Compare von Mehren and Trautman (1966) and Twitchell (1988). In practice, most American cases invoke specific jurisdiction over the corporation.
25. We argued that place of the sale is the optimal default for products liability cases: see chapter 5, p. 83 *supra*.
26. See, e.g., Brilmayer et al. (1987, pp. 739-740). Brand (1998, p. 151) says that the focus of the U.S. Supreme Court's jurisdiction decisions has not been on the connection between the court and the cause of action, but 'on the nexus between the defendant and the court claiming jurisdiction.'
27. Brilmayer (1989), Brilmayer et al. (1987).
28. Brilmayer (1989), relying on Hirschman (1970).
29. See chapter 3, p. 36 *supra*.
30. See Ayres and Gertner (1989, p. 98), Korobkin (1998, pp. 673-675).
31. This conclusion varies from our earlier analysis in Whincop and Keyes (1998c).
32. Under the Brussels and Lugano Conventions, this is the sole forum for these cases: arts. 7-15.
33. *Dunbee Ltd v. Gilman & Co. (Aust.) Pty Ltd* (1968) 70 S.R. (N.S.W.) 219, *Compagnie d'Armement Maritime S.A. v. Compagnie Tunisienne de Navigation S.A.* [1971] A.C. 572. Cf. *Acrow (Automation) Ltd v. Rex Chainbelt Inc.* [1971] 1 W.L.R. 1676.
34. Shavell (1982).
35. [1897] A.C. 22. *Salomon* had nothing to do with a corporate group. It concerned the rights of the creditors to proceed against Mr Salomon, when they had contracted with Salomon & Co. Ltd. This difference is important, as it comes down to enforcing the terms of real contracts on one hand, and respecting the property rights allocated between corporate groups by non-contractual unilateral acts on the other: Whincop (1998c).
36. Blumberg (1983), Brilmayer and Paisley (1986), Fawcett (1988, pp. 663-665).
37. Classic examples can be found in income tax cases. For instructive comparisons, compare *Deane v. F.C.T.* (1982) 82 A.T.C. 4112 with *Investment & Merchant Finance Corp. Ltd v. F.C.T.* (1971) 125 C.L.R. 249. A Tax Commissioner may have greater coercive power to penetrate disguises than the average plaintiff.

38. Sommer (1990).
39. Hansmann and Kraakman (1990). Our comments should be taken to apply to jurisdiction, not the substantive act of lifting the veil or enforcing shareholder liability, although the issues are practically very similar (Brown 1992).
40. See, e.g., LoPucki (1999), Rasmussen (1997), Trautman et al. (1993), Westbrook (1991).
41. LoPucki (1999). We adopt LoPucki's comparison of universalist and territorialist approaches.
42. LoPucki (1999), referring to LoPucki and Whitford (1991) and Eisenberg and LoPucki (1998). Cf. Rasmussen and Thomas (2000).
43. Westbrook (1996, p. 2533) refers to this as 'modified' universalism.
44. Rasmussen (1997). The paper internationalises his general contractual approach to bankruptcy in Rasmussen (1992).
45. Creditors will also desire a prohibition on the corporation taking assets out of the jurisdiction (LoPucki and Warren 1998, pp. 301, 305).
46. That is, a creditor indebted to a corporation with assets in Canada and England would otherwise need to file two claims, one in each jurisdiction.
47. Ayres and Gertner (1989).

10 Beyond the Nation State

Pragmatism Revisited

In chapter 1, we claimed we would develop a pragmatic theory of private international law. We said there that such an attempt at theorisation would need to do three things. First, it would need to refer to the theory underlying substantive law areas. Second, it would emphasise party interests, not state interests, since the former are more tractable and more justifiable. Third, our approach was to be transactional, focusing on how conflicts rules affect decision making and strategic behaviour. To be pragmatic, a theory needs to minimise reliance on excessively conceptual or metaphysical methods — it must look forward, not backward.

Our approach has an inherent tension, given its forceful advocacy of party interests and its neglect of state interests. Some will find this unpragmatic, either because much of the analysis lies in an economic theory of behaviour the assumptions of which are not pragmatic, or because the neglect of the state is an unrealistic representation of modern democracies where government intervention is a fact of life. We answer this criticism in two ways. First, we have advocated interest positivism as a method which permits governments to favour the collective 'good' over party interests. Those regulations will take away the rights of parties to privately order their relations if they are sufficiently explicit in their intention to do so. In practice, a state *cannot* have more than that since attempts to do presuppose the acquiescence of other states in the export of the first state's regulatory policy. Second, most of our analysis is not controversial. Fritz Juenger favours party autonomy in contract cases and Lea Brilmayer prefers territorial approaches to pro-forum approaches in torts cases, even though both dislike economic consequential analysis. Even our differences from interest analysis are easy to exaggerate if one looks at exceptional cases, in the manner that lawyers do. Our theory is wrong if experience proves that the prescriptions of another theory do a better job, not because its assumptions are unrealistic.

The clearest influence of pragmatism on our analysis is the attempt to move the debates away from the extreme positions — that rules can only ever be limited to the stock in trade of vested rights theorists, and that differentiation between cases demands that we eschew attempts to give ex ante content to choice of law method. Thus, our approach to choice of law in contract cases, market torts, and relational torts is designed to partition cases into smaller groups where there may be greater homogeneity in preferences. Party autonomy is not desirable simply for liberal reasons, but because it provides an opportunity to limit the consequences of rules that are sometimes wrong. Contracting need not take on negative overtones if lawmakers take an intelligent approach to contract formation. Thus, economic theory allows us to build simpler legal principles which economise on information costs of the parties and adjudication costs, while taking advantage of superior information where it exists. Conversely, although economic theory focuses on deterrence in non-market torts cases, it seems likely that ex post selection of the law will not influence accident prevention one way or the other. Territorial approaches to these cases reduce inefficient forum choices, while their greater predictability favours risk averse parties who seek to make optimal insurance decisions.

This approach demonstrates our claims — it uses economic theory in a pragmatic way to formulate clearer ways of resolving conflicts cases. This approach is strongly transactional given its tendency to partition cases along transactional lines, and its preference for resolving choice of law problems by agreement.

Our approach to jurisdiction, and to choice of law issues where jurisdictional concerns are paramount, recognises that the law sometimes reflects the interests of the forum. State interests dominate the traditional equation between state sovereignty and jurisdiction, an approach which is at odds with the need to select efficient forums for litigation. In the twentieth century, common law systems have moved away from these approaches by liberalising the rules on the exercise of special jurisdiction, and by qualifying the forum's wider competence with more expansive approaches to declining jurisdiction. More contingent definitions of a plaintiff's right to continue in the forum are desirable because they correct inefficient forum choices, and because they may facilitate jurisdictional trade or settlement. We have shown how this might serve party interests. We have emphasised the importance of jurisdictional trade, both pre-contractually (by way of jurisdiction clauses) and at the time of disputes. Again, theory clarifies how courts can serve party welfare in jurisdictional problems, without becoming entangled in awkward metaphysical questions.

The remainder of this chapter looks forward into private international law's future, and how our theorisation may assist future problem solving.

Weak States, Strong Federations

Private international law is not limited to choice of law issues, but the existence of choice of law creates many of the most interesting problems. If choice of law problems were self-resolving, or if substantive law did not differ between states, only issues of jurisdiction would remain — and they would be less complex since plaintiffs would seek forums that minimised their costs, rather than award-maximising forums. The continued existence of such conflicts depends on the significance and momentum of two forces at work in society. One is globalisation. Given the amount of commerce and intercourse between nations, global solutions to problems are being urged. One thinks of environmental and trade problems first in this respect,[1] but there is substantial enterprise at work on unifying private law. Active here are the U.N. Commission on International Trade Law (UNCITRAL), the International Institute for the Unification of Private Law (UNIDROIT), the Hague Conference on Private International Law, the International Chamber of Commerce, and other regional bodies.[2]

The second force is a pressure towards localisation within sovereign states. This is obvious in federations. The desire for greater local power can be seen across the common law world. Examples include the Blair government's commitment to greater self-determination within the United Kingdom, the adoption in Australia of measures designed to reduce the so-called 'fiscal imbalance' between the states' taxing powers and their spending responsibilities, and political backlash in the United States against the federal government.

Sitting somewhere between globalisation and localisation, unitary states and the federal governments of federations have surrendered bits of their autonomy to form supranational federal systems operating at a range of levels. Substantive unification is often not the primary aim of these arrangements. Some are designed to decrease frictions in trade and intercourse, and the minimisation of bias in local laws and institutions. Good examples are the North American Free Trade Agreements and Closer Economic Relations between Australia and New Zealand.

These two forces — which one commentator has concatenated in an horrific neologism, 'glocalisation'[3] — are transforming the concept of the 'strong state' as it has been known for centuries following the Treaty of Westphalia.[4] Decades ago, commentators predicted the demise of federalism in the global age and the strengthening of federal governments. Only the latter were expected to rise to the demands of the coming age.[5]

But, in the event, the strong state has ceded sovereign power either to subordinate units in the polity, or to other sovereigns.

Explanations for these trends are difficult. The reasons for localisation are varied. Relevant factors include efficiency considerations and changes in interest group dynamics. Tom Ulen has suggested that the superiority of national solutions to ones provided by states may diminish over time, if there are changes in technology and social preferences.[6] For example, as technology changes, scale economies may be attainable at state level. Changed preferences, as regards, say, pollution, may decrease the need for a national solution to problems of cross-border externalities, since the likelihood of a negotiated solution may be higher. Supranational groupings may reflect these negotiated arrangements at a higher level. If that is so, the sub-national and supra-national movements are not inconsistent, but respond to different types of problems.

Public choice factors may also explain the different trends. On its face, public choice theory predicts the pre-emption of state authority by national law in all areas of shared competence, since federal regulators can earn rents from supplying such laws to those demanding them.[7] If there is one thing better than a deal cut at a national level, it is a deal cut at an international level. Paul Stephan demonstrates the influence of interest groups on various proposals for uniform laws.[8] The more extensive the deal, the harder it is to avoid. As we have said, legislative attempts to constrain choices of foreign law are constrained by the willingness of foreign forums to enforce the parties' agreements. If, however, the foreign forum's substantive law is the same, the mandatory rule's status is genuinely international and difficult to avoid.

On the other hand, public choice theorists have offered some reasons why federal regulators may defer to state law.[9] These include the existence of 'jurisdiction-specific' investments by interest groups in local regulation, which have low opportunity costs if federal law pre-empts state law. This is a standard explanation for Delaware's success in the market for corporate charters. State interest groups, such as the corporate bar in Delaware, have invested heavily in expertise concerning local law, and share their state's determination to ensure its pre-eminence.[10] State law may also be preferred where the solution that maximises political support varies between states; federal regulators may be better off doing nothing in these cases.

Approaches within federations may vary markedly. The American approach to federalism celebrates its competitive quality, for which substantial efficiency claims have been made. The Australian approach to federalism in private law has not been a competitive one, perhaps because of different incentives,[11] perhaps because cooperative solutions are easier to negotiate between six states than fifty. A dismal view has been taken of contractual choices of law as a device for avoiding local mandatory laws.[12]

One peculiar Australian development is the High Court's decision that provisions of the cross-vesting legislation, which conferred state jurisdiction on federal courts was unconstitutional.[13] This decision, based on a literal reading of the constitution, astonished many, as the legislation was acclaimed as a landmark in cooperative federalism, because it decreased litigation costs associated with conflictual issues. The decision is especially problematic in corporate and family law, and raises the spectre of complex jurisdictional questions. One of us has proposed a solution for corporate law by which corporations pre-commit to a forum by choosing a state of incorporation.[14]

Our theory of private international law has implications for federalism issues. First, quite apart from interest group effects, uniform law may impede efficient contracting. Even if rules are defaults, the lack of choice may restrict opting out because of learning externalities associated with contract terms.[15] In other words, different substantive laws create networks of observed contractual provisions, so that choice between those laws expands the effective domain of choice. Uniform laws should ideally be formulated in menu format, from which choices may be made, in a way that telescopes the pre-unification range of national laws.

We should not ignore the possibilities of races to the bottom which enable states to externalise the costs of their laws or of the productive operations within their territory. However, uniform law may not be the best solution to races to the bottom. Sometimes, a federal choice of law rule might be a preferable strategy. We do not want to ignore the advantages of uniform law, which may include decreases in search costs and solutions to coordination problems. Federal law may have particular attractions where contracting costs are not uniform. In these circumstances, parties with low transaction costs may contract around inefficient law choices or insist on other rights, but parties with high transaction costs may not. Examples include involuntary and trade creditors in bankruptcy situations.[16] There has been relatively little enthusiasm for state-based bankruptcy.[17] This may reflect expectations of the relative susceptibilities of federal and state law-making processes to undesirable interest group influences. State legislatures in the United States are not held in high regard.[18]

Second, a reinvigorated federal system must ascertain how it will handle choice of law problems since conflicts arise more frequently. Our analysis favours contracting parties' rights to choose the law applicable to their relation, in the absence of externality issues or contract process problems. Some constitutions have scope for the protection for these provisions.[19] On the other hand, as Kobayashi and Ribstein argue, states, initially at least, may have common incentives not to enforce choices of law and jurisdiction because they diminish the scope of political deals cut at the state level.[20] U.S. law took longer to accommodate contractual choices of law than English law did.

In torts cases, we argued that the rule in *Phillips v. Eyre* may have some appeal in cases involving foreign countries but little in intra-federation cases. Federations should enable lower costs and fewer errors in the application of 'foreign' law. Thus, a strict *lex loci delicti* rule is appealing where the *locus delicti* is clear. A similar argument seems to follow for jurisdiction cases. It may be preferable to use more rule-like jurisdiction principles. The costs of litigating in another state should often not be exorbitantly higher than in one's home state, given the existence of lower-cost travel and national law firms. It is therefore harder to justify flexibility in jurisdiction allocation on grounds of fairness to the defendant where the alternative forum is within the federation. Jurisdictional trade remains a means for correcting errors in the rules. This explains the approach in the Brussels and Lugano Conventions, but, once again, the imprecise Australian approach to cross-vesting seems anomalous. The imprecise U.S. approach that assesses a defendant's contacts with a forum to determine the existence of jurisdiction might also be improved by a rule-like approach.

Conflicts of Law and the Internet[21]

The Internet has aroused the interests of legal scholars like few other phenomena. A vast literature is growing up on the Internet's implications for intellectual property, securities, constitutional law, crime, and many other areas. Conflicts have not been ignored either.[22] Theorising the effect of the Internet on normative analyses of private international law resembles a scientific crisis for the established paradigms for research in international law, arguably interest analysis. It also gives an opportunity for alternative theories to demonstrate their superior analytical power.

A Scientific Crisis

Initially, scholars found the Internet so revolutionary that it overwhelmed existing legal and regulatory theories.[23] Some scholars were attracted to the borderless quality of the Internet, either for Utopian or libertarian reasons.[24] Others displayed much ingenuity in deriving regulatory solutions by analogy with such phenomena as the medieval *lex mercatoria*, maritime law, and Antarctica.[25] More recently, scholars have argued that although some new solutions may be needed, they can be accommodated within existing approaches to regulation and conflicts of law.[26]

A crucial issue that lies between the insurgents and the apologists is the relevance of territorial sovereignty. There is an argument that by providing such close links between citizens in different nations, the Internet renders national boundaries and distance irrelevant. It is typically unclear where resources are located, which places a veil of anonymity between the parties. The old dichotomy between territorial and extraterritorial laws dissolves.[27] Jack Goldsmith maintains that states are still capable of regulating Internet users within their jurisdiction, and enforcing their laws against those whose actions have effect there.[28] Although, in the latter case, the law will involve some element of extraterritoriality, the exorbitance of such laws is often substantially limited by the need for judgment enforcement. Goldsmith dismisses the argument that the international accessibility of the Internet may result in irreconcilable regulation if states assert their territorial sovereignty. In addition to the emerging technology which permits the control of content flows geographically, a content provider need only be concerned with laws that can be enforced against it. There is also some evidence that courts recognise the fact that their orders would externalise costs. In *Macquarie Bank Ltd v. Berg*, Simpson J. refused to grant an interlocutory injunction restraining the publication of allegedly defamatory material on the Internet. The judge acknowledged that a court had discretion to restrain conduct occurring outside the jurisdiction. However, Simpson J. recognised the impossibility of limiting the effect of the injunction to the state of New South Wales because of the international accessibility of the Internet. An injunction would 'superimpose the law of [this state] relating to defamation on every other state, territory and country of the world'.[29]

Instances of a more active approach can be found in recent American cases dealing with Internet jurisdiction. For example, in *Inset Systems, Inc. v. Instruction Set, Inc.*,[30] a court held in a trademark infringement case that it had jurisdiction over a company based out of the state. The basis of jurisdiction was that its Web site directed advertising into all states. That sufficed for the solicitation of business under the state long arm statute. The court held that since issues of state law arose the state had an interest in litigating the case. Other cases have also held that a Web site, which in-state residents may access, may suffice for the assertion of jurisdiction.[31] Sometimes, the nature of the Web site matters — placing information on the Internet may not suffice, but more interactive sites which permit the exchange of information may suffice.[32] Thus, in several cases, courts have held that they do *not* have jurisdiction simply because of the in-state accessibility of a site.[33] One court has stated that to hold otherwise would 'eviscerate the personal jurisdiction requirement as it currently exists'.[34]

The approach of U.S. courts to jurisdiction in cases involving contracts is also revealing. In *CompuServe, Inc. v. Patterson*,[35] a court found that Ohio had jurisdiction over a Texas resident. The defendant had registered shareware for sale through a facility on the plaintiff's server, based in Ohio. Ohio residents had bought it. The shareware agreement specified that it was governed by Ohio law. The defendant alleged a trademark infringement, leading the plaintiff to seek a declaratory judgment in Ohio. Of particular importance to the finding was the fact that the defendant had thought to market a product through the plaintiff's server. More problematic is the case of *Resuscitation Technologies, Inc. v. Continental Health Care Corp.*[36] The plaintiff, an Indiana corporation, advertised an investment opportunity on the Internet, to which the defendant responded. Despite extensive communication, a contract was not entered, leading the plaintiff to bring suit in Indiana. The defendant's claim that the court did not have jurisdiction was not upheld. It did not matter that the plaintiff, not the defendant, had initiated contact with its Internet advertisement. Negotiations were focused on Indiana. The parties' object was to transact business and develop the plaintiff's enterprise in Indiana. The court made the curiously parochial comment that social policies are furthered if an in-state business is allowed to seek capital without fearing that litigation arising from the suit will be in another jurisdiction.[37] A narrower approach is discernible in *Pres-Kap, Inc. v. System One, Direct Access, Inc.*[38] In that case, a corporation based in New York had used the database facility of the plaintiff located in Florida. A Florida court did not think it reasonable that a user could be haled into court wherever the database fortuitously happens to be located.

Will Existing Theories Survive?

What can we say about the durability of extant conflictual paradigms, in light of such approaches to the law? First, one's view of the cases should be informed by pragmatic considerations, since there is a risk of discerning non-existent grand principles. For example, the expansive tendencies in some of the cases may reflect their intellectual property origins. The Internet expands opportunities for the infringement of intellectual property rights. Expansive reading of long-arm statutes may be a necessary deterrent if those rights are to have any content.[39] However, there is a danger in analogising these cases to, say, a products liability suit arising out of a sale effected by the Internet. Typically, one would not want to deter product sales as one wants to deter trademark infringements. To bring out a theme of chapter 9, a consequential approach based on the nature of the dispute is superior to one which resolves issues in terms such as presence. The meaning of presence is likely to be exceedingly hard to ascertain in cases in which the Internet is involved. One pervasive problem is the lack of necessary correspondence between a business's head office and its domain name. A 'dot com' is as likely to be located in the Cayman Islands as in New York. Conventional approaches to defining presence will make the jurisdiction of a court underinclusive; attempts to update it, such as referring to solicitation of business, run the opposite risk.

Second, the Internet increases the proliferation of government interests by bringing the world much closer together. To return to the example of the products liability suit, the place where the buyer lives has an interest in seeing that its residents are compensated for injuries they suffer. The place where the vendor conducts (real) business has an interest in seeing that predictable, reconcilable standards apply to those conducting business within the forum. To these interested forums, we might add the places where each of the parties' Internet service providers carry on their business — or the place the relevant server is located, or the place the buyer connects if that is not his usual place of residence. A case might be made out for each. If so, the methodology for resolving true conflicts becomes more important. Currie's pro-forum method is even more solicitous of forum shopping when the number of interested states multiplies. Kramer's attempt to resolve interpretation issues purposively is compromised by the fact that only recent legislation will even *contemplate* Internet transactions.

Similar problems arise from attempts to condition the application of laws on concepts of fairness. The defendant's domicile remains fair to the defendant, but the obvious problem is the unfairness caused to the plaintiff if, as may often be true, the Internet obscures that domicile. The use of concepts of voice and exit is also complicated. For reasons already observed, exiting a state may practically require the exiting of the Internet.[40] In the twenty-first century, if not now, a party's vote in the democratic process may be vastly less important than his or her rights to communicate via, and to have access to, the Internet.[41] That form of communication may become the true yardstick of voice. Voice may then become practically circular in its implications for Internet cases.

Third, our arguments reinforce our approach to contracts statutes set out in chapter 4. The Internet facilitates the avoidance of at least some mandatory rules, given the ability for parties to relocate servers and businesses to jurisdictions in which the mandatory rule will not have effect. If this is so, courts should not read down choice of law or forum agreements without clear legislative imprimatur: the long run benefits from doing so are minimal.

Policy and Pragmatism in Internet Conflicts

The Internet lends itself well to the resolution of choice of law and jurisdiction problems by contract. Some of the jurisdiction cases we considered above show that on-line contracts provide for applicable law and forum.[42] A number of scholars addressing the relationship between intellectual property rights and contracts in a digitised Internet environment have commented favourably on the capacity of contracts to solve the dilemmas created in this environment.[43] The Internet permits contracts between the owner of the rights and users where these contracts were never previously possible.

The usual objections to such contracts can be made — that information costs are high, that consumers lack the sophistication to understand them, and so on. But there may be reason to think that these concerns are weaker, not stronger. The availability of search engines increases the scope for comparison shopping, and thus competition on price and non-price terms. Web sites which enable comparison shopping are thriving. The future may see the development of Web sites (perhaps by consumer organisations) providing information on relevant features of national laws and of the costs of and delays in litigation in a country's courts that enable consumers to make more informed contracting decisions. Sellers and other service providers may provide hypertext links to such sites as a means of enabling customers to verify the fairness of the terms offered. Internet service providers may seek to differentiate themselves from competitors by providing that information to their members. As information costs fall, we may find that sellers provide the terms that customers value most highly, as economists have always claimed they would.[44]

The principal difficulty is ascertaining the applicable procedure-settling law. As we explained in chapter 3, this is necessary to ascertain issues of form and notice. This is particularly problematic in Internet contexts, because of unique issues of form, such as recognition of digital signatures. Yet, the conventional means adapted to procedure-settling are difficult to use, since they refer to the place of contracting. The place of contracting is not obvious. It seems to require a rule which can function as a focal point. In chapters 3 and 5, we catalogued the faults of alternative bases for setting choice of law defaults. These hold equally for Internet contracts. For example, simple rules are likely to be even more unrepresentative given the variety of contracts that may be formed. The problem with more tailored methods is that the information a court might use for optimal tailoring may not be observable at the time of contracting, given the anonymity of aspects of the Internet. A buyer may not know where the seller's principal placer of business is since domain names are no guide to physical loci. If this is so, the applicable law will be unclear. This will have adverse affects on the operation of product markets and may protract litigation. Our advocacy of (relatively) complex rules, decided on the basis of contract types, is affected by similar problems. Where the place of a transaction is implicated in a choice of law rule, as for product sales, the Internet may preclude the use of such factors if those factors are not common knowledge.

In chapter 9, we considered a similar problem of jurisdiction rules for contracts with corporations. We suggested the possibility of using a default that would be adverse to the party whose function it would typically be to supply the standard form terms of an agreement. Such a default might compel that party to propose a specific term. In much the same way, for choice of law questions, one might supplement our preferred rules with a further proviso that if the information required for the choice of law rule is not common knowledge between the parties,[45] the plaintiff could invoke the law of his place of domicile. This would induce term offerors to specify the place of contracting or to offer explicit choice of law clauses. The rule functions as a tax on the party in the best position to fill a gap in contracts, the judicial resolution of which will involve high error costs.

Similar approaches might be used to resolve forum questions. Jurisdiction problems are, however, harder than choice of law questions. The fundamental problem is that the Internet exacerbates the disparity between the costs of entering transactions and the costs of litigating them. The former decrease; the latter do not. The greater the capacity the Internet has to bring parties together, the greater the risk that disputes require high litigation costs for at least one of the parties. For instance, a forum clause or a jurisdiction rule directing litigation in Connecticut may be unproblematic when most custom comes from New England, but not where the custom is global. Thus, the Internet creates greater heterogeneity in forum preferences amongst contracting parties. Of itself, this is not a problem. Rational parties will assess their costs of litigating in the selected forum, discounted by the probability of litigation. That will lead them to choose providers with lower-cost forum choices. But a great deal depends on the ability of customers to make realistic estimates of their litigation costs and the probability of suit.

Several authors have described the nascence of Internet-based arbitration as a possible solution to these problems.[46] This is an appealing prospect intuitively, and one likely to reinforce the tendency towards party interests and away from government interests in choice of law.[47] Its ultimate success remains to be seen. Arbitration is a good example of a network good — its attractiveness to contracting parties depends on the extent to which others make use of it. Wider use will establish the quality of arbitration, the norms which underlie it, and so on. Only the future will provide these answers. Much also depends on the extent to which Internet-based arbitral awards are capable of being enforced.

The logical question, in light of the earlier part of this chapter, is the relevance of federalism and globalisation to the responsibility for regulating the Internet. An enduring feature of the literature is the apparent need for unified solutions, international ones being preferred to national ones, national ones being preferred to state ones.[48] This conclusion needs to be seen in context. The Internet raises a number of unique issues. Appropriate procedural rules are an example. Some new substantive areas of law have arisen, such as intellectual property rights in digitised works, domain names, or issues regarding the administration of the Internet itself.[49] But that is far from exhausting the stock of legal rules. Much of the law of property and obligations applies as well to Internet transactions as to any other. Thus, a claim that the Internet compels harmonisation of the law is insupportable. As we have said, there is much value in diversity.

The primary contributions harmonisation may make are, first, the provision of the sorts of rules for areas where substance is less important than coordination. These include the procedural rules that apply to form and disclosure on Internet transactions. They also include evidentiary principles (for instance, the admission to proof of matter located on the Internet) and other presumptions used in private law, such as ascertaining the *situs* of relevant property and the places where contracts are formed. Second, consistency in approaches to choice of law is also important. The penalty default we have outlined depends, as we said in chapter 3, on substantial uniformity if it is to have effect. Third, a range of technological issues may need harmonisation, but these are outside the parameters of this book. Fourth, there is substantial room for cooperation in developing comparisons between the laws and procedure of different jurisdiction to facilitate the reduction of information costs for parties needing to make comparisons between different contract terms. This approach to the Internet fits well with our discussions of contracts, torts, and property, suggesting the superiority of our approach in the face of this apparent crisis.

Conclusion

The twentieth century has seen great changes in the relations between states, and between states and individuals. At one level, competition has diminished. The collapse of ideology has seen greater cooperation between states in place of armed conflict, and the rise of the modern welfare state has taken the sharp edge off market incentives. At another level, competition is not hostile to cooperation, since much of the economic agenda in globalisation has been the enhancement of markets in world trade, and since many domestic institutions respond to market forces.

Informed choice is at the core of both competition and cooperation. We have demonstrated the value of choice in this work. We have emphasised how private international law has substantially preserved choice for citizens and firms, so serving liberal and economic objectives. In so doing, it serves both competitive and cooperative purposes. Scholars however have not done half as well, preferring conceptualism to pragmatism, erring in the specification of the appropriate unit of analysis, and neglecting or obfuscating the consequences of the rules they advocate. If the conflict of laws has a future, much of its scholarship does not. We hope that this book foreshadows modes of future scholarship. Our theory has explained the major trends in private international law, such as the endorsement of party autonomy, the movement from simple rules to complexity, contingent allocations of jurisdiction, and the development of exceptions to major rules, such as *Phillips v. Eyre* and *Moçambique*. Thus, we stake a claim to explain much current doctrine, while demonstrating various instances in which either excessive conceptualism or goals inconsistent with efficiency caused the doctrine to take undesirable paths. Our analysis makes clear normative claims, which are susceptible of formal proof or empirical tests. Our analysis focuses on the transaction as the crucial unit for analysis, rather than on the metaphysical apparatus on which other theories build. Only experience will tell us whether our approach is sound or not, but as pragmatists, we do not ask for any more.

Notes

1. Chapter 7 shows that environmental problems are by no means irrelevant to private international law.
2. For an analysis of these bodies, see Stephan (1997, 1999).
3. Courchene (1993).
4. Cf. Krasner (1999).
5. See, e.g., Laski (1939).
6. Ulen (1998).
7. Ibid., 939.
8. Stephan (1999).
9. Macey (1990).
10. Macey and Miller (1987), Romano (1985).
11. In corporate law, Australia has no franchise tax which deflates competition for incorporations (Whincop 1999a).
12. *Kay's Leasing Corp. Pty Ltd v. Fletcher* (1964) 116 C.L.R. 124.
13. *Re Wakim; ex parte McNally; Re Wakim; ex parte Darvall; Re Brown; ex parte Amann; Spinks v. Prentice* (1999) 31 A.C.S.R. 99.
14. Whincop (1999c).
15. Klausner (1995), Kahan and Klausner (1997). See chapter 3, p. 37 *supra*.
16. We use a similar argument to justify territoriality in multinational bankruptcies: see chapter 9, p. 182 *supra*.
17. Skeel (1994). Cf. Rasmussen and Thomas (1999).
18. Mashaw (1997, p. 60).
19. See, e.g., Constitution of the United States, art. I, s. 10, Butler and Ribstein (1995, ch. 2).
20. Kobayashi and Ribstein (1999).

21. This section is based on ideas in Whincop (1999d). We have resisted the desire to coin further neologisms and call this section 'Cyberconflicts'.
22. See, e.g., Burnstein (1996), Goldsmith (1998a), Gooch (1998), Reindl (1998), Salbu (1998), Wille (1998), Wilske and Schiller (1997).
23. Geist (1998) demonstrates a maturation effect in Internet scholarship.
24. See, e.g., Hardy (1994), Johnson and Post (1996).
25. See, e.g., Burnstein (1996), Mefford (1997).
26. Goldsmith (1998), Reindl (1998). Although not explicitly concerned with the Internet, see also Bradley (1997).
27. Burnstein (1996), Gibbons (1997), Johnson and Post (1996).
28. Goldsmith (1998a).
29. [1999] N.S.W.S.C. 526 § 14.
30. 937 F. Supp. 161 (D. Conn. 1996).
31. The following cases involve trademark infringements: *Heroes, Inc. v. Heroes Foundation*, 958 F. Supp. 1 (D.D.C. 1996), *Maritz, Inc. v. Cybergold, Inc.*, 947 F. Supp. 1328 (E.D. Mo. 1996), *Zippo Manufacturing Co. v. Zippo Dot Com, Inc.*, 952 F. Supp. 1119 (W.D. Pa. 1997). For discussion, see Wilske and Schiller (1997). See also *Playboy Enterprises, Inc. v. Chuckleberry Publishing, Inc.*, 939 F. Supp. 1032 (S.D.N.Y. 1996).
32. *Zippo Manufacturing Co.*, 952 F. Supp. 1119, 1124.
33. See, e.g., *I.D.S. Life Ins. Co. v. Sun America, Inc.*, 958 F. Supp. 1258 (N.D. Ill. 1997), *McDonough v. Fallon McElligott, Inc.*, 40 U.S.P.Q.2d 1826 (S.D. Cal. 1996), *Bensusan Restaurant Corp. v. King*, 937 F. Supp. 295 (S.D.N.Y. 1996).
34. *McDonough*, 40 U.S.P.Q.2d 1826, p. 1828.
35. 89 F.3d 1257 (6th Cir. 1996).
36. 1997 WL 148567 (S.D. Ind. 1997).
37. Ibid. *5.
38. 636 So.2d 1351 (Fla. Dist. Ct. App. 1994).
39. Reindl (1998).
40. Cf. Goldsmith (1998b).
41. Nelson Mandela has observed that '[i]n the 21st century, the right to communicate will be the main human right'. (Quoted in Selin 1996, p. 365.)
42. See, e.g., *CompuServe, Inc. v. Patterson*, 89 F.3d 1257 (6th Cir. 1996), Almaguer and Baggott (1998, p. 740).
43. See, e.g., Hardy (1995), Merges (1996, 1997), O'Rourke (1997). Cf. Cohen (1998).
44. Katz (1990a), A. Schwartz (1988).
45. A matter is not common knowledge simply because it is known to both parties. Something is common knowledge only if both parties know the information, each party knows that the other party knows the information, each party knows that the other party knows that each party knows the information, and so on: Ayres and Nalebuff (1997). Here, the place of contracting would only be

common knowledge if the information was explicitly disclosed or formed part of the contract.

46. See generally Almaguer and Baggott (1998), Gibbons (1997, pp. 532-539), Katsch (1996), Mefford (1997).
47. Ware (1999).
48. See generally Salbu (1998).
49. Geist (1998).

Bibliography

Alchian, A.A. (1965), 'Some Economics of Property Rights', *Il Politico*, **30**, 816-829.

Alchian, A.A. (1975), 'Some Implications of Recognition of Property Right Transaction Costs', Economics Department, U.C.L.A., discussion paper.

Alden, R.C. (1987), 'Modernizing the Situs Rule for Real Property Conflicts', *Texas Law Review*, **65**, 585-633 (student author).

Almaguer, A.E. and Baggott, R.W. III (1998), 'Shaping New Legal Frontiers: Dispute Resolution for the Internet', *Ohio State Journal on Dispute Resolution*, **13**, 711-748.

Amar, A.R. (1989), 'Law Story', *Harvard Law Review*, **102**, 688-720.

American Law Institute (1994), *Complex Litigation Project: Statutory Recommendations and Analysis*, American Law Institute, Philadelphia.

Anton, A.E. (1956), 'The Introduction into English Practice of Continental Theories on the Conflict of Laws,' *International and Comparative Law Quarterly*, **5**, 534-541.

Atiyah, P. (1979), *The Rise and Fall of Freedom of Contract*, Clarendon Press, Oxford.

Australian Law Reform Commission (1992), Report No 58: *Choice of Law*, Australian Law Reform Commission, Sydney.

Ayres, I. (1992), 'Making a Difference: The Contractual Contributions of Easterbrook and Fischel', *University of Chicago Law Review*, **59**, 1391-1420.

Ayres, I. (1993), 'Preliminary Thoughts on Optimal Tailoring of Contractual Rules', *Southern California Interdisciplinary Law Journal*, **3**, 1-20.

Ayres, I. (1998), 'Protecting Property with Puts', *Valparaiso University Law Review*, **32**, 793-831.

Ayres, I. and Balkin, J.M. (1996), 'Legal Entitlements as Auctions: Property Rules, Liability Rules, and Beyond', *Yale Law Journal*, **106**, 703-750.

Ayres, I. and Gertner, R. (1989), 'Filling Gaps in Incomplete Contracts: An Economic Theory of Default Rules', *Yale Law Journal*, **99**, 87-130.

Ayres, I. and Gertner, R. (1992), 'Strategic Contractual Inefficiency and the Optimal Choice of Legal Rules', *Yale Law Journal*, **101**, 729-773.

Ayres, I. and Nalebuff, B. (1997), 'Common Knowledge As A Barrier to Negotiation', *UCLA Law Review*, **44**, 1631-1659.

Ayres, I. and Talley, E. (1995a), 'Solomonic Bargaining: Dividing an Entitlement to Facilitate Coasean Trade', *Yale Law Journal*, **104**, 1027-1117.

Ayres, I. and Talley, E. (1995b), 'Distinguishing Between Consensual and Nonconsensual Advantages of Liability Rules', *Yale Law Journal*, **105** 235-253.

Baird, D., Gertner, R. and Picker, R. (1995), *Game Theory and the Law*, Harvard University Press, Cambridge.

Baxter, W.F. (1963), 'Choice of Law and the Federal System', *Stanford Law Review*, **16**, 1-42.

Beale, J. (1935), *A Treatise on the Conflict of Laws*, Baker, Voorhis & Co., New York.

Beales, H., Craswell, R. and Salop, S.C. (1981), 'The Efficient Regulation of Consumer Information', *Journal of Law & Economics*, **24**, 491-539.

Bebchuk, L.A. (1984), 'Litigation and Settlement under Imperfect Information', *Rand Journal of Economics*, **15**, 404-415.

Bebchuk, L.A. (1988), 'Suing Solely to Extract a Settlement Offer', *Journal of Legal Studies*, **17**, 437-450.

Bebchuk, L.A. (1989), 'Limiting Contractual Freedom in Corporate Law: The Desirable Constraints on Charter Amendments', *Harvard Law Review*, **102**, 1820-1860.

Bebchuk, L.A. and Shavell, S. (1991), 'Information and the Scope of Liability for Breach of Contract: The Rule of Hadley v. Baxendale', *Journal of Law, Economics & Organization*, **7**, 284-312.

Becker, G.S. (1983), 'A Theory of Competition Among Pressure Groups for Political Influence', *Quarterly Journal of Economics*, **98**, 371-400.

Bell, A.S. (1995), 'The Negative Declaration in Transnational Litigation', *Law Quarterly Review*, **111**, 674-695.

Bell, A.S. (1996), 'Jurisdiction and Arbitration Agreements in Transnational Contracts, Part II', *Journal of Contract Law*, **10**, 97-119.

Bell, A.S. and Gleeson, J. (1997), 'The Anti-Suit Injunction', *Australian Law Journal*, **71**, 955-975.

Bell, P.W. (1990), 'Analyzing Tort Law: The Flawed Promise of Neocontract', *Minnesota Law Review*, **74**, 1177-1249.

Benjamin, J. (1998), 'Determining the Situs of Interests in Immobilised Securities', *International & Comparative Law Quarterly*, **47**, 923-934.

Berle, A. and Means, G. (1932), *The Modern Corporation and Private Property*, Macmillan, New York.

Bermann, G.A. (1990), 'The Use of Anti-Suit Injunctions in International Litigation', *Columbia Journal of Transnational Law*, **28**, 589-631.

Bernstein, L. (1996), 'Merchant Law in a Merchant Court: Rethinking the Code's Search for Immanent Business Norms', *University of Pennsylvania Law Review*, **144**, 1765-1821.

Black, B.S. (1990), 'Is Corporate Law Trivial?: A Political and Economic Analysis', *Northwestern University Law Review*, **84**, 542-597.

Bliesener, D.H. (1994), 'Fairness and Choice of Law: A Critique of the Political Rights-Based Approach to the Conflict of Laws', *American Journal of Comparative Law*, **42**, 687-710.

Blumberg, P. (1983), *The Law of Corporate Groups: Procedural Problems in the Law of Parent and Subsidiary Corporations*, Little Brown, Boston.

Borchers, P.J. (1997), 'Back to the Past: Anti-Pragmatism in American Conflicts Law', *Mercer Law Review*, **48**, 721-726.

Bradley, C.A. (1997), 'Territorial Intellectual Property Rights in an Age of Globalism', *Virginia Journal of International Law*, **37**, 505-585.

Brand, R.A. (1998), 'Tort Jurisdiction in a Multilateral Convention: The Lessons of the Due Process Clause and the Brussels Convention', *Brooklyn Journal of International Law*, **24**, 125-155.

Bratton, W.W. (1989), 'The "Nexus of Contracts" Corporation: A Critical Appraisal', *Cornell Law Review*, **74**, 407-465.

Briggs, A. (1990), 'The Formation of International Contracts', *Lloyds Maritime & Comparative Law Quarterly*, 192-204.

Briggs, A. (1997), 'The Unrestrained Reach of an Anti-Suit Injunction: A Pause for Thought', *Lloyds Maritime & Comparative Law Quarterly*, 90-102.

Brilmayer, L. (1980a), 'Interest Analysis and the Myth of Legislative Intent', *Michigan Law Review*, **78**, 392-431.

Brilmayer, L. (1980b), 'How Contacts Count: Due Process Limitations on State Court Jurisdiction', *Supreme Court Review*, 77-120.

Brilmayer, L. (1985), 'Governmental Interest Analysis: A House Without Foundations', *Ohio State Law Journal*, **46**, 459-481.

Brilmayer, L. (1989), 'Rights, Fairness, and Choice of Law', *Yale Law Journal*, **98**, 1277-1319.

Brilmayer, L. (1995), *Conflict of Laws*, 2nd ed., Little Brown, Boston.

Brilmayer, L., Haverkamp, J., Logan, B., Lynch, L., Neuwirth, S. and O'Brien, J. (1987), 'A General Look at General Jurisdiction', *Texas Law Review*, **66**, 723-783.

Brilmayer, L. and Paisley, K. (1986), 'Personal Jurisdiction and Substantive Legal Relations: Corporations, Conspiracies, and Agency', *California Law Review*, **74**, 1-40.

Brown, D.G. (1992), 'Jurisdiction Over a Corporation on the Basis of the Contacts of an Affiliated Corporation: Do You Have to Pierce the Corporate Veil' *Cincinnati Law Review*, **61**, 595-622.

Buckley, F.H. (ed) (1999), *The Fall and Rise of Freedom of Contract*, Duke University Press, Durham.

Buckley, F.H. and Ribstein, L.E. (2000), 'Calling a Truce in the Marriage Wars, *University of Illinois Law Review*, **75**, forthcoming.

Burnstein, M.R. (1996), 'Conflicts on the Net: Choice of Law in Transnational Cyberspace', *Vanderbilt Journal of Transnational Law*, **29**, 75-116.

Butler, H.D. and Ribstein, L.E. (1995), *The Corporation and the Constitution*, A.E.I. Press, Washington.

Calabresi, G. and Melamed, A.D. (1972), 'Property Rules, Liability Rules, and Inalienability: One View of the Cathedral', *Harvard Law Review*, **85**, 1089-1128.

Carrington, P.D. and Haagen, P.H. (1996), 'Contract and Jurisdiction', *Supreme Court Review*, 331-402.

Castel, J.-G. (1994), *Canadian Conflict of Laws*, 3rd ed., Butterworths, Toronto.

Cavers, D.F. (1933), 'A Critique of the Choice of Law Problem', *Harvard Law Review*, **47**, 171-208.

Cavers, D.F. (1965), *The Choice of Law Process*, University of Michigan Press, Ann Arbor.

Charny, D. (1991), 'Competition among Jurisdictions in Formulating Corporate Law Rules: An American Perspective on the "Race to the Bottom" in the European Communities', *Harvard International Law Journal*, **31**, 423-456.

Cheshire, G.C. (1965), *Private International Law*, 7th ed., Butterworths, London.

Choi, S.J. and Guzman, A.T. (1998), 'Portable Reciprocity: Rethinking the Reach of Securities Laws', *Southern California Law Review*, **71**, 903-951.

Clarkson, C.M.V. and Hill, J. (1997), *Jaffey on the Conflict of Laws*, Butterworths, London.

Coase, R.H. (1937), 'The Nature of the Firm', *Economica*, **4**, 386-405.
Coase, R.H. (1960), 'The Problem of Social Cost', *Journal of Law & Economics*, **3**, 1-41.
Coffee, J.C. (1986), 'Understanding The Plaintiff's Attorney: The Implications Of Economic Theory For Private Enforcement Of Law Through Class And Derivative Actions', *Columbia Law Review*, **86**, 669-727.
Cohen, J.E. (1998), 'Lochner in Cyberspace: The New Economic Orthodoxy of "Rights Management"', *Michigan Law Review*, **97**, 462-563.
Coleman, J. (1992), *Risks and Wrongs*, Cambridge University Press, New York.
Coleman, J., Heckathorn, D. and Maser, S. (1989), 'A Bargaining Theory Approach to Default Provisions and Disclosure Rules in Contract Law', *Harvard Journal of Legal & Public Policy*, **12**, 639-709.
Collins, L. (ed) (1993), *Dicey and Morris on the Conflict of Laws*, 12th ed., Sweet & Maxwell, London.
Collins, L. (1992), 'Negative Declarations and the Brussels Declaration', *Law Quarterly Review*, **109**, 545-549.
Cook, W.W. (1933), '"Substance" and "Procedure" in the Conflict of Laws', *Yale Law Journal*, **42**, 333-358.
Cook, W.W. (1942), *The Logical and Legal Basis of the Conflict of Laws*, Harvard University Press, Cambridge.
Cooter, R.D. (1996), 'Decentralized Law for a Complex Economy: The Structural Approach to Adjudicating the New Law Merchant', *University of Pennsylvania Law Review*, **144**, 1643-1696.
Cooter, R.D. and Rubinfeld, D.L. (1989), 'Economic Analysis of Legal Disputes and Their Resolution', *Journal of Economic Literature*, **27**, 1067-1097.
Courchene, T. (1993), 'Glocalisation, Institutional Evolution and the Australian Federation' in Galligan, B. (ed), *Federalism and the Economy: International, National and State Issues*, Federalism Research Centre, Australian National University, Canberra.
Craswell, R. (1991), 'Passing On the Costs of Legal Rules: Efficiency and Distribution in Buyer-Seller Relationships', *Stanford Law Review*, **43**, 361-398.
Crawford, V.P. (1982), 'A Theory of Disagreement in Bargaining', *Econometrica*, **50**, 607-637.

Croley, S.P. and Hanson, J.D. (1993), 'Rescuing the Revolution: The Revived Case for Enterprise Liability', *Michigan Law Review*, **91**, 683-797.

Currie, B. (1963), *Selected Essays on the Conflict of Laws*, Duke University Press, Durham.

Dane, P. (1987), 'Vested Rights, "Vestedness," and Choice of Law', *Yale Law Journal*, **96**, 1191-1275.

Daniels, R.J. (1991), 'Should Provinces Compete? The Case for a Competitive Corporate Law Market', *McGill Law Journal*, **36**, 130-190.

Davies, M. (1995), 'Too Little Imagination or Too Much? *Phillips v. Eyre* Revisited Yet Again', *Torts Law Journal*, **3**, 273-298.

Davies, M. (1996), 'What Exactly is the Australian Choice of Law Rule in Torts Cases?', *Australian Law Journal*, **70**, 711-722.

Delaume, G.R. (1981), 'The European Convention on the Law Applicable to Contractual Obligations: Why a Convention?', *Virginia Journal of International Law*, **22**, 105-121.

Demsetz, H. (1967), 'Towards a Theory of Property Rights', *American Economic Review*, **57**, 347-359.

Demsetz, H. (1972), 'Wealth Distribution and the Ownership of Rights', *Journal of Legal Studies*, **1**, 223-232.

Dicey, A.V. (1896), *Digest of the Law of England with Reference to the Conflict of Laws*, Stevens and Sons, London.

Diggins, J.P. (1994), *The Promise of Pragmatism: Modernism and the Crisis of Knowledge and Authority*, University of Chicago Press, Chicago.

Diver, C. (1983), 'The Optimal Precision of Administrative Rules', *Yale Law Journal*, **93**, 65-109.

Donohue, J.J., III (1991), 'Opting for the British Rule, or if Posner and Shavell Can't Remember the Coase Theorem, Who Will?', *Harvard Law Review*, **104**, 1093-1119.

Downes, A. (1957), *An Economic Theory of Democracy*, Harper, New York.

Drury, R.R. (1998), 'The Regulation and Recognition of Foreign Corporations: Responses to the "Delaware Syndrome"', *Cambridge Law Journal*, **57**, 165-194.

Dutson, S. (1996a), 'The Territorial Application of Statutes', *Monash University Law Review*, **22**, 69-89.

Dutson, S. (1996b), 'International Products Liability Litigation: The Territorial Application of Part VA of the *Trade Practices Act* 1974 (Cth) and Part I of the *Consumer Protection Act* 1987 (UK)', *Monash University Law Review,* **22**, 244-288.

Dworkin, R.M. (1967), 'The Model of Rules', *University of Chicago Law Review*, **35**, 14-46.

Dworkin, R.M. (1980), 'Is Wealth a Value?', *Journal of Legal Studies*, **9**, 191-226.

Dworkin, R.M. (1991), 'Pragmatism, Right Answers and True Banality' in Brint, M. and Weaver, W. (eds), *Pragmatism in Law and Society*, Westview Press, Boulder.

Easterbrook, F.H. (1983), 'Statutes' Domains', *University of Chicago Law Review*, **50**, 533-552.

Easterbrook, F.H. (1984), 'The Supreme Court, 1983 Term: The Court and the Economic System', *Harvard Law Review*, **98**, 4-60.

Easterbrook, F.H. (1985), 'Method, Result, and Authority: A Reply', *Harvard Law Review*, **98**, 622-629.

Easterbrook, F.H. and Fischel, D.R. (1984), 'Mandatory Disclosure and the Protection of Investors', *Virginia Law Review*, **70**, 669-715.

Easterbrook, F.H. and Fischel, D.R. (1991), *The Economic Structure of Corporate Law*, Harvard University Press, Cambridge.

Edwards, W. and Von Winterfeldt, D. (1986), 'Cognitive Illusions and Their Implications for the Law', *Southern California Law Review*, **59**, 225-276.

Ehrenzweig, A.A. (1951), *Negligence Without Fault*, University of California Press, Berkeley.

Ehrenzweig, A.A. (1956), 'The Transient Rule of Personal Jurisdiction: The "Power" Myth and Forum Conveniens', *Yale Law Journal*, **65**, 289-314.

Ehrenzweig, A.A. (1960), 'The Lex Fori — Basic Rule in the Conflict of Laws', *Michigan Law Review*, **58**, 637-688.

Ehrenzweig, A.A. (1962), *A Treatise on the Conflict of Laws*, West Publishing, St. Paul.

Ehrlich, I. and Posner, R.A. (1974), 'An Economic Analysis of Legal Rulemaking', *Journal of Legal Studies*, **3**, 257-282.

Eisenberg, M.A. (1995), 'The Limits of Cognition and the Limits of Contract', *Stanford Law Review*, **47**, 211-259.

Eisenberg, T. and LoPucki, L.M. (1998), 'Shopping for Judges: An Empirical Study of Venue Choice in the Bankruptcy Reorganization of Large, Publicly Held Companies', *Cornell Law Review*, **84**, 967-1003.

Ellickson, R.C. (1989), 'Bringing Culture and Human Frailty to Rational Actors: A Critique of Classical Law and Economics', *Chicago–Kent Law Review*, **65**, 23-55.

Epstein, R.A. (1973), 'A Theory of Strict Liability', *Journal of Legal Studies*, **2**, 151-204.

Epstein, R.A. (1988), 'The Political Economy of Product Liability Reform', *American Economic Review*, **78**, 311-315.

Epstein, R.A. (1995), *Simple Rules for a Complex World*, Harvard University Press, Cambridge.

Epstein, R.A. (1997), 'A Clear View of *The Cathedral*: The Dominance of Property Rules', *Yale Law Journal*, **106**, 2091-2120.

Eskridge, W.N. (1990), 'The New Textualism', *UCLA Law Review*, **37**, 621-691.

Fama, E.F. (1980), 'Agency Problems and the Theory of the Firm', *Journal of Political Economy*, **88**, 288-307.

Fama, E.F. and Jensen, M.C. (1983a), 'Separation of Ownership and Control', *Journal of Law & Economics*, **26**, 301-325.

Fama, E.F. and Jensen, M.C. (1983b), 'Agency Problems and Residual Claims', *Journal of Law & Economics*, **26**, 327-349.

Farrell, J. (1987), 'Information and the Coase Theorem', *Journal of Economic Perspectives*, **1**, 113-129.

Fawcett, J.J. (1982), 'Is American Governmental Interest Analysis the Solution to English Tort Choice of Law Problems?', *International & Comparative Law Quarterly*, **31**, 150-166.

Fawcett, J.J. (1988), 'A New Approach to Jurisdiction over Companies in Private International Law', *International & Comparative Law Quarterly*, **37**, 645-667.

Fawcett, J.J. (1990), 'Evasion of Law and Mandatory Rules in Private International Law', *Cambridge Law Journal*, 44-62.

Fawcett, J.J. (1995), *Declining Jurisdiction in Private International Law*, Clarendon Press, Oxford.

Fentiman, R. (1992), 'Foreign Law in English Courts', *Law Quarterly Review*, **108**, 142-156.

Fletcher, G.P. (1972), 'Fairness and Utility in Tort Theory', *Harvard Law Review*, **85**, 537-573.

Forsyth, C. (1998), 'Characterisation Revisited: An Essay in the Theory and Practice of the English Conflict of Laws', *Law Quarterly Review*, **114**, 141-161.

Fox, M. (1999), 'Retaining Mandatory Securities Disclosure: Why Issuer Choice is not Investor Empowerment', *Virginia Law Review*, **85**, 1335-1419.

Friedman, L. (1965), *Contract Law in America: a Social and Economic Case Study*, University of Wisconsin Press, Madison.

Friedman, M. (1953), 'The Methodology of Positive Economics', in Friedman, M. (ed), *Essays in Positive Economics*, University of Chicago Press, Chicago.

Fruehwald, S. (1996), 'A Multilateralist Method of Choice of Law', *Kentucky Law Journal*, **85**, 347-403.

Fudenberg, D. and Tirole, J. (1991), *Game Theory*, MIT Press, Cambridge.

Fuller, L. (1941), 'Consideration and Form', *Columbia Law Review*, **41**, 799-824.

Garner, M. (1989), 'Formation of International Contracts — Finding the Right Choice of Law Rule', *Australian Law Journal*, **63**, 751-760.

Garnett, R. (1999), 'Stay of Proceedings in Australia: A "Clearly Inappropriate" Test?', *Melbourne University Law Review*, **23**, 30-64.

Geist, M.A. (1998), 'The Reality of Bytes: Regulating Economic Activity in the Age of the Internet', *Washington Law Review*, **73**, 521-574.

Geistfeld, M. (1994), 'The Political Economy of Neocontractual Proposals for Products Liability Reform', *Texas Law Review*, **72**, 803-847.

Gergen, M. (1988), 'Equality and the Conflict of Laws', *Iowa Law Review*, **73**, 893-934.

Gibbons, L.J. (1997), 'No Regulation, Government Regulation, or Self-Regulation: Social Enforcement or Social Contracting for Governance in Cyberspace', *Cornell Journal of Law and Public Policy*, **6**, 475-551.

Gilmore, G. (1974), *The Death of Contract*, Ohio State University Press, Columbus.

Gilson, R. and Kraakman, R. (1984), 'The Mechanisms of Market Efficiency', *Virginia Law Review*, **70**, 549-644.

Goetz, C.J. and Scott, R.E. (1985), 'The Limits of Expanded Choice: An Analysis of the Interactions Between Express and Implied Contract Terms', *California Law Review*, **73**, 261-322.

Goldsmith, J.L. III (1989), 'Interest Analysis Applied to Corporations: The Unprincipled Use of a Choice of Law Method', *Yale Law Journal*, **98**, 597-616.

Goldsmith, J.L. III (1998a), 'The Internet and the Abiding Significance of Territorial Sovereignty', *Indiana Journal of Global Legal Studies*, **5**, 475-491.

Goldsmith, J.L. III (1998b), 'Against Cyberanarchy', *University of Chicago Law Review*, **65**, 1199-1250.

Gooch, J.C. (1998), 'The Internet, Personal Jurisdiction, and the Federal Long-Arm Statute: Rethinking the Concept of Jurisdiction', *Arizona Journal of International and Comparative Law*, **15**, 635-657.

Gordon, J.N. (1989), 'The Mandatory Structure of Corporate Law', *Columbia Law Review*, **89**, 1549-1598.

Gordon, J.N. and Kornhauser, L.A. (1985), 'Efficient Markets, Costly Information and Securities Research', *New York University Law Review*, **60**, 761-849.

Graveson, R.H. (1962), 'Philosophical Aspects of the English Conflict of Laws', *Law Quarterly Review*, **78**, 337-370.

Guzman, A.T. (2000), 'Choice of Law: New Foundations', unpublished paper.

Haddock, D.D., Macey, J.R., and McChesney, F.S. (1987), 'Property Rights in Assets and Resistance to Tender Offers', *Virginia Law Review*, **73**, 701-746.

Hadfield, G. (1990), 'Problematic Relations: Franchising and the Law of Incomplete Contracts', *Stanford Law Review*, **42**, 927-992.

Hadfield, G. (1994), 'Judicial Competence and the Interpretation of Incomplete Contracts', *Journal of Legal Studies,* **23**, 159-184.

Hansmann, H. and Kraakman, R. (1991), 'Towards Unlimited Shareholder Liability for Corporate Torts', *Yale Law Journal*, **100**, 1879-1934.

Hardy, I.T. (1994), 'The Proper Legal Regime for "Cyberspace"', *University of Pittsburgh Law Review*, 993-1055.

Hardy, I.T. (1995), 'Contracts, Copyright and Preemption in a Digital World', *Richmond Journal of Law & Technology*, **1**, 2, <http://www.richmond.edu/jolt/v1i1/hardy.html>

Harris, J. (1997), 'Recognition of Foreign Judgments at Common Law — The Anti-Suit Injunction Link', *Oxford Journal of Legal Studies*, **17**, 477-498.

Harris, J. (1998), 'Choice of Law in Tort — Blending in with the Landscape of the Conflict of Laws', *Modern Law Review*, **61**, 33-55.

Hay, B.L. (1992), 'Conflicts of Law and State Competition in the Product Liability System', *Georgetown Law Journal*, **80**, 617-652.

Hirschman, A. (1970), *Exit Voice and Loyalty*, Harvard University Press, Cambridge.

Horlacher, H.M (1991), 'The Rome Convention and the German Paradigm: Forecasting the Demise of the European Convention on the Law

Applicable to Contractual Obligations', *Cornell International Law Journal*, **27**, 173-201.

Huber, P.W. (1988), Liability: The Legal Revolution and its Consequences, Basic Books, New York.

James, W. (1968), 'Pragmatism's Conception of Truth' in McDermott, J.J. (ed), *The Writings of William James*, Modern Library, New York.

Jensen, M.C. and Meckling, W.H. (1976), 'Theory of the Firm: Managerial Behaviour, Agency Costs, and Ownership Structure', *Journal of Financial Economics*, **3**, 305-360.

Johnson, D.R. and Post, D. (1996), 'Law and Borders: The Rise of Law in Cyberspace', *Stanford Law Review*, **48**, 1367-1402.

Johnston, J.S. (1990), 'Strategic Bargaining and the Economic Theory of Contract Default Rules', *Yale Law Journal*, **100**, 615-663.

Johnston, J.S. (1995), 'Bargaining Under Rules Versus Standards', *Journal of Law, Economics & Organization*, **11**, 256-281.

Johnston, J.S. (1996), 'The Statute of Frauds and Business Norms: A Testable Game Theoretic Model', *University of Pennsylvania Law Review*, **144**, 1859-1912.

Jolls, C., Sunstein, C.R., and Thaler, R.H. (1998), 'A Behavioral Approach to Law and Economics', *Stanford Law Review*, **71**, 1471-1550.

Juenger, F.K. (1984), 'A Page of History', *Mercer Law Review*, **35**, 419-460.

Juenger, F.K. (1993), *Choice of Law and Multi-State Justice*, Martinus Nijhoff, Dordrecht.

Juenger, F.K. (1994), 'The Complex Litigation Project's Tort Choice-Of-Law Rules', *Loyola Law Review*, **54**, 907-924.

Juenger, F.K. (1997), 'Contract Choice of Law in the Americas', *American Journal of Comparative Law*, **45**, 195-208.

Juenger, F.K. (1998), 'A Hague Judgments Convention', *Brooklyn Journal of International Law*, **24**, 111-123.

Kahan, M. (1992), 'Securities Laws and the Social Costs of "Inaccurate" Stock Prices', *Duke Law Journal*, **41**, 979-1044.

Kahan, M. and Klausner, M. (1997), 'Standardization and Innovation in Corporate Contracting (or "The Economics of Boilerplate")', *Virginia Law Review*, **83**, 713-770.

Kahneman, D., Knetsch, J.L., and Thaler, R.H. (1990), 'Experimental Tests of the Endowment Effect and the Coase Theorem', *Journal of Political Economy*, **98,** 1325-1348.

Kaplow, L. (1992), 'Rules Versus Standards: An Economic Analysis', *Duke Law Journal*, **42**, 557-629.

Kaplow, L. and Shavell, S. (1995), 'Do Liability Rules Facilitate Bargaining? A Reply to Ayres and Talley', *Yale Law Journal*, **105**, 221-233.

Kaplow, L. and Shavell, S. (1996), 'Property Rules Versus Liability Rules: An Economic Analysis', *Harvard Law Review*, **109**, 715-790.

Katsch, M.E. (1996), 'Dispute Resolution in Cyberspace', *Connecticut Law Review*, **28**, 953-979.

Katz, A.W. (1987), 'Measuring the Demand for Litigation: Is the English Rule Really Cheaper?', *Journal of Law, Economics & Organization*, **3**, 143-176.

Katz, A.W. (1990a), 'The Strategic Structure of Offer and Acceptance: Game Theory and the Law of Contract Formation', *Michigan Law Review*, **89**, 215-295.

Katz, A.W. (1990b), 'Your Terms or Mine: The Duty to Read the Fine Print in Contracts', *Rand Journal of Economics*, **21**, 518-537.

Kelly, D.St.L. (1974), *Localising Rules in the Conflict of Laws*, Woodley Press, Adelaide.

Kennedy, D. (1976), 'Form and Substance in Private Law Adjudication', *Harvard Law Review*, **89**, 1685-1778.

Kincaid, P. (1996), 'Justice in Tort Choice of Law', *Adelaide Law Review*, **18,** 191-212.

Klausner, M. (1995), 'Corporations, Corporate Law, and Networks of Contracts', *Virginia Law Review*, **81**, 757-852.

Klein, B., Crawford, R. and Alchian, A.A. (1978), 'Vertical Integration, Appropriable Rents, and the Competitive Contracting Process', *Journal of Law & Economics*, **21**, 297-326.

Klein, B. and Leffler, K.B. (1981), 'The Role of Market Forces in Assuring Contractual Performance', *Journal of Political Economy*, **89**, 615-641.

Kobayashi, B.H. and Ribstein, L.E. (1999), 'Contract and Jurisdictional Freedom' in Buckley, F.H. (ed), *The Fall and Rise of Freedom of Contract*, Duke University Press, Durham.

Kogan, T. (1987), 'Toward a Jurisprudence of Choice of Law: The Priority of Fairness over Comity', *New York University Law Review*, **62**, 651-714.

Korobkin, R.B. (1998), 'The Status Quo Bias and Contract Default Rules', *Cornell Law Review*, **83**, 608-687.

Korobkin, R.B. and Guthrie, C. (1997), 'Psychology, Economics, and Settlement: A New Look at the Role of the Lawyer', *Texas Law Review*, **76**, 77-141.

Kozyris, P.J. (1981), 'Reflections on Allstate — The Lessening of Due Process on Choice of Law', *University of California Davis Law Review*, **14**, 889-906.

Kozyris, P.J. (1987), 'Choice of Law for Products Liability: Whither Ohio?', *Ohio State Law Journal*, **48**, 377-385.

Kramer, L. (1985), 'The Myth of the Unprovided For Case', *Virginia Law Review*, **75**, 1045-1074.

Kramer, L. (1990), 'Rethinking Choice of Law', *Columbia Law Review*, **90**, 277-345.

Krasner, S.D. (1999), *Sovereignty: Organized Hypocrisy*, Princeton University Press, Princeton, 1999.

Krier, J.E. and Schwab, S.J. (1995), 'Property Rules and Liability Rules: The Cathedral in Another Light', *New York University Law Review*, **70**, 440-483.

Kuhn, T.S. (1970), *The Structure of Scientific Revolutions*, 2nd ed., University of Chicago Press, Chicago.

Kunreuther, H. (1976), 'Limited Knowledge and Insurance Protection', *Public Policy*, **24**, 227-261.

Landes, W.M. (1971), 'An Economic Analysis of the Courts', 14 *Journal of Law & Economics*, **14**, 61-107.

Landes, W.M. and Posner, R.A. (1987), *The Economic Structure of Tort Law*, Harvard University Press, Cambridge.

Laski, H.J. (1939), 'The Obsolescence of Federalism', *New Republic*, **3**, 367-369.

Lee, S. (1995), 'Title to Foreign Real Property in Transnational Money Claims', *Columbia Journal of Transnational Law*, **32**, 607-672.

Lee, S. (1997a), 'Jurisdiction Over Foreign Land: A Reappraisal', *Anglo-American Law Review*, **26**, 273-329.

Lee, S. (1997b), 'The Ok Tedi River: Papua New Guinea or the Parish of St. Mary Le Bow in the Ward of Cheap?', *Australian Law Journal*, **71**, 602-618.

Leflar, R.A. (1966), 'Choice-Influencing Considerations in Conflicts Law', *New York University Law Review*, **41**, 267-327.

Llewellyn Davies, D.J. (1937), 'The Influence of Huber's *De Conflictu Legum* on English Private International Law', *British Year Book of International Law*, 49-78.

LoPucki, L.M. (1994), 'The Unsecured Creditor's Bargain', *Virginia Law Review*, **80**, 1887-1965.

LoPucki, L.M. (1999), 'Cooperation in International Bankruptcy: A Post-Universalist Approach', *Cornell Law Review*, **84**, 696-762.

LoPucki, L.M. and Whitford, W.C. (1991), 'Venue Choice and Forum Shopping in the Bankruptcy Reorganization of Large, Publicly Held Companies', *Wisconsin Law Review*, 11-63.

LoPucki, L.M. and Warren, E.M. (1998), Secured Credit: A Systems Approach, 2nd ed., Aspen, New York.

Lorenzen, E. (1947), *Selected Articles on the Conflict of Law*, Yale University Press, New Haven.

Macey, J.R. (1986), 'Promoting Public-Regarding Legislation Through Statutory Interpretation: An Interest Group Model', *Columbia Law Review*, **86**, 223-268.

Macey, J.R. (1990), 'Federal Deference to Local Regulators and the Economic Theory of Regulation: Toward a Public-Choice Explanation of Federalism', *Virginia Law Review*, **76**, 265-291.

Macey, J.R. and Miller, G.P. (1987), 'Toward an Interest-Group Theory of Delaware Corporate Law', *Texas Law Review*, **65**, 469-523.

Macey, J.R. and Miller, G.P. (1992), 'The Canons of Statutory Construction and Judicial Preferences', *Vanderbilt Law Review*, **45**, 647-672.

Macneil, I.R. (1974), 'The Many Futures of Contract', *Southern Californian Law Review*, **47**, 691-816.

Macneil, I.R. (1978), 'Contracts: Adjustments of Long-Term Economic Relations Under Classical, Neoclassical and Relational Contract Law', *Northwestern University Law Review*, **72**, 854-901.

Mashaw, J.L. (1997), *Greed, Chaos, and Governance: Using Public Choice to Improve Public Law*, Yale University Press, New Haven.

McConnell, M.W. (1988), 'A Choice-of-Law Approach to Products-Liability Reform' in Olson, W. (ed), *New Directions in Liability Law*, Academy of Political Science, New York.

Mefford, A. (1997), 'Lex Informatica: Foundations of Law on the Internet', Indiana Journal of Global Legal Studies, **5**, 211-237.

Merges, R.P. (1996), 'Contracting Into Liability Rules: Intellectual Property Rights and Collective Rights Organizations', *California Law Review*, **84**, 1293-1393.

Merges, R.P. (1997), 'The End of Friction? Property Rights and Contract in the "Newtonian" World on On-line Commerce', *Berkeley Technology Law Journal*, **12**, 115-136.

Morris, J.H.C. (1951), 'The Proper Law of the Tort', *Harvard Law Review*, **64**, 881-895.

Morse, C.G.J. (1989), 'Products Liability in the Conflict of Laws', *Current Legal Problems*, 167-195.

Mullenix, L.S. (1988), 'Another Choice of Forum, Another Choice of Law: Consensual Adjudicatory Procedure in Federal Court', *Fordham Law Review*, **57**, 291-373.

North, P.M. (1993), 'Contract as a Tort Defence in the Conflict of Laws' in North, P. (ed), *Essays in Private International Law*, Clarendon Press, Oxford.

North, P.M. and Fawcett, J.J. (1992), *Cheshire and North's Private International Law*, 8th ed., Butterworths, London.

Nygh, P. (1995a), *Conflict of Laws in Australia*, 6th ed., Butterworths, Sydney.

Nygh, P. (1995b), 'The Reasonable Expectations of the Parties as a Guide to Choice of Law in Contract and in Tort', *Recueil des Cours*, **251**, 268-400.

O'Hara, E.A. (2000), 'Opting Out of Regulation: A Public Choice Analysis of Contractual Choice of Law', *Vanderbilt Law Review*, **53**, forthcoming.

O'Hara, E.A. and Ribstein, L.E. (1997), 'Interest Groups, Contracts and Interest Analysis', *Mercer Law Review*, **48**, 765-774.

O'Hara, E.A. and Ribstein, L.E. (2000), 'From Politics to Efficiency in Choice of Law', *University of Chicago Law Review*, **67**, forthcoming.

Olson, M. (1971), *The Logic of Collective Action: Public Goods and the Theory of Groups*, 2nd ed., Harvard University Press: Cambridge.

Opeskin, B.R. (1996), 'The Use of Choice of Law Rules in Statutes Affecting Contracts: A Note on the Insurance Contracts Act 1984', *Journal of Contract Law*, **10**, 231-243.

O'Rourke, M.A. (1997), 'Copyright Preemption After the *ProCD* Case: A Market-Based Approach', *Berkeley Technology Law Journal*, **12**, 53-91.

Orts, E.W. (1995), 'The Legitimacy of Multinational Corporations' in Mitchell, L.E. (ed), *Progressive Corporate Law*, Westview Press, Boulder.

Owen, D.G. (1992), 'The Fault Pit', *Georgia Law Review*, **26**, 703-724.

Peltzman, S. (1976), 'Toward a More General Theory of Economic Regulation', *Journal of Law & Economics*, **19**, 211-240.

Polinsky, A.M. (1980), 'Resolving Nuisance Disputes: The Simple Economics of Injunctive and Damage Remedies', *Stanford Law Review*, **32**, 1075-1112.

Polinsky, A.M. (1989), *An Introduction to Law and Economics*, 2nd ed., Little Brown, Boston.

Polinsky, A.M. and Rubinfeld, D.L. (1988), 'The Deterrent Effect of Settlements and Trials', *International Review of Law & Economics*, **8**, 109-116.

Posner, R.A. (1973), 'An Economic Approach to Legal Procedure and Judicial Administration', *Journal of Legal Studies*, **2**, 399-458.

Posner, R.A. (1983), 'Statutory Interpretation — in the Classroom and in the Courtroom', *University of Chicago Law Review*, **50**, 800-822.

Posner, R.A. (1985), *The Federal Courts: Crisis and Reform*, Harvard University Press, Cambridge.

Posner, R.A. (1990), *The Problems of Jurisprudence*, Harvard University Press, Cambridge.

Posner, R.A. (1993), 'What Do Judges and Justices Maximize (The Same Thing as Everyone Else Does)', *Supreme Court Economic Review*, **3**, 1-41.

Posner, R.A. (1995), *Overcoming Law*, Harvard University Press, Cambridge.

Posner, R.A. (1996), *Law and Legal Theory in England and America*, Clarendon Press, Oxford.

Posner, R.A. (1997), 'Wealth Maximization and Tort Law: A Philosophical Inquiry' in Owen, D. (ed), *Philosophical Foundations of Tort Law*, Clarendon Press, Oxford.

Posner, R.A. (1998a), *Economic Analysis of Law*, 5th ed., Aspen, New York.

Posner, R.A. (1998b), 'Rational Choice, Behavioral Economics, and the Law', *Stanford Law Review*, **50**, 1551-1575.

Priest, G.L. (1985), 'The Invention of Enterprise Liability: A Critical History of the Intellectual Foundations of Modern Tort Law', *Journal of Legal Studies*, **14**, 461-533.

Priest, G.L. (1987), 'The Current Insurance Crisis and Modern Tort Law', *Yale Law Journal*, **96**, 1521-1590.

Priest, G.L. and Klein, B. (1984), 'The Selection of Disputes for Litigation', *Journal of Legal Studies*, **13**, 1-55.

Pryles, M.C. (1972), 'The Basis of Adjudicatory Competence in Private International Law', *International & Comparative Law Quarterly*, **21**, 61-80.

Pryles, M.C. (1988), 'Judicial Darkness on the Oceanic Sun', *Australian Law Journal*, **62**, 774-791.

Rabin, R.L. (1996), 'Law for Law's Sake', *Yale Law Journal*, **105** 2261-2283.

Radin, M. (1987), 'Market Inalienability', *Harvard Law Review*, **100**, 1849-1937.

Rakoff, T. (1983), 'Contracts of Adhesion: An Essay In Reconstruction', *Harvard Law Review*, **96**, 1173-1284.

Ramsay, I.M. (1990), 'Company Law and the Economics of Federalism', *Federal Law Review*, **19**, 169-202.

Rasmussen, R.K. (1992), 'Debtor's Choice: A Menu Approach to Corporate Reorganization', *Texas Law Review*, **72**, 51-121.

Rasmussen, R.K. (1997), 'A New Approach to Transnational Insolvencies', *Michigan Journal of International Law*, **19**, 1-36.

Rasmussen, R.K. and Thomas, R.S. (2000), 'Timing Matters: Forum Shopping by Insolvent Corporations', *Northwestern University Law Review*, **94**, forthcoming.

Rawls, J. (1971), *A Theory of Justice*, Oxford University Press, Oxford.

Reindl, A.P. (1998), 'Choosing Law in Cyberspace: Copyright Conflicts on Global Networks', *Michigan Journal of International Law*, **19**, 799-871.

Ribstein, L.E. (1993), 'Choosing Law by Contract', *Journal of Corporation Law*, **18**, 245-300.

Ribstein, L.E. (1994), 'Delaware, Lawyers, and Contractual Choice of Law', *Delaware Journal of Corporate Law*, **19**, 999-1025.

Robertson, A.H. (1939), 'A Survey of the Characterization Problem in the Conflict of Laws', *Harvard Law Review*, **52**, 747-772.

Romano, R. (1985), 'Law as a Product: Some Pieces of the Incorporation Puzzle', *Journal of Law, Economics & Organization*, **1**, 225-283.

Romano, R. (1993), *The Genius of American Corporate Law*, AEI Press, Washington.

Romano, R. (1996), 'Corporate Law and Corporate Governance', *Industrial & Corporate Change*, **5**, 277-339.

Romano, R. (1998), 'Empowering Investors: A Market Approach to Securities Regulation', *Yale Law Journal*, **107**, 2359-2430.

Rogerson, P.J. (1990), 'The Situs of Debts in the Conflict of Laws — Illogical, Unnecessary and Misleading', *Cambridge Law Journal*, **49**, 441-460.

Rorty, R. (1989), *Contingency, Irony, Solidarity*, Cambridge University Press, New York.

Rose, C.A. (1988), 'Crystals and Mud in Property Law', *Stanford Law Review*, **40**, 577-610.

Rosenberg, D. and Shavell, S. (1985), 'A Model in Which Suits Are Brought for Their Nuisance Value', *International Review of Law & Economics*, **5**, 3-13.

Rubin, P.H. (1993), *Tort Reform by Contract*, AEI Press, Washington.

Rubin, P.H. (1999), 'Courts and the Tort-Contract Boundary in Product Liability', in Buckley, F.H. (ed), *The Fall and Rise of Freedom of Contract*, Duke University Press, Durham.

Rubin, P.H., Calfee, J.E. and Grady, M.F. (1997), '*BMW v. Gore*: Mitigating the Punitive Economics of Punitive Damages', *Supreme Court Economic Review*, **5**, 179-216.

Salbu, S.R. (1998), 'Who Should Govern the Internet?: Monitoring and Supporting a New Frontier', *Harvard Journal of Law & Technology*, **11**, 429-480.

Schauer, F. (1991), *Playing by the Rules: A Philosophical Examination Of Rule-Based Decisionmaking In Law And In Life*, Clarendon Press, Oxford.

Schelling, T. (1960), *The Strategy of Conflict*, Harvard University Press, Cambridge.

Schwartz, A. (1988), 'Proposals for Products Liability Reform: A Theoretical Synthesis', *Yale Law Journal*, **97**, 353-419.

Schwartz, A. (1992), 'Relational Contracts in the Courts: An Analysis of Incomplete Agreements and Judicial Strategies', *Journal of Legal Studies*, **21**, 271-318.

Schwartz, A. (1993), 'The Default Rule Paradigm and the Limits of Contract Law', *Southern California Interdisciplinary Law Journal*, **3**, 390-419.

Schwartz, A. and Scott, R.E. (1995), 'The Political Economy of Private Legislatures', *University of Pennsylvania Law Review*, **143**, 595-654.

Schwartz, A. and Wilde, L. (1979), 'Intervening in Markets on the Basis of Imperfect Information: A Legal and Economic Analysis', *University of Pennsylvania Law Review*, **127**, 630-682.

Schwartz, G. (1981), 'The Vitality of Negligence and the Ethics of Strict Liability', *Georgia Law Review*, **15**, 963-1005.

Schwartz, G. (1994), 'Reality in the Economic Analysis of Tort Law: Does Tort Law Really Deter', *UCLA Law Review*, **42**, 377-444.

Schwartz, G. (1997), 'Mixed Theories of Tort Law: Affirming Both Deterrence and Corrective Justice', *Texas Law Review*, **75**, 1801-1834.

Selin, S. (1996), 'Governing Cyberspace: The Need for an International Solution', *Gonzaga Law Review*, **32**, 365-388.

Shavell, S. (1980), 'Damage Measures for Breach of Contract', *Bell Journal of Economics*, **11**, 466-489.

Shavell, S. (1982), 'Suit, Settlement, and Trial: A Theoretical Analysis under Alternative Methods for the Allocation of Legal Costs', *Journal of Legal Studies*, **11**, 55-81.

Shavell, S. (1987), *Economic Analysis of Accident Law*, Harvard University Press, Cambridge.

Shreve, G.R. (1996), 'Choice of Law and the Forgiving Constitution', *Indiana Law Journal*, **71**, 271-296.

Skeel, D.A. Jr. (1994), 'Rethinking the Line Between Corporate Law and Corporate Bankruptcy', *Texas Law Review*, **72**, 471-557.

Solimine, M.E. (1989), 'An Economic and Empirical Analysis of Choice of Law', *Georgia Law Review*, **24**, 49-93.

Sommer, J.A. (1990), 'The Subsidiary: Doctrine Without a Cause', *Fordham Law Review*, **59**, 227-281.

Spence, A.M. (1975), 'Monopoly, Quality, and Regulation', *Bell Journal of Economics*, **6**, 417-429.

Stephan, P.B. (1997), 'Accountability and International Lawmaking: Rules, Rents and Legitimacy', *Northwestern Journal of International Law & Business*, **17**, 681-735.

Stephan, P.B. (1999), 'The Futility of Unification and Harmonization in International Commercial Law', *Virginia Journal of International Law*, **39**, 743-797.

Stout, L. (1988), 'The Unimportance of Being Efficient: An Economic Analysis of Stock Market Pricing and Securities Regulation', *Michigan Law Review*, **87**, 613-709.

Sugden, R. (1993), 'The Contractarian Enterprise' in Gauthier, D. and Sugden, R., *Rationality, Justice and the Social Contract*, Harvester Wheatsheaf, London.

Sunstein, C.R. (1989), 'Interpreting Statutes in the Regulatory State', *Harvard Law Review*, **103**, 405-508.

Sunstein, C.R., (1997), 'Behavioral Analysis of Law', *University of Chicago Law Review*, **64**, 1175-1195.

Sunstein, C.R. and Ullmann-Margalit, E. (1998), 'Second-Order Decisions', University of Chicago Working Papers in Law & Economics (2nd) No. 57.

Sykes E.I. and Pryles, M.C. (1991), *Australian Private International Law*, 3rd ed., Law Book Company, Sydney.

Symeonides, S.C. (1997), 'Resolving Six Celebrated Conflicts Cases Through Statutory Choice-of-Law Rules', *Mercer Law Review*, **48**, 837-869.

Telser, L. (1980), 'A Theory of Self-enforcing Agreements', *Journal of Business*, **53**, 27-44.

Tiebout, C.M. (1956), 'A Pure Theory of Local Government Expenditures', *Journal of Political Economy*, **64**, 416-424.

Trachtman, J. (1997), 'Externalities and Extraterritoriality: The Law and Economics of Prescriptive Jurisdiction' in Bhandari, J.S. and Sykes, A.O., (eds.), *Economic Dimensions in International Law*, Cambridge, Cambridge University Press.

Trakman, L. (1980), 'The Evolution of the Law Merchant: Our Commercial Heritage: Ancient and Medieval Law Merchant (part I)', *Journal of Maritime Law & Commerce*, **12**, 1-24.

Trautman, D.T., Westbrook, J.L. and Gaillard, E. (1993), 'Four Models for International Bankruptcy', *American Journal of Comparative Law*, **41**, 573-625.

Tversky, A. and Kahneman, D. (1982), 'Judgment Under Uncertainty: Heuristics and Biases', in Kahneman, D., Slovic, P., and Tversky, A. (eds.), *Judgment Under Uncertainty*, Cambridge University Press, New York.

Twerski, A. (1971), 'Enlightened Territorialism and Professor Cavers — The Pennsylvania Method', *Duquesne Law Review*, **9**, 373-421.

Twitchell, M. (1988), 'The Myth of General Jurisdiction', *Harvard Law Review*, **101**, 610-681.

Ulen, T.S. (1998), 'Economic and Public-Choice Forces in Federalism', *George Mason University Law Review*, **6**, 921-951.

Von Mehren, A.T. and Trautman, D. (1966), 'Jurisdiction to Adjudicate: A Suggested Analysis', *Harvard Law Review*, **79**, 1121-1179.

Von Mehren, A.T. (1998), 'Enforcing Judgments Abroad: Reflections on the Design of Recognition Conventions', *Brooklyn Journal of International Law*, **24**, 17-29.

Ware, S.J. (1999), 'Default Rules From Mandatory Rules: Privatizing Law Through Arbitration', *Minnesota Law Review*, **83**, 703-754.

Watts, R.L. and Zimmerman, J.L. (1983), 'Agency Problems, Auditing and the Theory of the Firm', *Journal of Law & Economics*, **26**, 613-633.

Weinrib, E.J. (1983), 'Toward a Moral Theory of Negligence Law', *Law & Philosophy*, **2**, 37-62.

Welling, B. and Heakes, E.A. (1980), 'Torts and Foreign Immovables Jurisdiction in Conflict of Laws', *University of Western Ontario Law Review*, **18**, 295-315.

West, C. (1989), *The American Evasion of Philosophy: A Genealogy of Pragmatism*, University of Wisconsin Press, Madison.

Westbrook J.L. (1991), 'Theory and Pragmatism in Global Insolvencies: Choice of Law and Choice of Forum', *American Bankruptcy Law Journal*, **65**, 457-490.

Westbrook J.L. (1996), 'The Lessons of Maxwell Communication', *Fordham Law Review*, **64**, 2531-2541.

Whincop, M.J. (1997a), 'Of Fault and Default: Contractarianism as a Theory of Anglo-Australian Corporate Law', *Melbourne University Law Review*, **21**, 187-234.

Whincop, M.J. (1997b), 'A Relational and Doctrinal Critique of Shareholders' Special Contracts', *Sydney Law Review*, **19**, 314-335.

Whincop, M.J. (1997c), 'Nexuses of Contracts, the Authority of Corporate Agents, and Doctrinal Indeterminacy: From Formalism to Law and Economics', *University of New South Wales Law Journal*, **20**, 274-310.

Whincop, M.J. (1997d), 'Overcoming Corporate Law: Instrumentalism, Pragmatism, and the Separate Legal Entity Concept', *Company & Securities Law Journal*, **15**, 414-434.

Whincop, M.J. (1998a), 'Of Dragons and Horses: Filling Gaps in Pre-Incorporation Contracts', *Journal of Contract Law*, **12**, 217-235.

Whincop, M.J. (1998b), 'Forum Shopping Duty Free: The Law and Economics of Anti-Suit Injunctions After CSR v Cigna', *Canberra Law Review*, **5**, 77-94.

Whincop, M.J. (1999a), 'The Political Economy of Corporate Law Reform in Australia', *Federal Law Review*, **27**, 77-120.

Whincop, M.J. (1999b), 'The Recognition Scene: Game Theoretical Issues in the Recognition of Foreign Judgments', *Melbourne University Law Review*, **23**, 416-439.

Whincop, M.J. (1999c), 'Trading Places: Thoughts on Federal and State Jurisdiction in Corporate Law After *Re Wakim*', *Company & Securities Law Journal*, **17**, 11-29.

Whincop, M.J. (1999d), 'Choice of Law, Jurisdiction and the Internet: A Policy Analysis, *National Law Review*', **3,** 10, <http://www.nlr.com.au/articles/whincop/whincop.htm>

Whincop, M.J. (2000a), 'Conflicts in the Cathedral: Towards a Theory of Property Rights in Private International Law', *University of Toronto Law Journal*, **50**, 41-73.

Whincop, M.J. (2000b), 'Choice of Forum, the Stay Application, and Jurisdictional Trade: An Economic Model of International Litigation', unpublished paper.

Whincop, M.J. (2000c), 'Three Positive Theories of International Jurisdiction', *Melbourne University Law Review*, **24**, forthcoming.

Whincop, M.J. and Keyes, M.E. (1997), 'Putting the "Private" Back Into Private International Law: Default Rules and the Proper Law of the Contract', *Melbourne University Law Review*, **21**, 515-543.

Whincop, M.J. and Keyes, M.E. (1998a), 'Statutes' Domains in Private International Law: An Economic Theory of the Limits of Mandatory Rules', *Sydney Law Review*, **20**, 435-456.

Whincop, M.J. and Keyes, M.E. (1998b), 'Economic Analysis of Conflict of Laws in Torts Cases: Discrete and Relational Torts', *Melbourne University Law Review*, **22**, 370-395.

Whincop, M.J. and Keyes, M.E. (1998c), 'The Nexus of Forums: A Contractual Theory of Jurisdiction Over Corporations', *University of New South Wales Law Journal*, **21**, 681-711.

Whincop, M.J. and Keyes, M.E. (1999), 'The Market Tort in Private International Law', *Northwestern Journal of International Law & Business*, **19**, 215-271.

Whincop, M.J. and Keyes, M.E. (2000), 'Towards an Economic Theory of Private International Law', *Australian Journal of Legal Philosophy*, **25**, 1-35.

Wille, D. (1999), 'Personal Jurisdiction and the Internet: Proposed Limits on State Jurisdiction over Data Communications in Tort Cases', *Kentucky Law Journal*, **87**, 95-201.

Williamson, O.E. (1985), *The Economic Institutions of Capitalism*, Free Press, New York.

Williamson, O.E. (1988), 'Corporate Governance and Corporate Finance', *Journal of Finance*, **43**, 567-591.

Williamson, O.E. (1996), *The Mechanisms of Governance*, Oxford University Press, New York.

Wilske, S. and Schiller, T. (1997), 'International Jurisdiction In Cyberspace: Which States May Regulate The Internet?', *Federal Communications Law Journal*, **50**, 117-178.

Wilson, J. (1997), 'Anti-Suit Injunctions', *Journal of Business Law*, 424-437.

Winter, R.K. Jr (1977), 'State Law, Shareholder Protection, and the Theory of the Corporation', *Journal of Legal Studies*, **6**, 251-292.

Yntema, H.E. (1953), 'The Historic Bases of Private International Law', *American Journal of Comparative Law*, **2,** 297-317.

Index